Jeffrey A. Gill

The Christian Pastor's Manual

A Selection of Tracts on the Duties, Difficulties, and Encouragements of the Christian Ministry

Compiled by
Rev. John Brown
Minister of the Gospel, Edinburgh

Edited by Dr. Don Kistler

Soli Deo Gloria Publications
. . . for instruction in righteousness . . .

Soli Deo Gloria Publications
A division of Soli Deo Gloria Ministries, Inc.
P. O. Box 451, Morgan, PA 15064
(412) 221-1901/FAX 221-1902
www.SDGbooks.com

*

*

ISBN 1-57358-136-4

Library of Congress Cataloging-in-Publication Data

The Christian pastor's manual / compiled by John Brown; edited by Don
Kistler
    p. cm.
  Originally published: Edinburgh : David Brown, 1826.
    ISBN 1-57358-136-4 (hardcover : alk. paper)
    1. Pastoral theology. I. Brown, John, 1784-1858. II. Kistler, Don.
    BV4011.3.C47 2003
    253–dc21

                2003003587

Contents

The Evil and Danger of Neglecting Souls

by
Dr. Phillip Doddridge

"If thou forbear to deliver them that are drawn unto death, and those that are ready to be slain; if thou sayest, 'Behold, we knew it not,' doth not He that pondereth the heart consider it? And He that keepeth thy soul, doth not he know it? And shall not He render to every man according to his works?"

Proverbs 24:11–12

For the explication of these words, I would offer three plain and obvious remarks:

1. The omission which is here charged as so displeasing to God, though immediately referring to men's natural lives, must surely imply that the neglect of their souls is much more criminal. The text strongly implies that we shall be exposed to guilt and condemnation before God by forbearing to deliver those who are drawn unto death and those who are ready to be slain. This must directly refer to innocent persons, brought into visible and extreme danger by some oppressive enemy either by the sudden assault of a private person or by some unjust prosecution under forms of law; it may particularly extend to cases where we have reason to believe that a capital sentence has been passed, in consequence of false witness, detected before execution is done. It was allowed among the Jews that if

1

any person could offer anything in favor of a prisoner after sentence was passed, he might be heard before execution was done; and therefore it was usual (as the Mishnah says) that when a man was led to execution, a crier went before him and proclaimed, "This man is now going to be executed for such a crime, and such and such are witnesses against him; whoever knows him to be innocent, let him come forth and make it appear." And if the neglect of that is (as you see it is) represented as highly criminal, it must be a much more heinous crime, by any neglect of ours, to permit the ruin of men's souls without endeavoring after their recovery when they are, as it were, drawn away to the extreme danger of eternal death, and are ready to be slain by the sword of divine justice.

2. The text seems to suppose that men would be ready to excuse themselves for this neglect. It is true indeed that at the first sight of a miserable object we naturally find a strong impulse to endeavor to relieve it. Our hearts, as it were, spring in our bosoms and urge us forward to exert ourselves on such an occasion, which seems to be intimated by that word which we render "forbear," which often signifies to check, restrain, and hold back a person from what he is eager to do; but the wise man intimates that there may be danger of suppressing these generous impulses of the soul on the first view of the object, of suffering our charity to cool, and then of searching out apologies for our inactivity. You may be ready to say, "Behold, I knew it not. I did not particularly see the danger. I did not, however, apprehend it to be so extreme; or, I did not know the innocence of the person in danger; or, if I did believe it, I knew not how to deliver him. I did not think the

interposition of such a person as myself could be of any importance in such an affair. I was sorry to see innocence overborne and weakness oppressed, but I was myself too weak to contend with the mightier oppressor; too poor, too ignorant, or too busy to meddle in an affair where those who were much my superiors were concerned, and had determined the case. I had no obligation to the person in danger. I had no concern with him nor anything to do to embarrass myself with his affairs." If these excuses are just, it is well.

3. Nevertheless, the text supposes that these excuses might often be overruled by an appeal to men's consciences, as in the sight of God. "Doth not He that pondereth the heart consider it?" It is as if he had said, "It is an easy thing to excuse omissions so that a fellow creature shall have nothing to reply; but whoever you are who reads these words, I charge you to remember that it is comparatively a very little matter to be judged of man's judgment. He who judges you is the Lord; it is He who ponders the heart. He weighs in a most accurate balance all its most secret sentiments. I therefore cut off all chicane and trifling debate at once by placing you in His presence, and laying open your conscience there. You can answer me, but can you answer the heart-searching God?

"Does not He, the great Father of spirits, see in every instance how inferior spirits conduct themselves? Does He not precisely know the situation in which your heart was at the very moment in question? You say that you did not know it, but He is witness whether you indeed did or did not know it. And He also sees all the opportunities and advantages which you had to know it, all the hints which might have been traced out to open a more explicit and particular knowledge, every glimpse which you had when you were (like the priest, when he spied at a distance the wounded traveler) passing by on the other side, and perhaps affecting to look the contrary way."

Nor was it in vain that the wise man renewed his expostulation in a different form: "He that keepeth thy soul, doth not He know it?" It is as if he had said, "Consider God as keeping your own soul, as holding it in life, as preserving your spirit by His continued visitation. Oh, you who neglect the life of your brother, must He not be highly displeased with that neglect? May He not reasonably expect that while He, the Lord of Heaven and earth, condescends to become your guardian, you should learn from Him, and be according to your ability and in your sphere, a guardian to the whole human race, and should endeavor, in every instance, to ward off danger from the life, from the soul of your brother!"

And that these thoughts may enter into your mind with all their weight, it is added once more in this pointed form of interrogation, "Will not He render to every man according to his works?" I appeal to your own heart, is He not a being of infinite moral as well as natural perfections? And will He not, as the Judge of all the earth, do right? Would He not have remembered and rewarded your generous care for the preservation of the miserable creature in question? And, on the other hand, will He not reckon with you for such a failure? Human laws, indeed, cannot punish such neglects; but the supreme Legislator can and will do it. Think of these things, and guard against such fatal negligence in every future instance. Think of them, and humble yourself deeply before God for every past instance in which such guilt has been incurred.

God is my witness that I do not mean to insinuate the least disrespectful thought with regard to any one of you. Nevertheless, permit me to say without offense (for I say it in the fear of God, and with the sincerest deference and friendship to you) that I am afraid that the extensive and important obligations of the ministerial office are not generally considered and remembered among us as they ought to be. I apprehend that much more might be done for the honor of God and the good of souls than is commonly done, even by those who, in the main, have a principle of true religion in their hearts; by those who keep up the exercise of public worship in a regular and honorable manner, and appear not only irreproachable in their conversation, but, if considered as in private life, bringing forth the fruits of righteousness. The learned, the wise, the virtuous, the pious minister is, I hear, often negligent of a considerable part of his trust and charge, and thereby fails to deliver, as he might, those who are drawn unto death, and perhaps are just ready to be slain.

To awaken our spirits, therefore, from that insensibility, in this respect, into which they are so ready to fall, I shall take the liberty briefly to consider what excuses we may be most ready to offer for neglecting the souls of men. Second, I will seriously represent the great evil of that neglect in the sight of God, notwithstanding all those excuses. After that I shall add a few hints, by way of reflection, as time permits.

I shall first consider what excuses we may be ready to make for neglecting to do our utmost for the salvation of men's souls.

1. We must do something considerable for that purpose. We must take care for their instruction in public, reading the Word of God to them when they are assembled together in His house, explaining and enforcing it in our expositions and sermons; presenting prayers and praise to God in their name, and, at proper seasons, administering the sacraments in such a manner as we judge most agreeable to the institution of our Lord Jesus Christ.

And so far indeed it is well; and a most wise and gracious appointment of our blessed Redeemer it is that such ordinances should be administered on solemn stated days, and by men appropriated to that employment. In consequence of this, such knowledge is dispersed as is, through the divine blessing, effectual for the salvation of many souls. I am not afraid to say that this would make the Christian ministry, even in the hands of ignorant, careless, and vicious men, a blessing to the nation where it is settled, as long as reading the Scriptures, and almost any kind of prayers in an intelligible language, are a part of divine service in their assemblies. Much more will it be so in the hands of wise, sober, and religious men.

But while we are thus pleading our diligence and care in the administration of public ordinances, it will be kindness to ourselves seriously to ask our own hearts, at least, how they are administered. It is a very important trust to have the management of men's religious hours committed to us, their season of social worship being, comparatively, so short, and so infinitely momentous. I think that we almost, as it were, put our own lives in our hand while we undertake it, and may justly tremble on the view of that awful account which we are to give of it.

I hope, sirs, we have the testimony of our own consciences before God that we do not, on these solemn occasions, content ourselves with cold essays on mere moral subjects, however acute, philosophical, or polite; nor that we make it our main business, in our sermons, to seek the ornament of elegant words, the refinements of criticism, or the nice arrangement of various complex and abstruse argumentations. When we speak in the name and presence of God to immortal creatures on the borders of eternity, I hope we entertain our hearers with plain, serious, and lively discourses on the important doctrines of Christianity, in their due connection and their relation to each other, in such a manner as we, on mature consideration, do verily believe may have the most effectual tendency to bring them to God through Christ, and to produce and promote in their hearts, through the divine blessing, the great work of regeneration and holiness. I hope and trust that God is our witness, and that the people of our charge are witnesses, that not one of those who diligently attend on our ministry, though but for a few succeeding Sabbaths, can fail to learn the way of salvation as exhibited in the gospel; that we speak of it as those who are in earnest and do, from our very souls, desire to answer the great ends of our ministry in the prosperity of the Redeemer's kingdom, and in the eternal happiness of those invaluable souls whom He has committed to our care. Otherwise we may incur great and fatal guilt, though public worship may be constantly and decently carried on, and though a reasonable proportion of time is employed in it, with numerous and attentive auditories, to whom we may be as the lovely song of one who has a pleasant voice, while in the ears of God, for want of that fervent charity which should dictate and animate all, we are but as sounding brass or as a tinkling cymbal.

But granting, as I would willingly suppose, and as with relation to you, my brethren, I do firmly believe that all these reflections can be answered with satisfaction—here is indeed a part of your duty honorably formed, and an important part of it too—but is that part, though ever so important, to be substituted for the whole? The diligent inspection of our flock, pastoral visits, the observation of the religious state of families, personal exhortations, admonitions, and cautions by word or letter, as prudence shall direct, catechizing children, promoting religious associations among the younger and the elder people of our charge, and the strict and resolute exercise of discipline in the various churches over which we preside—are these not parts of our office? Will we say it with our dying breath? Will we maintain before the tribunal of Christ that they did not belong to the Christian ministry? And, if not, will our care of other parts of it be allowed as sufficient excuse before Him for our total omission of these? We have preached and prayed and administered the sacraments. These things we should indeed have done; and when we had taken the care of congregations upon us, we could hardly avoid it. But surely our own conscience will, now or hereafter, tell us that we ought not to have left the others undone.

2. But we may, perhaps, for a while elude the conviction by pleading that the care of particular persons more properly belongs to others, and especially to

heads of families, who have more opportunities of being serviceable to those under their charge, and indeed
have the most immediate concern for them. It certainly
does. But does it belong to them alone? Or if it did, do
not they belong to us and to our care? And is it not the
part of every superior officer of a society to see to it that
the subaltern officers are careful and diligent in the
discharge of their duty? And in this case, are we to take
it for granted that, in our respective congregations,
heads of families are so diligent automatically that they
pray in their families; that they read the Scriptures and
other good books there, especially on the evening of
the Lord's day; that they catechize their children and
solemnly press upon them, and upon their servants, the
serious care of practical religion? Are we to conclude
without any further inquiry that all this is done, and
done in so diligent and so prudent a manner that there
is no need of any particular exhortations, instructions,
or admonitions from us? Would to God there were any
one congregation in the whole kingdom of which this
might reasonably be presumed to be the case! But if it
were indeed so, would not our concurrence with these
wise and pious heads of families, in so good but so difficult a work, encourage and strengthen them to prosecute it with greater cheerfulness and vigor? Would it
not quicken both their cares and their endeavors? And
might it not, by the divine blessing, promote the success of them? Might it not gain on the minds of children and servants to see that we do not think it beneath
us to tenderly care for their souls? And might not our
tender and condescending regards to them in private,
by convincing them how well we mean them, render
our public labors more acceptable and useful to them?

Now, we well know that the children and servants of
the present generation are the hopes of the next, as
they are probably those who, in their turns, will be parents and governors of families whose children and servants, when they arise, will in one way or another feel
the happy or unhappy consequences of our fidelity or
neglect.

3. And when such affairs are in question, shall we allow ourselves to plead that we have so much other
business, and such various engagements of a different
kind, that we cannot possibly attend to these things?
But give me leave, my brethren, to observe that the
question here is not whether we can find out other
agreeable ways of filling up our time, but whether those
other ways are more important, and whether that different manner of employing it is more acceptable in
the sight of God, and will turn to a better account in
that great day when our conduct is to be finally re-
viewed by Him. We must indeed have our seasons of
recreation, and our seasons of study; but it will easily
appear that no regards to either of these will vindicate
or excuse our neglect of the private duties we owe to our
flock in giving diligence to know their state, and in being careful to teach them not only publicly, but from
house to house.

Recreation, to be sure, can afford no just apology for
neglecting this duty since to follow this employment
prudently might be made a kind of recreation from the
labors of a sedentary and studious life. "A grave and
sincere recreation!" you will perhaps say. Grave indeed I
will acknowledge it to be, but not therefore, to a serious
mind, less delightful. So much of those two noblest and
sweetest exercises of the soul, devotion and benevo-

lence, would naturally mingle with these pious cares and tender addresses as would renew the strength which had been exhausted in our studious hours, and the manly, shall I say, or rather the God-like joy it would administer would quite discountenance that which we find in the gay indulgences of a humorous and facetious conversation—though I see no necessity of forbidding that at proper intervals, so far as its cheerfulness is consistent with wisdom and religion. And I am sure that if we can turn our seasons of recess from study to so profitable an account as would be answered by the duties which you know I have now in view, it will be a most happy art, well becoming one who is truly prudent, and would therefore husband his time to the best purposes for eternity. In this view, it is evident that the smallest fragments of it, like the dust of gold, are too valuable to be lost.

The greatest portion of time to be given to our studies will, no doubt, be urged as a yet more material excuse; but here it is obvious to reply that a prudent care in the duties I am now recommending is very consistent with our employing a great deal of time in study, and particularly with our giving it what I hope we shall always learn to value and redeem, namely our morning hours, to which some of the evening may also be added. And if these will not generally suffice, give me leave to ask, what are those important studies that would thus engross the whole of our time, excepting what is given to devotion and to what is generally called recreation?

I have had some little taste of the pleasures of literature myself, and have some reason to hope I shall not be suspected of any prejudice against it; nor am I at all inclined to pass those contemptuous censures on the various branches of it in which ignorance and sloth are often, with strange stupidity, or with yet stranger assurance, seeking—and, it may be, finding—a refuge; but on such an occasion I must freely say that I fear many things, which employ a very large portion of our retired time, are studied as rather polite amusements to our own minds than as things which seem to have any apparent subservience to the glory of God and the edification of our flock. Consequently, I fear, they will stand as articles of abatement, if I may so express it, in our final account; and, when they come to be made manifest, they will be found works that shall be burned, as being no better, in the divine esteem, than wood, hay, and stubble, however beautifully they may have been varnished or gilded over.

Let me here, in particular, address myself to my younger brethren, with a frankness which may be to them more excusable, while I urge them to a Christian self-denial in this area, where perhaps it may be, of all others, the most difficult. I do not apprehend persons of your approved character to be in danger of any other kind of luxury or intemperance; but there is, if you will permit me so to call it, a sort of refined, intellectual luxury, with regard to which I am jealous over you, lest you should be seduced into it, or, rather, lest some of you be already ensnared by its specious charms.

I would not, my young friends, be so severe and cruel as to desire that you be denied that high and elegant entertainment which a person of genius and taste will find in the masterly writings of the ancient orators, historians, and poets, or in those polite and elegant pieces which our own and other modern languages may afford, from which the wise man and the Christian will learn many things of solid use, as well as matters of most delightful amusements. Neither would I pretend to forbid some mathematical and philosophical researches into which you are initiated in your academic course, and with which you will do well to retain and improve your acquaintance in the progress of life, both to strengthen your rational faculties by that strenuous exercise and to improve your knowledge of the works of God. These will appear great, wonderful, and delightful in proportion to the degree of sagacity and diligence with which they may be searched out; but it is one thing to taste of these poignant and luscious fruits, and another to feed and live upon them; one thing to make the most noble and substantial parts of them our entertainment and refreshment, and quite another to make their circumstantial curiosities the chief business of our study, and the favorite subjects of our most attentive inquiry. That true greatness and elevation of mind which the gospel is so admirably calculated to produce would teach us a much sublimer science; and if, for the sake of these little things, we neglect to pray for those whom God has committed to our care, to inquire into their religious state, and to pursue them with suitable applications and addresses, the time will come when we shall assuredly own that we dearly purchased the most refined pleasures they could possibly give us—not to say how much greater and nobler pleasure we even now give up while our duty is neglected.

Oh, my brethren, let us consider how fast we are passing through this dying life which God has assigned us, in which we are to manage concerns of infinite moment; how fast we are passing on to the immediate presence of our Lord, to give our account to Him.

You must judge for yourselves, but permit me to say that, for my own part, I would not, for ten thousand worlds, be that man who, when God shall ask him at last how he has employed most of his time while he continued as a minister in His church and had the care of souls, should be obliged to reply, "Lord, I have restored many corrupted passages in the ancient classics, and illustrated many which were before obscure. I have cleared up many intricacies in chronology or geography; I have solved many perplexed cases in algebra; I have refined astronomical calculations and left behind me many sheets on these curious and difficult subjects, where the figures and characters are ranged with the greatest exactness of truth. These are the employments in which my life has been worn out, while preparations for the pulpit, or ministering in it, did not demand any immediate attendance." Oh, sirs, as for the waters which are drawn from these springs, however sweetly they may taste to a curious mind that thirsts for them, or to an ambitious mind which thirsts for the applause they sometimes procure, I fear there is often reason to pour them out before the Lord with rivers of penitential tears, like the blood of souls which have been forgotten while these trifles have been remembered and pursued.

Nor am I without my fears that a great deal of studious time is lost in an overly artful composition of sermons, and in giving them such polish and ornament as does not conduce to their usefulness, nor in any way balance the labor employed in the work. If we do not diligently watch over our hearts, this will be an incense offered to our own vanity, which will render our sacrifice less acceptable to God, however we and our hearers may be delighted with the perfume.

Greater plainness and simplicity of speech might often be more useful to the bulk of our audience, and perhaps more acceptable too. Moreover, on the whole, it might be at least equally beautiful; for all who are not children in understanding know that there is a natural and manly kind of eloquence arising from a deep sense of the subject and an ardent love for the souls of our hearers, which is of all others the most to be desired and esteemed. And though such discourses may be attended with some little inaccuracies, and may want something of the varnish which exacter preparation might set on, yet, surely, where a habit of speaking is formed by proper application and the materials of a sermon are well digested in the mind, it will rise above a reasonable contempt. And if, where more exact preparation is made, a care to preserve those niceties of composition deadens the manner of the delivery, and takes off either its solemnity, its vigor, or its tenderness, I cannot but apprehend it as injurious to the character of the orator as to that of the Christian. The most celebrated speakers, in judicial courts and in senates, have in all nations and ages pursued the method I now recommend; and the most acceptable preachers have successfully attempted it.

On the whole, permit me to say, it would be a fateful thing to barter away the souls of our people for the highest and justest reputation of speaking well; yet I fear there are many who, in this view, do it for naught, and have not, in any sense, increased their wealth by the price. But perhaps, after all, the most plausible excuse may be that which I have reserved as the last I shall mention now.

4. The attempts I am proposing might displease those who attend upon our ministry, upon which account it may seem, both with respect to them and ourselves, a necessary precaution of prudence to decline them. This is the lion in the street which we often plead, slothful as we too naturally are, for staying within doors when our duty calls us abroad on these charitable errands. But I hope that, on a nearer approach, it will not be found so fierce or so invincible as a timorous imagination paints it.

I think, brethren, we make a very unfavorable representation of the temper and character, not to say of the breeding and understanding, of our people when we so readily take it for granted that they will be displeased with us for addressing those exhortations to them in private which they seem so desirous of receiving from us in public. Let us ask our own consciences, would they all be displeased? If not, the displeasure it might give to some can be no excuse for neglecting it with regard to others; and are we indeed so miserable as to be situated among whole congregations in whom ignorance, pride, and profaneness prevail to such a degree that a minister who would be welcome among them, if he came only as a common visitant, should be looked upon with contempt or indignation when he came expressly as a friend to their eternal interest, and would step a little out of the common way for their salvation?

If this were really our case, who would not say with the prophet, "Oh, that I had in the wilderness a lodging-place of wayfaring men, though it were but such a wretched cave as travelers find in a desert, that I might leave my people, and go from them; for they are all an assembly of treacherous men!" Treacherous men indeed, if, while they call themselves Christians and Protestants, they should think themselves injured and affronted by the exhortations of their ministers when they would warn every man, and teach every man in all wisdom, that they might present them perfect in Christ. But, blessed be God, bad as the world is, there is no room to imagine this to be the case, or anything like it. Perhaps, while we are delaying, and coldly deliberating about it, many lively Christians under our care are earnestly praying that God may put such a thing into our hearts. And should we attempt it, I doubt not but they would receive us as angels of God, or even as Christ Himself. Their love for us would be more abundantly confirmed, and their heart cemented in closer bonds then they have yet known; and many others would at least own that we acted in character, and maintained a more apparent consistency of behavior, if the affair were properly conducted.

Did we indeed pretend to control them in the management of their temporal affairs, or to exercise a lordly dominion over their faith and their consciences, they might justly be displeased; or did we craftily demand that they should lay open to us the secrets of their breasts in confession, their suspicions would be pardonable and their resentments reasonable. But it must be great malice and folly to suspect any design of that infamous nature from our visiting them as pastors, with pious exhortations and affectionate prayers, as those who are concerned for them and their children and servants, that their souls may prosper and be in health. A solicitude for the health of their bodies is esteemed friendship and gratitude, and inquiries concerning it seem but common decency. And can it offend them to find that we are solicitous about that welfare which is indefinitely more important and, by virtue of our office, our peculiar charge?

Yes, you will say, in one instance it will displease; for when we are obliged to blame anything which we see amiss in them, their pride will naturally take fire on such an occasion. And perhaps those whom we have thought our best friends will become our enemies if we venture to tell them such disagreeable truths as fidelity may extort in some circumstances. This is, after all, the main difficulty; and, as I cannot wonder if it impresses our minds, I pray God to forgive the perverseness of those who make it so great. Yet surely it is possible to manage reproof so that, in most instances, it shall oblige rather than provoke. If we tell our hearers of their faults privately, and if we do it with tenderness and respect; if we show by our manner of speaking that what we say proceeds from a humble fear lest we should displease God, betray our trust, and injure their souls by neglect; if at the same time our behavior to them is as it surely should be, constantly obliging; if we do our utmost, so far as truth and justice will permit, to guard and shelter their character in the world, and bring our complaints of them to none but themselves—bad as the world is, I believe few will quarrel with us upon this account. But we shall see, as Solomon observed, that he who rebukes a man will afterwards find more favor than he who flatters with his tongue.

But supposing the worst that can happen, that folly and wickedness should prevail so far over all the tender and prudent address of the friend and the pastor as to render us evil for so great a good, and hatred for so generous and so self-denying an instance of love, how could that hatred be expressed? Seldom in any more formidable manner than by withdrawing from our ministry, and discontinuing what they have done for our support; for the revilings of persons of such a character can seldom hurt any but themselves.

Now I hope, brethren, that we shall always retain so much of a manly (not to say Christian) spirit as to choose to retrench some of our expenses, to forego some of the entertainments of life, to cast ourselves and our families on providence, or even, if it were necessary, to subsist in an honest and creditable poverty by the daily labor of our own hands, much rather than meanly to crouch to such haughty sinners and sacrifice duty, honor, and conscience to the arrogance of their petulant temper. Let us fear God as we ought, and we shall find nothing to fear from them; but we should be willing to imitate the fidelity and courage of John the Baptist, though the wrath of a king might be provoked by it, and imprisonment or martyrdom might be its reward.

I hope such considerations as these may effectually obviate the excuses which indolence or cowardice may be ready to form for our neglect of men's souls, especially when we go on to consider the great evil of that neglect, as it appears in the sight of God, notwithstanding all these excuses, or any of the like kind, with which we may endeavor to make it palatable.

But who can fully represent it, as it appears to His capacious and all-penetrating view! What human mind can conceive the infinite evil! It is not, sirs, a subject on which to display the wantonness of wit or the colorings of artificial harangue; a terrible kind of solemnity attends it, and I attempt the display of it with fear and trembling. If it seems a light matter to us to forbear to deliver those who in this sense are drawn unto death, those who are thus ready to perish, consider, my brethren (and, oh, may my own conscience always consider) what the death of the soul is! How many wretched souls are continually dying around us! What gracious provision God has made to prevent it, and what peculiar obligations we are under to labor to the utmost to preserve their lives!

Let us think what the death of the soul is. The Apostle James intimates that it is a thought of great importance when he says, "He that shall turn a sinner from the error of his ways shall save a soul from death." It is as if he had said, "Do but reflect what that is, and you will find your success is its own reward." We well know that to save a soul from death is not merely to prevent the extinction of its being, though even that would be much, but to prevent its positive, its lasting, its eternal misery. It is to prevent its being slain by the pointed and flaming sword of divine justice.

It is a tragic spectacle to behold a criminal dying by human laws, even where the methods of execution are gentle (as, through our leniency they generally are among us); and I doubt not but it would grieve us to the heart to see any who had been under our ministerial care in that deplorable circumstance. But, oh, how much more deeply must it pierce our very souls to see them led forth to that last dreadful execution, with those of whom Christ shall say, "As for these Mine enemies, who would not that I should reign over them, bring them forth, and slay them before Me!" Oh, how will it wound us to hear the beginning of those cries and wailings which must never end! How shall we en-

dure the reflection, "These wretches are perishing forever, in part because I would not take any pains to attempt their salvation!" Is it so strange a supposition
then that some, once under our ministry, may then perish in our sight? Would to God that it were only less
probable!

But, on the contrary, let us consider how many
souls, precious and immortal as they are, seem to be
continually dying around us! Are there but few that
miscarry? Let Peter inform us, when he says that "the
righteous are scarcely saved." Yea, let our Lord Himself
inform us when He says, "Strait is the gate and narrow
is the way that leadeth unto life, and few there be that
find it; whereas wide is the gate and broad is the way
that leadeth to destruction, and many there be that go
in thereat" (Matthew 7:13–14).

We grieve to see epidemic distempers prevailing
around us; we are ready, as providence calls us, to visit
the sick and the dying, and could take little pleasure in
our health if we did not endeavor to succor them as we
have opportunity. But let us look around and see
whether that distemper which threatens the death of
souls is not epidemic indeed. With all the allowances
which that charity can make which believes all things
and hopes all things, which it can with any shadow of
reason do, must we not own that there are many marks
of eternal death on many, and that there are many
more in whom we can see nothing which looks like a
token of spiritual life? So that the best we can say of
them is that possibly there may be some latent sparks of
it concealed in the heart which as yet produce no effect
to the honor of their profession or the benefit of the
world. In the meantime, sinners are spreading the

infection of their infidelity and their vices far and wide, as if, like some illustrious wretches who have been miscalled "heroes," they accounted the destruction of numbers their glory. Can we behold such a contagion spreading itself even in the Christian church, which ought to be healthful as the regions of paradise, and not bitterly lament it before God? Can we seriously lament it, and not endeavor its redress?

This is so especially when we consider what a gracious provision God has made to prevent their death. Is there not indeed balm in Gilead? Is there not a Physician there, even this glorious gospel of the blessed God, whose efficacy we have so often heard of and seen! And shall they yet perish! Adored are the riches of divine grace; we know (and it is infinitely the most important part of all our knowledge) that there is a rich and free pardon proclaimed to all who will sue for it and accept the benefit in a proper, that is, a grateful manner—for cordial acceptance and real gratitude are all it demands. One would expect that the tidings should be as life to the dead; but we see how coldly they are received, how shamefully they are slighted, how generally, yea, how obstinately they are rejected. And what is the consequence? Refusing to believe on the Son of God, they "shall not see life, but the wrath of God abideth on them," with an additional weight of vengeance, as it well may.

Now, is not this enough to make our very hearts bleed to think that immortal souls aggravate their guilt and ruin! Instead of being anything the better for this delightful message of peace and grace, they should be forever the worse for it, and should have reason to wish throughout all eternity that they had never seen the

faces nor heard the voices of those who brought it, but
had been numbered among the sinners of Tyre and
Sidon, of Sodom and Gomorrah.

If we do not, on the express authority of our Lord,
believe this to be the case with regard to impenitent
sinners under the gospel, we are not Christians of even
the lowest class; but if we do believe it, and are not affected with it so far as to endeavor their recovery, I do
not see how any regard to our own temporal interest, or
that of others, can entitle us to the character of either
prudence or humanity, even though we had not been
distinguished by a public office in the church, but had
passed through life in the station of the obscurest
among our hearers.

But it is impossible to do justice to my argument if I
do not urge the consideration of the peculiar obligations we are under to endeavor the preservation of
souls, not only in virtue of our experience as Christians,
but of our office as ministers. If we were only to consider our experiences as Christians, if we have anything
more than the empty name, that consideration might
certainly afford us a very tender argument to awaken
our compassion for the souls of others. We know what
it is ourselves to be upon the brink of destruction, and
in that sad circumstance to obtain mercy; and shall we
not extend mercy to others? We have looked to Jesus
that we might live; and shall we not point Him out to
them? We have tasted that the Lord is gracious; and
shall we not desire to communicate the same happy relish of His grace to all about us? He has magnified the
riches of His pardoning love toward us; and shall we
not, with David, resolve that we will endeavor to teach
transgressors His ways, and labor to promote the

conversion of sinners unto Him? Even now He is keeping our souls, and His visitation preserves our spirits;
and, as it is by His grace that we are what we are, it is by
having obtained help from Him that we continue unto
this day. And shall His grace daily bestowed upon us be
in vain? Shall we not have compassion on our fellow
servants, as the Lord continually has pity on us?

But our office as ministers completes the obligation, when we consider the view in which the Word of
God represents that office, and the view in which we
ourselves have received it. As for the former of these, we
are all acquainted with those representations; and it is
greatly to be wished, for our own sake and that of our
people, that they may be very familiar to our minds. Let
us often listen with becoming attention to the blessed
God as speaking to us in those words which He once
addressed to the prophet Ezekiel, that faithful approved
servant of the Lord: "Son of man, I have made thee a
watchman to the house of Israel; therefore, hear the
word at My mouth, and give them warning for Me.
When I say to the wicked, 'Thou shall surely die,' and
thou givest him no warning, nor speakest to warn the
wicked from his evil ways to save his life, the same
wicked man shall die in his iniquity; but his blood will
I require at thine hand." And with apparent reason may
the sentinel be punished for the desolation which the
enemy makes while, instead of watching, he sleeps.

We are elsewhere represented as men of God, as soldiers of Jesus Christ, as made overseers or bishops by
the Holy Ghost, as under-shepherds in subordination
to Christ, the great Shepherd and Bishop of souls. And
should not the thought, gentle as it is, awaken us to
diligent inspection over the sheep He has committed

to our care? Otherwise, we are but images of shepherds, as it is represented in those lively and awful words of God by Zechariah, which I think might strike terror and trembling into many who, in the eye of the world, may seem the happiest of their brethren: "Woe to the idol-shepherd that leaveth the flock." The sword of divine vengeance which, by his negligence, he has justly incurred "shall be upon his arm, and upon his right eye," upon that eye which should have watched over the flock, and that arm which should have been stretched out for its rescue. So that he shall be deprived of those capacities that he abused, and be made miserable in proportion to that abuse; for "his arm shall be clean dried up, and his right eye shall be utterly darkened." Such we know are the pathetic views which the Scripture gives us of our office, and of the guilt and danger attending the neglect.

I might, if my time would admit, farther urge the views with which we have ourselves received our office and engage in it. Most of us, when we undertook the pastoral charge, solemnly recorded our vows before God, that we would "endeavor, with all diligence and zeal, to attend to the services of this holy function; that we would be instant in season and out of season, and labor to discharge the private as well as public duties of the ministerial life."

These vows of God are upon us, and every ordination of any of our brethren at which we assist adds a farther and solemn obligation to them. Let us therefore take the greatest care that we do not deal deceitfully and unfaithfully with both God and man. For it is most evident that though the neglect of immortal souls is very criminal in every rational creature, it is most of all

so in us who have so deliberately and so publicly undertaken the charge of them.

It would indeed, in this case, not only be cruelty to
them, but the basest treachery and ingratitude to our
great Lord, who has lodged such a trust in our hands, a
trust which evidently lies so near His heart. Having redeemed His people with His own blood, He commits
them to our care; and having acquired for Himself the
most tender claim to our love that can be imagined, He
graciously requires this evidence of it, that we should
feed His sheep, yea, His lambs—so putting our office in
the most amiable and tender view, and bringing in every sentiment of grateful friendship to excite our diligence in it.

However we may regard it, I doubt not but our
blessed Redeemer considers it as the greatest favor and
the highest honor He could have conferred upon us
that, being returned to His throne in the heavens, He
should choose us to negotiate His cause and interest
on earth, and should consign over to our immediate
care that gospel He brought down from heaven, and
those souls which He died to save; and that He should
make it the delightful labor of our life to follow Him in
His own profession and employment—to be, of all our
fellow creatures, His most immediate representatives
and, in humble subordination to Him, saviors of men.
Does not the very mention of it cause our hearts to glow
with a fervent desire and generous ambition of answering so high a confidence? Could any one of us endure
the thought of betraying it?

How could we, in that case, lift up our faces before
Him when we shall, as we certainly must, see Him eye to
eye! Yes, my brethren, let us every hour recollect it; our

Master will ere long come and reckon with us. He will
"render to every man according to his works," as my
text expresses it, in exact harmony with the language of
the New Testament; and which of us would not then
wish to appear before Him as those who have been
faithfully attached to His cause, and have distinguished
themselves by a zeal for His service? Shall we then, any
of us, repent of our activity in so good a work? Shall we
wish that we had given more of our time to the pursuit
of secular interest, or the curiosities of literature, and
less to the immediate care of souls? Oh, my brethren,
let us be wise in time! We have but one life to spend on
earth, and that a very short one too. Let us make the
best of it, and lay it out in such kind of employments as
we verily believe will give us the most satisfaction in the
closing moments of it, and when eternity is opening
upon us. It is easy to form plausible excuses for such a
conduct, but our own hearts and consciences would
answer us, if we would seriously ask them what the
course of life in the ministerial office is which will
then afford the most comfortable review, and, through
the riches of divine grace, the most pleasing prospect.

I now proceed to the further application of these
things in some practical inferences from them. You
have all, I doubt not, preceded me in reflecting on the
reason we have to humble ourselves deeply in the presence of the blessed God, while we remember our faults
this day. I do not indeed at all question but that many
of us have set before our people life and death, and
have in our public address urged their return to God by
the various considerations of terror and of love which
the thunders of Mount Sinai and the grace of Mount
Zion have taught us. We have on great occasions visited

them, and entered into some serious discourse with
them, and have often, and I would hope more or less
daily, borne them on our hearts before God in our season of devout retirement. Blessed be God that in these
instances we have, in any degree, shown ourselves faithful! It must give us pleasure in the review; but, oh, why
have not our prayers been more frequently presented
and more importunately enforced? Why have we not
been more serious and more pressing in our private address to them, and more attentive in our contrivances,
if I may so express it, to catch them* in the net of the

---

* On June 30, 1741, a meeting of ministers had been held at
Denton, Huntingdonshire, and after that a private conference, in
which Dr. Doddridge presented hints of a scheme for the revival of
religion, which was approved not only at the Denton conference,
but also by some of the most eminent of the London ministers of
different denominations, and at a meeting of ministers which was
held at Northampton the August following. Then it was agreed to
take them into a more particular consideration in a conference at
the next assembly, to be held at Kettering, on the 15th of October.
To that conference this discourse was introductory. The result was
that the scheme was approved with a few other particulars which
had not before occurred, and measures were taken to carry them
into execution. As they were printed originally with the discourse in
the form of resolutions, we attach them here:

1. That it may tend to the advancement of religion, the ministers of this association, if they have not already done it, should
agree to preach one Lord's day on family religion, and another on
secret prayer; and that the time should be fixed, in humble hope
that concurrent labors, connected with concurrent petitions to the
throne of grace, may produce some happy effect.

2. That it is proper that pastoral visiting should be more
solemnly attended to, and that greater care should be taken in personal inspection than has generally been used; and, that it may
conduce to this good end, each minister should take an exact sur-

vey of his flock and note down the names of the heads of families, the children, the servants, and other single persons in his audience, in order to keep proper memorandums concerning each, that he may judge the better of the particulars of his duty with regard to everyone, and may observe how his visits, exhortations, and admonitions correspond to their respective characters and circumstances.

3. That consequent on this survey it will be proper, as soon as possible, and henceforth at least once a year, to visit, if it is practical, every head of a family under our ministerial care, with a solemn charge to attend to the business of religion in their hearts and houses, watching over their domestics in the fear of the Lord, we, at the same time, professing our readiness to give them all proper assistance for this purpose.

4. That it will be highly expedient, immediately, or as soon as may be, to set up the work of catechizing in one form or another, and to keep to it stately for one half of the year at least; and that it is probable that future counsels may ripen some scheme for carrying on this work in a manner which tends greatly to the propagation of real, vital, catholic Christianity in the rising generation.

5. That there is reason to apprehend there are in all our congregations some pious and valuable persons who live in a culpable neglect of the Lord's Supper; and that it is our duty particularly to inform ourselves who they are, and to endeavor by our prayers to God, and our serious address to them, to introduce them into communion (to which I question not we shall all willingly add), cautiously guarding against anything in the methods of admission which may justly discourage sincere Christians of a tender and timorous temper.

6. That it is to be feared there are some, in several of our communions at least, who behave in such a manner as to give just offense; and that we may be in great danger of making ourselves partakers of other men's sins if we do not seek to reason with them; and that, if they will not reform, or if the crime is notorious, we ought, in duty to God and to them, and to all around us, solemnly to cut them off from our sacramental communion as a reproach to the church of Christ.

7. That it may, on many accounts, be proper to advise our

people to enter into little bands or societies for religious discourse and prayer, each consisting of six or eight, to meet for these good purposes once a week or a fortnight, as may best suit with their other engagements and affairs.

8. That it might be advisable, if it can be done, to select out of each congregation under our care a small number of persons remarkable for experienced prudence, seriousness, humility, and zeal, to act as a stated council for promoting religion in the said society; and that it would be proper they should have some certain times of meeting with each other and with the minister, to join their counsels and their prayers for the public good.

9. That so far as we can judge, it might, by the divine blessing, conduce to the advancement of these valuable ends that neighboring ministers in one part of our land and another (especially in this country) should enter into associations, to strengthen the hands of each other by united consultations and prayer; and that meetings of ministers might, by some obvious regulations, be made more extensively useful than they often are. In this regard it was further proposed (with unanimous approbation) that these meetings should be held at certain periodic times; that each member of the association should endeavor, if possible, to be present, studying to order his affairs so as to guard against unnecessary hindrances; that public worship should begin and end sooner than it commonly has done on these occasions; that each pastor preach at these assemblies in his turn; that the minister of the place determine who shall be employed in prayer; that after a moderate repast, to be managed with as little trouble and expense as may be, an hour or two in the afternoon be spent in religious conference and prayer, and in taking into consideration (merely as a friendly council, and without the least pretense to any right of authoritative decision) the concerns of any brother or any society which may be brought before us for our advice; and, finally, that every member of this association shall consider it as an additional obligation upon him to endeavor to be, so far as he justly and honorably can, a friend and guardian to the reputation, comfort, and usefulness of all his brethren.

10. That it may be proper to enter into some further measures to regulate the admission of young persons into the ministry. I will

gospel? Let us ask our own consciences this day, as in the presence of God, if there is not reason to apprehend that some who were once our hearers, and it may be our dear friends too, have perished through our neglect, and are gone to eternal destruction for want of our more prudent, more affectionate, and more zealous care for their deliverance!

In these instances, my brethren, though it is dreadful to say it, yet it is most certain that we have been, in part, accessory to their ruin; we have reason to say, with trembling hearts and weeping eyes, "Deliver us from blood-guiltiness, from the blood of these unhappy souls, O God, thou God of our salvation!" And we have need, with all possible earnestness, to renew our application to the blood and righteousness of a Redeemer, not daring to mention any services of our own as a matter of confidence in His presence—however highly others may have esteemed them, who candidly look on

---

take leave to add one particular more which has since occurred to my thoughts, and which I here submit to your consideration, and to that of my other reverend brethren into whose hands they may fall, especially those of our own association:

11. Whether something might not be done in most of our congregations towards assisting in the propagation of Christianity abroad, and spreading it in some of the darker parts of our own land. In pursuance of which it is further proposed that we endeavor to engage as many pious people of our respective congregations as we can to enter themselves into a society, in which the members may engage themselves to some peculiar cares, assemblies, and contributions, with a regard to this great end. A copy of such an association I am endeavoring to introduce among my own people and several have already signed it. It is a feeble attempt; but if it were generally to be followed, who can tell what a harvest such a little grain might at length produce! May God multiply it a thousandfold!

the little we do, and perhaps make more charitable excuses for our neglect than we ourselves can dare to urge before God.

Let the remembrance of these things be for a lamentation; and while it is so, let us seriously consider what methods are to be taken to prevent such things for the time to come.

They who have perished have perished forever, and are far beyond the reach of our labors and our prayers; but multitudes to this day surround us who stand exposed to the same danger, and on the very brink of the same ruin. And besides these dying sinners, who are the most pitiful objects which the eye of man or God beholds on this earth of ours, how many languishing Christians demand our assistance (or, if they do not expressly demand it, appear so much the more to need it)! Let us look around, my brethren, on the churches under our immediate care, and say whether the face of them is such as becomes the societies of those whom the Son of God has redeemed with His own blood, and of those who call themselves the disciples and members of a once crucified and now glorified Jesus. Is their whole temper and conduct formed upon the model of His gospel? Are they such as we would desire to present before the presence of His glory? What is wanting cannot be numbered; and perhaps we may be ready to rashly conclude that what is crooked cannot be made straight. Nevertheless, let us remember that it is our duty to attempt it, as prudently, as immediately, and as resolutely as we can. Many admirable advices for that purpose our fathers and brethren have given us; particularly Mr. Watts, in the first part of his *Humble Attempt for the Revival of Religion,* and Mr. Some in his sermon on the same subject. These are excellent treatises which, reduced into practice, would soon produce the noblest effects.

That those important instructions may be revived and accommodated to present circumstances, with such additions as those circumstances require, we are this day, having united our prayers to unite our counsels. I will not anticipate what I have to offer to your consideration in the more private conference on which we are quickly to enter. To form proper measures will be comparatively easy; to carry them strenuously into execution will be the greatest exercise of our wisdom and piety. May proportionable grace be given to animate us, and to dispose those who are committed to our care to fall in with us, in all our attempts for the honor of God and for their edification and comfort!

Preaching Christ

by
Rev. John Jennings

Professing ourselves to be Christians, I hope that we are satisfied, upon careful and rational inquiry, that the religion of Jesus comes from God, and that it is a most glorious dispensation, no less for the sublime wonders of its doctrine than the divine purity of its precepts. Now in all the peculiar glories of this religion, Christ is interwoven like Phidias's name in the shield itself, so that preaching Christ and preaching the gospel are, in Scripture style, synonymous terms.

To preach Christ, therefore, is our charge, our business, and our glory. But who is sufficient for these things? Give me leave, then, my dear brethren and friends, to remind myself and you what regard a minister should have to our Redeemer in his preaching.

Let us make Christ the end of our preaching. If we seek principally to please men, then we are not the servants of Christ. If we look no farther than our own reputation or temporal advantage, appropriating our talents to our own private use, how shall we make our accounts to our divine Master?

Our ultimate end should be the personal glory of Christ. That the glory of Christ as God is the ultimate end of the gospel, none can doubt; so that it is said of this divine Person, "All things are for Him as well as by Him." Is He not worth ten thousand of us? Is He not of more worth than the world, the only begotten Son of God, whom the highest angels adore? Now if the glory of Christ's person is the principal end in the divine schemes and actions, it should also be our highest view and design.

Again, as the glory of Christ's person should be our ultimate end, so the advancement of His kingdom of grace among men should be our subordinate end. The immediate design of the gospel is the recovery of fallen creatures to holiness and happiness. Christ has come into the world to save sinners, and He sends us to preach His gospel in order "that men might live soberly, righteously, and godly, looking for the blessed hope." We should not think it enough to inform, to amuse, to please, to affect, but we must aim further to bring them to trust in Christ, to be penitent and holy; and every subject must be managed with this view. And let it be our great care, on a speculative subject, still to keep the end in view, and apply it practically.

Let us by all means endeavor to save precious souls, but yet aim at a higher end, that we ourselves may be a sweet savor of Christ unto God; and then, though we miss our secondary end, and are not, as we could wish, "the savor of life unto life" to any great number, yet in being "the savor of death unto death to them that perish," we shall be the instruments of glorifying the justice and long-suffering of Christ, and be witness for God that there has been a prophet among them. Our primary end is answered; our labor is with the Lord, and we in the meantime are supported "though Israel be not gathered," for the Word shall not return empty.

Nay, further, it is not enough that the strain of our preaching is adapted to the true design of the gospel, but we must at heart sincerely intend it; otherwise, though our discourses are unexceptionable and others are saved through our ministry, yet if our designs are wrong and base we shall be castaways.

Let Christ be the matter of our preaching. Let us display the divine dignity and loveliness of His person as God manifest in the flesh; let us unfold His mediatorial office, the occasion, the design, and purport of His great undertaking; remind our hearers of the particulars of His incarnation, life, death, resurrection, ascension, and intercession; set forth the characteristics He bears as a prophet, priest, and king; as a shepherd, captain, advocate, and judge. Let us demonstrate the sufficiency of His satisfaction, the tenor and excellence of the covenant confirmed with and by Him, our justification by His righteousness, adoption through our relationship to Him, sanctification by His Spirit, our union with Him as our Head, and safe conduct by His providence; let us show how pardon, grace, and glory accrue to the elect through His suretyship and sacrifice, and are dispensed by His hand. Let us declare and explain His most holy laws in His name, and teach the people whatever duties He has commanded to God, our neighbor, and ourselves; quicken the saints to duty, raise their hopes, establish and comfort their souls by the exceedingly great and precious promises of the gospel, which in Him are "yea and amen." I give but short and imperfect hints of these things, and refer to the apostolic writings, which are made up of discourses on these and such like topics.

Let a continual regard to Christ distinguish our sermons on any subject from discourses on mere natural religion. If we speak of the perfections of God, let us consider them as shining as His Son, "who is the brightness of His Father's glory, and the express image

of His person," and exemplified in His undertaking. If
we set forth gospel blessings and promises, let us consider them as purchased by a Savior's blood and distributed by His bounty; for "by His own blood He has
obtained eternal redemption, and from Him the whole
body is supplied." If we take notice of the providence of
God, let us not forget that "all power is given to Christ
in heaven and in earth," and that "He is head over all
things to the church." If by the terrors of the last
judgment we persuade men, let "the wrath of the Lamb"
be pronounced, while the reckoning is represented as
most dreadful for abused grace and a slighted Savior;
for "this is the condemnation." And when we are assisting the devotions of the people, the same regard to
Christ should be observed.

When we are discoursing on the subject of duty,
Christ, as the most powerful motive, is by no means to
be forgotten; for to persuade men to practical godliness
is one of the most difficult parts of a minister's work.
Men will hear a speculative discourse with a curious satisfaction, and attend to the displays of God's grace with
some joy; nay, a Felix may tremble when judgment is
preached. Many, indeed, will bear to hear of duty too;
but to induce them to practice it is much harder work.
Here we have need to call in all helps, and take all advantages which the gospel, as well as the light of nature, can furnish. In other discourses we are rather at-
tacking Satan's out-works, a blind and prejudiced understanding, whereas in practical subjects we may gain
the understanding on our side with some share of the
affections; but to subdue a perverse will in favor of practical Christianity is not so easy a thing that we can afford to spare any important motive or quickening

consideration.[1] But here I must be more particular in
explaining how we should regard Christ in preaching
duty.

We should represent duty as the fruit of faith in
Christ, and as love for Him. When by faith we behold a
crucified Jesus, do we not tremble at the severity of
God's justice, and hate those sins that occasioned His
sorrows? When we consider that by His stripes we are
healed, can we forbear to love Him who first loved us?
Shall we not live to Him who died for us? Can we have
the heart to crucify Him afresh?

From such actions of faith and outgoings of love
flows that divine temper which constitutes the new
creature and lays the foundation of all right gospel duties up to their fountainhead, so that the people may
learn that it is not outward reformation which will
stand the test in the day of judgment, but an inward
renewal of the soul; that "the tree must first be made

---

[1] In reference to what is advised in this and the following sections, a
younger preacher will do well to read, with devotion and care, those parts
of Mr. Matthew Henry's practical and incomparable *Exposition* which relate
to the subject he would preach upon. He will also find in the works of Mr.
Arthur Hildersham, specifically in his expositions of Psalm 51 and John 14,
an uncommon degree of sacred skill in recommending duty and practice
from Christian motives, worthy of assiduous imitation.

Perhaps this may be the most proper place to recommend a work
lately published, *A Practical View of the Prevailing Religious System of Professed
Christians in the Higher Middle Classes in This Country, Contrasted with Real
Christianity,* by William Wilberforce, a work which, for excellence of plan, a
strain of masculine eloquence, acuteness of discernment, and force of reasoning, and above all a spirit of sublime devotion, is not perhaps equaled in
our language. Nor is it a small part of its excellence that it represents duty,
according to our author's advice, as the fruit of faith and love, enforcing
obedience with motives respecting Christ, to be performed by His grace,
and acceptable through His merits. (Dr. Daniel Williams)

good, before there can be any good fruit," and that all must be done for Christ's sake, and flow from faith working by love.

Let us enforce duties with motives respecting Christ. As grateful love for Him should constrain us, fear of His wrath should awe us, if we would show ourselves to be the disciples and followers of Christ, and enjoy communion with Him; if we would promote His honor and interest, and possess joy and not confusion at His appearing. Not that we should neglect any motives which the light of nature can furnish, and are equal to the capacities of the people (for we have need enough of all); but if we go no further, our exhortations will want for the greatest part of their weight. We must beseech and exhort by the Lord Jesus.

Let us inculcate duties as to be performed by the grace of Christ, telling the people that our fruitfulness depends on our being engrafted into this vine; that there is no holy walk without being led by the Spirit, and that when we do good, it is not we, but the grace of God that is in us; that out of a sense of weakness we are to be made strong, through Christ strengthening us.

Let us consider all good works as acceptable through the merits of Christ, and remind our hearers that could we do all we would be but unprofitable servants, and that we must seek to be found at last not having our own righteousness, but that which is of God by faith.

Let us express ourselves in a style becoming the gospel of Christ, not with great swelling words of vanity, or in the style of the heathen sophists, or in words that man's wisdom teaches and that perhaps sound best in our own ears; but let us use great plainness of speech, and seek to find out such acceptable words as may best reach the understanding and affections of the bulk of our audience.

As for the affectionate part of a discourse, brethren, I suppose you allow, upon a view of ancient and modern learning, that the men of the east, and next to them the ancient Greeks, excelled in fire and works of imagination; and yet the moderns, inhabiting milder western climates, even the French, from whom on many accounts we should expect the most of this sort, produce but an empty flash in comparison with the solid heat of the ancients, and rather amuse us with little delicacies than by masterly strokes command our whole souls. Now the Scriptures are the noblest remains of what the east has produced, and much surpass the best of the Greeks in the force of their oratory. Let us, therefore, take their spirit and style, and thence borrow bold figures and allusions, strong descriptions, and commanding address to the passions; but I am preceded in all I would say on this important head by the Archbishop of Cambray's *Dialogues Concerning Eloquence*, which I am as little capable of improving upon as I am of commending them as they deserve.[2]

---

[2] The sublime Fenelon's *Dialogues on Eloquence* are deservedly mentioned by many writers of eminence with a sort of respect bordering on veneration; and no wonder, for such a union of the sublime and simple, of learning and familiarity, of judicious criticism and happy illustration, such unaffected humility and warm benevolence, delicate taste and solid sense, and above all, such reverence for sacred things, blended with a subject so often employed by human vanity and pride, are superior excellencies very rarely found.

Dr. Doddridge (*Family Expositor* on John 14:2), having alluded

And now, brethren, let me lay before you some reasons and motives to back this friendly admonition concerning preaching Christ.

1. It is the only way to have our labors accepted of Christ, and to have communion with Him in our work. Even Paul cries out, "Who is sufficient for these things?" With how much more reason may we do so! Does not our cheerful progress in our work depend on a divine influence, and the spirit dispensed by Christ? But if we take little notice of Him in our preaching, and do not distinguish ourselves from the moral philosophers of the Gentiles, how can we expect any more of this enlivening and encouraging presence of Christ than they had? Nay, we have less ground to expect it if we slight willfully so noble a revelation, with which they were never favored.

2. It is the only way to win souls to Christ, and to make them lively Christians. The success of the gospel is owing, certainly, no less to the power of its precepts. These peculiar motives of the gospel have all such a re-

---

to a beautiful observation of this author, says, "This is the remark of the pious Archbishop of Cambray, in his incomparable *Dialogues on Eloquence*; which, may God put into the hearts of our preachers often and attentively to read!" Another able judge on this subject thus expresses himself: "But what need I enter further into the detail of pulpit eloquence? If you want to see the whole machinery and apparatus of it displayed in the completest manner, I refer you to the great and good Prelate of Cambray's *Dialogues* on that subject; who was himself the justest critic, and one of the best models of eloquence that I know" (Fordyce's *Theodorus* [London 1755], p. 150). For a brief but striking depiction of the eloquence of Fenelon, see the Abbe Maury's *Principles of Eloquence,* section lv.

(Daniel Williams)

spect to Christ, that they are enervated if He is disregarded. The gospel is what God in His unfathomable wisdom has fixed upon as the grand means to reform mankind and save them; and He seems in honor concerned to crown it with greater success than any other scheme whatsoever. The preaching of Christ crucified is the power of God. If by suppressing a part we maim the gospel, we can expect, in the nature of things, but a very defective success. Nay, may we not fear that God's honor is concerned, in such a case, to blast us while we labor almost in vain?

Observation agrees with this theory. The great masters of reason, who have less regard for Christ in their preaching, may indeed have a charm for one of a hundred who have a taste for the beauties of fine reasoning, and are of use to them while the bulk of an audience is asleep. Alas! With what heart can we go on, entertaining two or three, while starving most of the souls in an audience? May we not also observe a happier effect of a strain prudently evangelical on Christians themselves: that they who sit under it are more lively, zealous, ready to do every good work, and heavenly minded than those Christians who have heard less of the gospel?

3. It is a direct imitation of the apostles of Christ. Christ Himself, while upon the earth, preached the gospel in parables, in a concealed manner, distantly, and with reserve. He could not so fully take the advantage of His resurrection, satisfaction, ascension, and the like, not yet done, made, or proved. He had many things to say which His disciples could not then bear; but He declared them afterward by His Spirit in His apostles. They therefore are the true pattern of our preaching now, after the mystery of redemption has

been brought to light and has its full evidence.

How then did the apostles preach Christ? It is end-less to attempt a full detail of particulars; any part of the apostolic writings is sufficient authority for our pur-pose; and therefore I have been sparing in quotations all along, as needless to those who will look into these writings with this view. And here we do not desire to in-sist upon any passages in their writings which may be supposed to be written for reasons peculiar to that age and country in which the apostles wrote, and in which perhaps we are not so much obliged to imitate them in our preaching; for what will remain, after all these are put out of account, will, I am satisfied, be as full to our purpose as those that are struck off.

I shall then, by way of specimen, select some of the apostles' discourses on moral duties, where we are most apt to forget Christ or a due respect to Him, so that it may at once appear that the apostles neither shunned the pressing of such duties nor disregarded Christ in treating them.

Honesty is pressed by these motives: "The unrigh-teous, thieves, and extortioners, shall not inherit the kingdom of God" (which, in the style of the New Testament, is Christ's kingdom of grace and glory); that Christians are converted by the Spirit of Christ, and justified by His righteousness. Chastity is enjoined as our bodies are members of Christ, as we are one spirit with Him, temples of the Holy Ghost, and bought with a price. Almsgiving is recommended as it brings a large tribute of praise to God for our subjection to the gospel of Christ, and as Christ became poor for our sakes. Evil speaking is forbidden because we were once foolish and wicked, but the grace of God has made the difference. Not for our righteousness, but of His free mercy He has regenerated us, and given us His Holy Spirit, through Jesus Christ, by whom we are justified and heirs of glory. Subjects are commanded to obey magistrates because the gospel has come, and we should put on Christ Jesus. Husbands are charged to love their wives as Christ loved the church. The obedience of wives is urged, because the husband is the head of the wife, as Christ is the Head of the church. Servants are exhorted to their duty as they would adorn the doctrine of Christ, because grace so teaches, and that they look for Christ's appearance, who gave Himself for us that we might be holy. Now what is there in these motives that is peculiar to one age or nation? Are not all these as good now as formerly? And are men so ready in their duty that we have no need of them?

Nay, it is worthy of observation that the apostles do not confine themselves to motives peculiarly adapted to the duty they are pressing, and which serve to enforce one duty rather than another; but, as you may see, when such proper motives are not at hand, they take, without any scruple, common or general ones, which will equally enforce any duty whatsoever.

And why should we not introduce the peculiarities of the gospel on all occasions as frequently as the apostles did? If our schemes of theology will not allow us, we have reason to suspect that we are in a different scheme from the apostles. Are we afraid that men will make perverse use of such doctrines as the apostles used for motives? The apostles chose to venture it, and why should not we? If we will not dare to preach such a gospel as may be perverted by men of corrupt minds to their own injury, we must not expect to be instruments of any good. If we are a savor unto life to some, we must expect to be the savor of death to others, or not preach at all.

I confess, even the Remonstrant (Arminian) scheme (which, I think, considerably sinks the doctrines of grace) allows room to regard Christ abundantly more than most preachers of that denomination do. I would meet them on their own principles; what hinders their frequently inculcating the merits of Christ, the depravity of our nature, the necessity of regeneration, the aids of grace, and union and communion with Christ? These topics, it were to be hoped, might have their effect. But, alas, how few of the Remonstrants apply to their advantage so much of the gospel as they hold and receive! And it makes me less inclined to this scheme that it so generally draws those who embrace it into a strain of preaching, even on practical subjects, so different from that of the apostles. And it inclines them, I know not how, to suppress those glorious motives (which yet their own principles might allow) by which the apostles enforced gospel duties.

4. Only in this way shall we deserve the name of Christian preachers. "Only" did I say; I am afraid this may sound too harsh. Come, let us put the matter as softly and candidly as common sense will allow us. So shall we most evidently or best deserve this honorable title.

While a preacher keeps off from the peculiarities of the gospel, and says nothing but what the light of nature would also suggest and authorize, a stranger might possibly doubt whether he is a Deist or a Christian. The question is like an imperfect mathematical problem which equally admits of different solutions.

Suppose the ghosts of Paul and Seneca should come, mere strangers, into an assembly where someone is haranguing the people in this abstract manner. I am apt to think that Seneca would claim him as a philosopher of his own sect and religion. Now if Paul should also make his claim to him as a minister of Christ, how could the question be decided without allowing Seneca to be a preacher of Christ also?

On the other hand, if a preacher insists upon even the peculiar and glorious truths of Christianity, but so unhappily manages them as not to lead people to holiness, and the imitation of Christ thereby, what is this in the grand and full purpose of preaching or in the ultimate design of the gospel? Such preachers are quite off that divine system which is calculated to destroy the works of the devil, and to teach men sobriety, righteousness, and godliness. It is not only Christ outside us whom we are to preach, but also Christ in us, and our putting on Christ Jesus by a holy heart and life.

If the Apostle James should come again and visit our churches, and hear such a preacher, he would imagine himself among such people as he writes against in his epistle; he would be apt, when the minister had finished, in his zeal for Christ, to take the text in hand again and supply what the preacher had omitted, the application, and to say to the auditors, "Know ye not that faith without works is dead?" If the preacher should here interrupt him, saying, "Hold, spare your pains; the Spirit of God will make the application and teach men holiness," would not James reply, "I and the rest of the apostles were taught to preach otherwise, and to give particular exhortations to duty; we judged we might as well leave it to the Spirit, without our pains, to reveal the doctrine as to instruct men in the practice of the gospel"?

Upon the whole, brethren, let it be our resolution to study and preach Christ Jesus. On this subject, there is room for the strictest reasoning and most sublime philosophy; it deserves, invites, and inspires the strongest fire of the orator. In extolling Christ, we cannot shock the most delicate taste by overly strained hyperboles. Here the climax may rise till it is out of sight; our imagery cannot be too strong and rich.

Should our Lord Himself appear and give you a charge at your entrance on the ministry, would He not say (as indeed He has said), "As the Father hath sent Me, so send I you to preach the kingdom of God, that every knee may bow to Me, and every tongue confess Me. Teach them to observe all things whatsoever I have commanded you; tell them that without Me they can do nothing, and that when they have done all, they are unprofitable servants, and must be found in My righteousness. Become all things to all men; seek words which the Holy Ghost teaches that you may gain souls and bring in My sheep, for whom I have laid down My life. If you love Me, feed My sheep. I have called you friends; do all in My name and for My honor. So I will be with you always; and if you thus watch for souls, you shall give up your account with joy at My appearing. This is the preaching which, though it seems foolish to many, shall prove the power of God. Cast forth the net on this side, and you may expect to catch many souls. Be followers of My apostles as they are of Me, and in My name you shall do wonders. If you preach Me, I and Mine shall therein rejoice; be not ashamed of My gospel and I will not be ashamed of you."

But to arrive at any tolerable perfection in preaching Christ is a work of time, the result of a careful perusal of the Scriptures, and studying the hearts of men. It requires the mortifying of the pride of carnal reason, a great concern for souls, and a humble dependence on the Spirit of God, with the lively exercise of devotion in our closets.

As for the reasoning part on the more agreed points of our religion, a young preacher sooner may get to considerable excellence; but the Christian orator is longer in finishing. We may soon get necessary truths into our own minds, and come at minds of our size and taste; but by proper motives and ways to reach the souls of a different make and turn, even the lowest of the vulgar, is what very few quickly arrive at. But let us not despair. If we thus regard the Lord Jesus in our ministrations, we may very reasonably expect the assistance of His Spirit, and then we shall be able to do all things, through Christ strengthening us.

Particular and Experimental Preaching

by
Rev. John Jennings

To rightly divide the Word of truth is the necessary care of a minister, if he would be approved of God and be "a workman that needeth not to be ashamed." And it is a skill worth studying for, and laboring to attain; our success and the good of souls depend upon it more than is commonly imagined.

No doubt you may have heard many honest people express their dissatisfaction with some preachers in such terms as these: "They go on constantly in a general way that does not come close to the heart; they do not reach my case and experience, and I am not edified by them." Their complaint is not altogether without meaning or reason, as I hope you will be convinced by and by.

To keep a little in view that passage of Scripture I have mentioned, dividing the Word may mean these four things: (1) going through the variety of gospel subjects; (2) declaring the whole counsel of God; (3) explaining the doctrines of grace; and (4) pronouncing the threatenings, promises, and duties of morality, and giving each its due proportion.

Some, who find that their thoughts flow most readily and affectionately on the doctrines of grace, and that by these they best command the affections of the hearers, are altogether upon them, and neglect to teach the people to observe what Christ has commanded them. I bear many of them witness that they have a zeal for God, but I wish it were more according to knowledge. They do not sufficiently consider that holiness is the very design of Christianity; and our preaching on other topics is in order the better to enforce duty and render men like Christ.

I am afraid, from what I have observed, that this strain of preaching will increase the number of those hearers whom our Savior describes by the stony ground in the parable of the sower; namely, such who, though full of notions and transient affections, and forward in professing, yet have an unsubdued will, no root in themselves, and bring forth no fruit to God. This strain, I fear, though it may seem to bring many toward Christ, will bring but a few safely to Him. Many of their hearers, with Christ much in their mouths, will prove to be but hypocrites, settled on their lees and slaves to lusts. Nor is this strain more happy for the uniform growth of the sincere Christian. They who sit under it are too frequently low, imperfect, and partial in practical goodness; distempered with conceit and preposterous zeal for words and phrases, and things of little or no consequence; perplexed and perplexing others with a thousand groundless scruples; children in understanding. And it would be happy were they so in malice too. But, alas, their narrowness of mind infects the heart with uncharitable affections.

Others, having not arrived at the relish of the doctrines of grace themselves, suppress them in their preaching, and are altogether on morality. They enforce it with no motives of the gospel, except some of those addressed to fear. These, if they are masters of much fire, may be convincing to some; but it fares with most of their converts as with the man in the parable, out of whom the unclean spirit went for a while, who, finding his house empty, returned with seven more— and the latter end of such is worse than the beginning. Or else the awakened hearer either takes up a proud dependence upon mistaken, external, and pharisaical righteousness, or, not being led by his teacher to Christ, he does not proceed or settle. Abiding long under the doubtful concern, he is wearied with it, weary of it, and comes to nothing, as seems to be the thought in Hosea: "Ephraim is an unwise son; he shall not stay long in the place of the breaking forth of children." Or, lastly, if any are truly converted under such a ministry, it is very usual that they are forced to desert it, to find richer and sweeter pasture for their souls.

Some of their hearers may possibly prefer this strain of preaching; but it does not thence follow that they are the better for it. To illustrate this remark, I will recite a paragraph out of *Remarkable Passages in the Life of a Private Gentleman:* "Spiritually searching discourses I did not so much savor as mere moral doctrines, though too immoral myself. The hopes I had conceived of the strength of my good resolutions rendered them grateful. Seneca's *Morals* I read with pleasure; Mr. Baxter's *Saint's Rest* frightened me; so after reading a few passages, I threw it by." Thus with regret he tells us what little profit he had in that way, of his fondness for which he was ashamed, when he came to be of Paul's mind, to count all dross and dung, that he might win Christ.

For putting a thought in several distinct views and lights, for different purposes and designs, the sacred writers are herein our pattern, and that not by chance, but for wise reasons. One view is designed to raise one affection, another view to excite another of a different sort; and, finally, one of the views is designed as an antidote against the poison which the corruption of men's hearts might draw out of the other.

For instance, the terms and way of our justification and salvation are frequently stated thus: "That we must be found in Christ, having on the righteousness which is of God by faith," and "we must be made the righteousness of God in Him." And this view is exquisitely adapted to humble us, to draw forth love and gratitude, and to encourage our hopes and dependence.

But lest this phraseology, if used alone, should beget security, at other times we are told that "by works a man is justified, and not by faith only," that "faith without works is dead," and that the inquiry at the last day shall be who has fed the hungry and clothed the naked.

And most commonly these two views are united in the same paragraph, so that one may prevent the ill consequences man's perverseness would draw from the other, as physicians, finding some dangerous effect likely to follow from a drug of sovereign virtue, mix some other drug with it to prevent the fatal consequences.

So we are said to be "elect according to the foreknowledge of God, through sanctification of the Spirit unto obedience, and sprinkling of the blood of Jesus." Again, we are told that by grace we are saved through faith, which is the gift of God, not of works; for we are His workmanship, created in Christ Jesus unto good works.

I may give another instance in the different ways the Scripture speaks of power and duty. Sometimes we are told that we cannot come to Christ unless the Father draws us, that without Christ we can do nothing, and that if we live, it is not we, but Christ who lives in us. Now these views tend to hide pride from man, to create a diffidence of ourselves, and to center our hopes and dependence on Christ; but lest the slothful and wicked servant should make his impotence his excuse, we are called upon to turn and make ourselves new hearts; we are exhorted to ask and we shall receive; and we are assured that God will give the Spirit to them who ask Him. And how happily are these two views united in this passage: "Work out your own salvation with fear and trembling; for it is God that worketh in you to will and to do."

Now, less skillful dividers of the Word deal entirely in one of these views and neglect the other; and while they are laboring to excite one good affection, they raise another of a bad tendency together with it. To this in part it is owing that there are so many low or distempered Christians. Nor is this partiality more happy in effecting the real conversion of sinners, who generally, under such management, are either left asleep, and settled in a fond conceit of their own righteousness, or else stumble at the rock of offense (in a different manner indeed from what the Jews did), thinking to find by Christ a way to heaven without holiness or moral honesty.

Preachers of the Word are to distinctly explain and enforce particular duties, and oppose particular sins. It is true that the whole scheme of gospel duty is deducible from the general headings of faith and love;

but, alas, most men's minds are slow, confused, and erroneous in long deductions; and it is our business to
lead them on in every step, and to show what particular
duties to God, our neighbor, and ourselves will flow
from these principles, and are necessary to make them
the man of God perfect. We must particularly teach
them to add to their faith virtue, knowledge, temperance, patience, godliness, brotherly kindness, and
charity, if we would not leave them blind and unfruit-
ful. And we should, in a particular manner, speak of the
fruits of the Spirit, such as love, joy, peace, long-suffering, gentleness, goodness, faith, meekness, and temperance, and at proper seasons explain and enforce
each of them. We should apply the lamp of the Word to
detect and disgrace all the particular works of darkness,
and to make manifest the fruits of the flesh, such as
adultery, lasciviousness, wrath, strife, seditions, here-
sies, envyings, murders, drunkenness, revelings, and
such like.

If I should read to a sick person a learned lecture on
the benefit of health, and exhort him to take care to recover it, but never inquire into the nature of his disease
or prescribe proper methods and medicines for the
cure, he would hardly acquiesce to have me for his
physician, or resign to me the care of his bodily health.
Nor is it a more likely way to the soul's health to rest in
mere general exhortations to holiness without distinctly handling the several branches thereof and the
opposite sins.

We ought to particularly apply to the various cases,
tempers, and experiences of the hearers. Besides many
thoughts suited in general to all cases, there might
properly arise in the application of most subjects

thoughts distinctly proper to the converted and unconverted; to notional hypocrites and mere moralists; to mourners, backsliders, and lazy Christians, and at various times to a much greater variety of characters and persons. Now such particular addresses, when the case is drawn in a lively manner, in the natural language of the sort of men intended, and judiciously and artfully treated, are the closest, most weighty, and most useful parts of the application.

That this is the true way of addressing an audience, to divide them into several classes and distinctly speak to each, will be plain if we look through the apostolic writings, and, I might add, the prophetic also, with this view. We shall find that both prophets and apostles frequently take care to distinguish the holy and the vile, the converted and the unconverted. As, for instance, to their knowledge and apprehension of things: "The natural man receiveth not the things of the Spirit; they are foolishness to him; he cannot know them; but the spiritual judge all things." As to their obedience to the law: "The carnal mind is enmity against God; it is not subject to God's law, nor can it be subject, or please God."

They particularly reprove scoffers and confute gainsayers: "Behold, ye despisers, and wonder, and perish." For instance, to those who denied or cavilled at the resurrection: "Thou fool, that which thou sowest is not quickened except to die." And to those who were for a faith without works: "Wilt thou know, vain man, that faith without works is dead?"

They address carnal, stupid sinners in an awful way; they denounce woe "to them that are at ease." Paul made Felix tremble, and Stephen called them "ye stiff-necked and uncircumcised."

They lead convinced sinners to Christ. To those who are inquiring they say, "If ye will inquire, inquire ye, return, come; turn to the stronghold; if the Lord hath torn, He will heal." Then, "Repent and be baptized in the name of the Lord Jesus for the remission of sins." And, "Believe on the Lord Jesus Christ."

They reason with the moralist, and those who "trust in themselves that they are righteous," showing that their righteousness is as filthy rags. "The law saith there is none righteous, but all the world are guilty before God; therefore, by the deeds of the law shall no flesh be justified; but the righteousness of God is manifested, that God might freely justify them that believe on Jesus. Therefore man is justified by faith; boasting is excluded by the law of faith. And ye received the Spirit by the hearing of faith; the gospel was before preached to Abraham; they that are of the works of the law are under the curse. But the law could not disannul the covenant confirmed before, but was a schoolmaster to bring us to Christ, that we might be justified by faith; they then that are Christ's are Abraham's seed, and heirs according to the promise."

They sharply rebuke and expose pretending hypocrites, showing them their abominations, detecting and confounding the wretches who delight to know God's way and hear His Word, but will not do it. As Peter said, "Thou hast no part in this matter; thy heart is not right in the sight of God." Or as James said, "Show me thy faith without thy works; devils believe and tremble."

They rouse and encourage Christians who have but little strength, and persuade them to make farther ad-

vances in religion, so that he who is feeble may be as
David. "Ye are dull of hearing; for the time ye ought to
have been teachers. Strong meat belongeth to them
that are of full age; therefore, leaving the first principles, let us go on to perfection."

They deal with the several sorts of distempered
Christians tenderly, and yet plainly and faithfully, particularly with those who idolize one minister and despise others, telling them it is not by might and power
of man, but by God's Spirit that the gospel is successful.
"While one saith, 'I am of Paul,' and another, 'I am of
Apollos,' are ye not carnal? Who is Paul or Apollos, but
ministers by whom ye believed? It is God that giveth the
increase. Paul, Apollos, Cephas, all are yours."

They endeavor to soften those of too rigid a temper,
exhorting them not to speak to the grief of those whom
God has smitten: "Ye ought rather to forgive and comfort him; I beseech you to confirm your love towards
him." "If a man be overtaken in a fault, restore him in
the spirit of meekness, considering lest thou also be
tempted." They talk roundly to those who are apt to
make God the author of sin, to those who say, "We un-
avoidably pine away in our iniquities, and how can we
then be saved?" As in James, "Let no man say I am
tempted of God; for God tempteth not any man."

Declining Christians are quickened, awakened, and
put in mind of the love of their espousals: "Be watchful,
and strengthen the things which remain, that are ready
to die."

They awfully warn those who are in danger of sin-
ning and falling back to perdition, telling them that
"the righteousness they have done will be remembered
no more," and that God's soul will have no pleasure in

them. "It is impossible for those who were once enlightened . . . if they fall away, to renew them again to
repentance, seeing they crucify the Son of God afresh."

They encourage the persecuted and afflicted, telling
them that when they pass through the fire and water,
God will be with them, and that when they are tried,
they shall come forth as gold, and be the Lord's in that
day when He makes up His jewels. "The sufferings of
this present time are not worthy to be compared with
the glory that shall be revealed." "We are compassed
with a cloud of witnesses; Jesus endured the cross, and
is set down at the right hand of the Majesty on high;
whom the Lord loveth He chasteneth, and that for our
profit; chastening yields the peaceable fruits of righteousness." And more particularly, those who lament
relations dead in Christ are told that they shall go to be
happy with them, though the dead shall not return:
"Sorrow not as do others that have no hope; for those
that sleep in Jesus will God bring with Him."

There are also particular lessons for strong
Christians. They are to be tender to the weak, and to be
public-spirited, so that as "Ephraim should not envy
Judah, so neither should Judah vex Ephraim." "Him
that is weak in the faith receive; let not him that eateth
despise him that eateth not; let none put a stumbling-
block in his brother's way; let not your good be ill spoken of. Hast thou faith? Have it to thyself. Bear the infirmities of the weak. Let everyone please his neighbor
for his good to edification. Knowledge puffeth up, but
charity edifieth. Let not your liberty be a stumbling-
block to the weak, nor through thy knowledge let thy
weak brother perish, for whom Christ died. If meat
make my brother to offend, I will eat no flesh while the

world stands." Again, they are told that a mark is set upon the men who deplore the sins of the times; and "a book of remembrance is written" for those who distinguish themselves by their piety in times of abounding wickedness. "Thou hast few names who have not defiled their garments; and they shall walk with Me in white, for they are worthy."

You find also a suitable portion for those who are groaning under corruption, who complain that they were "shapen in iniquity," and that their actual errors are past understanding. Although "I am carnal, sold under sin, and what I would I do not, and what I hate that I do; in my flesh dwells no good, and to perform good I find not, yea, with the flesh I serve the law of sin. Oh, wretched man that I am!" yet, "I consent to God's law, and delight in it after the inner man; it is not then I that do this evil, but sin that dwelleth in me. I thank God through Jesus Christ: with my mind I serve God's law, and God will deliver me from the body of this death." And they are told how God has laid on Christ our iniquities, and that He will be the Lord our righteousness and strength. "If any man sin, we have an advocate with the Father, Jesus Christ the righteous."

The humble and penitent, who are of a contrite spirit and tremble at God's Word, are comforted: "Ye were sorry indeed, it was but for a season." In other words, it was after a godly manner. "I rejoice in it; such sorrow worketh repentance not to be repented of; it wrought in you carefulness, fear, desire, zeal, and renewal; you have shown yourselves clear in this matter."

They who lack direction, and cry out, "Oh, that my ways were directed to keep Thy statutes!" are sent to God for counsel. "If any man lack wisdom, let him ask it of God, and it shall be given him."

The deceiver and the deceived (those of evil minds who seduce others, and those who are misled in the simplicity of their hearts) are to be distinctly and differently treated: "On some have compassion, and others save with fear."

As for those of the house of Israel in desertion, who mourn after the Lord, who walk in darkness and see no light, and say, "The Lord has forsaken me," there were, I believe, few, if any, in those days of the plentiful effusion of the Spirit, when the gospel church was in its infancy, and "a nation was to be born in a day." There were but few, I say, who had doubts about their sincerity. They had persecutions, distresses, and exercises of another sort and those were sufficient. I am apt to think such cases were also rare in the beginning of the reformation from popery; this seems to be the occasion of some of the first reformers confounding faith with assurance. However, there are laid up in the New Testament some proper hints of counsel for such as should in later times labor under the hidings of God's face; they are told to examine themselves, to beseech the Lord, to clear themselves of sin, to not faint in well-doing, and the like.

Brethren, from your acquaintance with the Scriptures, you will easily perceive that I could run this specimen much farther through the sacred writings; and if you peruse the writings of the most powerful and successful preachers, particularly the Puritan divines, you will see that they herein imitated the great leaders of the Christian profession, and were large in their particular application to several sorts of persons, suiting their discourses to all the variety of the hearts of men, and sorts and frames of Christians, according to the precepts of Christianity, and (I may add) of true oratory. In this way they found their own hearts warmed, and thus they reached the hearts of their hearers, while many were imagining the minister had been told of their case, and made the sermon for them. And so was verified that passage: "The Word of God is quick and powerful, a discerner of the thoughts and intents of the heart."

Now, what success can we reasonably expect if we do not take into close consideration the case of our several spiritual patients? If a man, professing to be a physician, should administer or prescribe one constant medicine for fevers, and another for consumptions, and so for other distempers, without considering the age, constitution, strength, and way of living of his patient, and not vary his method and medicines as those vary, we would hardly call this the regular practice of medicine. Nor can I think this general and undistinguishing way will be more safe or likely to answer its end in divinity than in medicine.

Now I rest persuaded, brethren, that the thing is so evident that you cannot but allow it is best to suit ourselves to all the variety of tempers and experience of the hearers, if it can be done. And I hope some thoughts may be successfully offered upon the way how this skill may be attained.

1. Above all, then, carefully study your own hearts, and preach over the ruder sketches of your sermons to yourselves first. By this means the correspondent workings of your own hearts and affections may furnish you with proper thoughts wherewith to apply closely to all whose temper, experience, and case are like your own;

for what is supplied to your imperfect notes out of the applicatory meditations of your own minds on the subject will very probably, according to the usual way of the Spirit, happily and powerfully reach those of the same make in like circumstances.

2. But, alas, one man's experience falls far short of all the variety of men's hearts, and of the Spirit's work; nay, those whose heads are turned for close and regular thought, and whose time has been spent in study and letters, as they go on more rationally and evenly in religion, have less variety of experience than many of a different mold and way of thinking. It will be needful then to look out of ourselves and take a large view in order to be acquainted with cases and tempers different from our own, and with such methods of the Spirit's work as we ourselves have never experienced but many others have. Now the best and original way of getting this acquaintance with men, and with God's workings in them (and, I may add, of Satan's workings also), is by conversing freely with the serious people of our flock.

I know your thoughts will present me with an objection. You will say, "This is most impractical, especially among persons of politeness and figure; these, alas, too rarely will use any such freedom with us, in laying open their hearts and communicating their experience to us, as may give us the needful information. If we ever do arrive at any acquaintance with the experience of Christians, little thanks are due to such as these. They expect that we should preach suitably to them, and that with as much reason as Nebuchadnezzar demanded of the wise men to interpret a dream they knew not. The middle and lower sort of people, indeed, are more unreserved with grave ministers of age and standing, but will hardly use the same freedom with young men."

To help you over this difficulty, I would observe that, as for polite persons and men of some thought and reading, your own experience, with the allowances and corrections a moderate skill in human nature will enable you to make, may lead you into happy conjectures at their way of thinking. Besides, in the time of their visitation, under some sore affliction, you will find them more communicative; and an hour's free discourse with such as can give a rational and intelligible account of themselves, in a season when they are disposed to do it, is as valuable and useful as it is rare and difficult to enter into.

3. Again, have an eye upon the serious youth, whom nature and providence have designed to place in a superior class, and especially at a time when the impressions of religion are new to them. You will find them more open than elder persons, if you court their intimacy and relieve their bashfulness. And if you can see into the heart of a youth, then, with the proper allowances for alterations that age and business will make, you may pretty well guess at their turn of mind in more advanced years.

4. With the generality of serious and more advanced Christians, there need not be so much nicety to get into such a spiritual intimacy with them as we desire. Laying aside nicety and ceremony, and getting into such a grave, good-natured way as our character requires, is more than halfway to our purpose. Where this is insufficient to encourage the people to freedom, lead them into it by communicating, first, either what you yourselves have experienced, under the name of a third person (if modesty or prudence should require it), or

else what you have learned from others, without betraying the confidence they have put in you. By these methods we shall seldom fail to draw serious people on to such a freedom as will be of use to them and ourselves. If we heartily go about it, we are pretty sure to succeed.

I may farther hint at a compendious way for gaining much knowledge of men's hearts in a little time. If you have any tolerable skill in the different tempers and complexions of mankind, distribute, in your thoughts, your people into classes according to their natural genius and temper, and select one of each class with whom to be more particularly acquainted; for among those whom nature has formed alike, you will find, upon further inquiry, a striking uniformity in the Spirit's work and way of proceeding with them.

I might also recommend a way of knowing these things secondhand from the most popular and experimental authors; but this way is far inferior to the other. We shall but faintly paint any phenomenon of the heart by copying another picture; it is infinitely preferable to do it from the life. Yet I would earnestly recommend the perusal of such authors as deal much in an experimental strain, and have been very successful in it, but with a different design, so that we may learn from them how to describe, in a discreet and lively manner, such cases as we ourselves have observed, and how to address properly to those cases, with the like thoughts and expressions, as have in the course of their preaching happily answered the end.

After all, rightly to divide the Word of truth with true wisdom is a matter of no small difficulty; but if we carefully and diligently go about it, with a zeal for our

Master's interest, and sensible of our own insufficiency, asking wisdom of God, we know He gives liberally, and will surely make us wise to win souls, to the honor of His name and our own rejoicing in the day of the Lord Jesus. To whom, with the Father and Holy Spirit, that one God whom we adore, be paid the highest honors and praises to eternal ages. Amen.

Pastoral Cautions

by
Rev. Abraham Booth

As you, my brothers, are now invested with the pastoral office in this church, and have requested me to address you on the solemn occasion, I shall endeavor to do it with all the freedom of a friend, and with all the affection of a brother—not as your superior, but as your equal.

The language of divine law on which I shall ground my address is that memorable injunction of Paul in his charge to Timothy, "Take heed to thyself" (1 Timothy 4:16).

Very comprehensive, salutary, and important is this apostolic precept. For it comes recommended to our serious and submissive regard as the language of a saint who was preeminent among the most illustrious of our Lord's immediate followers; as the advice of a most accomplished and useful minister of the gospel, when hoary with age, rich with experience, and almost worn down by arduous labors; and as the command of an apostle, who wrote by the order and inspiration of Jesus Christ. This divine precept I shall now take the liberty of urging upon you in various points of light.

1. Take heed to yourself, then, with regard to the reality of true godliness and the state of religion in your own soul. That you are a partaker of regenerating grace, I have a pleasing persuasion; that you have some experience of those pleasures and pains, of those joys and sorrows, which are peculiar to real Christians, I

make no doubt. But this does not supersede the necessity of the admonition. Make it your daily prayer and your diligent endeavor, therefore, to feel the importance of those truths you have long believed, of those doctrines you now preach. Often inquire at the mouth of conscience, "What do I experience of their comforting, reproving, and sanctifying power?" When you have been preaching the promises of grace or urging the precepts of duty, earnestly pray that their practical influence may appear in your own dispositions and conduct. Endeavor to realize the force, and to comply with the requisition of that precept, "Grow in grace, and in the knowledge of our Lord and Savior Jesus Christ."

In proportion as the principles of true piety are vigorous in your heart may you be expected to fill up the wide circumference of pastoral duty. For there is no reason to fear that a minister, if tolerably furnished with gifts, will be remarkably deficient or negligent in any known branch of pastoral obligation while his heart is alive to the enjoyments and to the duties of Christian character. It is from the pastor's defects, considered under the notion of a disciple, that his principal difficulties and chief dangers arise. For, my brothers, it is only on the permanent basis of genuine Christian piety that your pastoral character can be established, or appear with respectability, in the light of the New Testament. I call genuine Christian piety permanent because everything essential to it will abide and flourish in immortal vigor, whereas the pastoral office, though honorable and important when connected with true godliness, must soon be laid aside as being inconsistent with the heavenly state.

2. Take heed to yourself, lest you mistake an in-

crease of gifts for a growth in grace. Your knowledge of
the Scriptures, your abilities for explaining them, and
your ministerial talents in general may considerably increase by reading, study, and public exercise, while real
godliness is far from flourishing in your heart. For,
among all the apostolic churches, none seem to have
abounded more in the enjoyment of spiritual gifts than
the church at Corinth; yet few of them appear to have
been in a more unhappy state, or more deserving of reproof. I have long been of the opinion, my brothers,
that no professors of the genuine gospel have more
need to be on their guard against self-deception, respecting the true state of religion in their own souls,
than those who statedly dispense the gracious truth.
For as it is their calling and their business, frequently,
to read their Bibles, and to think much on spiritual
things, to pray and preach and often to converse about
the affairs of piety, they will, if not habitually cautious,
do it all *ex officio*, or merely as the work of their ministerial calling, without feeling their own interest in it.

To grow in love for God and in zeal for His honor in
conformity to the will of Christ, and in heavenly-mindedness, should be your first concern. Look well, therefore, to your internal character. For it is awful to think
of appearing as a minister without really being a Christian, or of anyone officially watching over the souls of
others who is habitually unmindful of his own immortal interest.

In the course of your public ministry, and in a great
variety of instances, you may perhaps find it impracticable to enter into the true spirit of a precept or of a
prohibition so as to reach its full meaning and its various applications without feeling yourself convicted by

it. In cases of this kind, you must fall under the conviction secretly before God, and pray over it with undissembled contrition. This is agreeable to that saying, "Thou that teachest another, teachest thou not thyself?" When ministers hardly ever make this practical application of their public admonitions and cautions, as if their own spiritual interests were not a concern to them, their consciences will grow callous and their situation, with regard to eternity, extremely dangerous. For, this being habitually neglected, how can they be considered as walking humbly with God, which, nevertheless, is of such essential importance in the Christian life that, without it, all pretenses to true piety are vain? Hence an author, of no small repute in the churches of Christ, says, "He who would go down to the pit in peace, let him keep up duties in his family and closet; let him hear as often as he can have opportunity; let him speak often of good things; let him leave the company of profane and ignorant men, until he has obtained a great reputation for religion. Let him preach, and labor to make others better than he is himself. In the meantime, if he neglects to humble his heart to walk with God in a manifest holiness and usefulness, he will fail of his end."

3. Take heed that your pastoral office does not prove to be a snare to your soul by lifting you up with pride and self-importance. Forget not that the whole of your work is ministerial, not legislative; that you are not a lord in the church, but a servant; that the New Testament attaches no honor to the character of a pastor except in connection with his humility and benevolence, his diligence and zeal, in promoting the cause of the great Shepherd; and that there is no character

upon earth which so ill accords with a proud, imperious, haughty spirit as that of a Christian pastor.

If not intoxicated with a conceit of your own wisdom and importance, you will not, when presiding in the management of church affairs, labor to have every motion determined according to your own inclination. For this would savor of ecclesiastical despotism, would be inconsistent with the nature and spirit of congregational order, and would be implicitly grasping at a much larger degree of power and responsibility than properly falls to your share.

Nor, if this caution is duly regarded, will you consider it as an insult on either your ministerial wisdom or your pastoral dignity if now and then one or another of your people, and even the most illiterate among them, should remind you of some real or supposed inadvertency or mistake either in doctrine or in conduct; no, not even if it be in blunt language and quite unfounded. For a readiness to take offense on such occasions would be a bar to your own improvement, perhaps, in articles of relatively greater importance. Nay, in such cases, to be soon irritated, though not inconsistent with shining abilities, nor yet with great success in the ministry, would, nevertheless, be an evidence of pride and of your being, as a Christian, in a poor, feeble state. For to be easily shoved out of the way, pushed down, as it were, with a straw, or caused to fall into sin by so feeble an impulse must be considered as an undoubted mark of a great spiritual weakness. For the health of the soul and the vigor of the spiritual life are to be estimated not by our knowledge and gifts, but by the exercise of Christian graces, in cheerfully performing arduous labors, in surmounting successive difficul-

ties, and in patiently bearing hardships for the sake of
Jesus. Yes, and in proportion to the degree of your spiritual health will be your meekness and forbearance under those improprieties of treatment by one and another of your people which you will undoubtedly meet.
On examining ourselves by this rule, it will plainly appear, I presume, that though many of us in this assembly might, with regard to the length of our Christian
profession, be justly denominated "fathers," yet, with
reference to spiritual stature and strength, we deserve
no better character than that of rickety children. Think
not, however, that I advise you always to tolerate ignorant, conceited, and petulant professors in making ex-
ceptions to your ministry, or in calling you to account
for your conduct without reason, and without good
manners; but endeavor, with impartiality and prudence,
to distinguish between cases of this kind. Then the
simple and sincere, though improperly officious, will
not be treated with resentful harshness, but with some
resemblance of what is beautifully denominated "the
meekness and gentleness of Jesus Christ." But, alas,
how poorly we imitate our perfect Pattern!

It is of such high importance that a pastor possess
the government of his own temper, and a tolerable
share of prudence when presiding in the management
of church affairs, that without these his general integrity, though undisputed, and his benevolence,
though usually considered as exemplary, will be in
danger of impeachment among his people. Nay, notwithstanding the fickleness and caprice of many private professors with regard to their ministers, it has
long appeared probable to me that a majority of those
uneasinesses, animosities, and separations which, to

the disgrace of religion, take place between pastors and their several churches may be traced either to the unchristian tempers, to the gross imprudence, or to the laziness and neglect of the pastors themselves.

4. Take heed to yourself respecting your temper and conduct in general. Everyone who calls himself a Christian should fairly represent, in his own dispositions and behavior, the moral character of Jesus. The conversation of every professor should not only be free from gross defects, it should be worthy of general imitation. But though each member of this church is under the same obligations to holiness as yourself, yet your spiritual gifts, your ministerial office, and your pastoral relationships suggest a variety of motives to holiness which your people do not possess. Make it your diligent concern, therefore, to set your hearers a bright example, formed on that perfect model, the temper and conduct of Jesus Christ.

Yes, my brothers, it is required that pastors, in their own persons and conduct, especially in the discharge of ministerial duties, give a just representation of the doctrine they preach, and of Him in whose name they dispense it. But, in order to do this, though in an imperfect manner, what integrity, benevolence, humility, meekness, and zeal for the glory of God; what self-denial and readiness for bearing the cross; what mortification of corrupt affections and inordinate desires for earthly things; what condescension and patience; what contempt of the world and heavenly-mindedness are necessary not only the Scripture declares, but the nature of the thing shows.

Persons who are not acquainted with the true nature and genius of evangelical doctrine will be always disposed to charge the gospel itself with having a strong tendency to encourage those immoralities which appear in the character of its professors, and especially of those who preach it. Hence an apostle says, "Giving no offense in anything, that the ministry be not blamed." For what can persons, otherwise uninformed, with more appearance of reason conclude than that the example of those who propagate the doctrine of salvation by grace through Jesus Christ is an authentic specimen of its genuine tendency in the hearts and lives of all those who believe and avow it? In the ministry of religious teachers, there is an implicit language which is commonly considered by their hearers as importing that what they do and are, if disgraceful, is the effect not of their natural depravity or particular temptations, but of their doctrinal principles. Hence the ministers of Christ are commanded in all things to show themselves patterns of good works; to be examples to believers in word, in conversation, in charity, in spirit, in faith, and in purity. Yes, my brothers, the honor and preferment to which our divine Lord calls His ministers are to give a just representation, in their own conduct, of the graces of His person and the holiness of His doctrine to others. For whatever apparently splendid advantages a man may have, with reference to the ministry, if they do not enable him the more effectually, in his Christian course and ministerial work, to express the humility, the meekness, the self-denial, and the zeal of the chief Shepherd, together with the holiness of the doctrine he teaches, they will redound but little to his account another day.

5. I will now adopt the words of our Lord and say, take heed and beware of covetousness. That evil turn of

heart which is here proscribed with such energy and such authority is, through the false names it assumes and the pleas which it makes, to be considered as extremely subtle and equally pernicious. It evidently stands opposed in Scripture to contentment with the allotments of providence, to spiritual mindedness, and to real piety. It is an extremely evil disposition of the heart of which, notwithstanding, very little account is made by the generality of those who profess the gospel of divine grace except when it procures the stigma of penuriousness or the charge of injustice. But whatever excuses or palliatives may be invented, either to keep the consciences of covetous professors quiet or to support a good opinion of others respecting the reality of their piety, the New Testament declares them unworthy of communion in a church of Christ, and classifies them with persons of profligate hearts and lives. The existence and habitual operation of this evil, therefore, must be considered as forming a character for hell. Nor need I inform you that, for a long course of ages, myriads of those who assumed the appellation of Christian ministers have been so notorious for an avaricious disposition, for the love of secular honors, and for the lust of clerical domination as greatly to promote infidelity and expose Christianity to contempt.

Take heed, then, and beware of covetousness. For neither the comfort, the honor, nor the usefulness of a man's life consists in the abundance of the things which he possesses. Let your conversation be without covetousness and, possessing the necessities of life, without being indebted to any man, be content with such things as you have; for He who governs the world has said, "I will never leave thee nor forsake thee." For as man's happiness does not consist in things but in thoughts, that abundance after which the carnal heart so eagerly pants is adapted to gratify not the demands of reason, much less the dictates of conscience, nor yet the legitimate and sober claims of appetite, but a fond imagination, pride of show, the love of secular influence, the lust of dominion, and a secret desire of lying as little as possible at the mercy of providence. I have somewhere seen it reported of Socrates, the prince of pagan philosophers, that on beholding a great variety of costly and elegant articles exposed to sale, he exclaimed, "How many things are here that I do not want!" So, my brothers, when on entering the abode of wealth we behold the stately mansion, the numerous accommodations, the elegant furniture, the luxurious table, the servants in waiting, and the fashionable finery of each individual's apparel, with what propriety and emphasis ought each of us to exclaim, "How many things are here which I do not want, which would do me no good, and after which I have no desire!" For we should not forget who it was who said, "With what difficulty shall a rich man enter the kingdom of heaven!"

I said, possess the necessities of life without being indebted to any man. For this purpose, resolutely determine to live, if practicable, within the bounds of your income, not only so as to keep out of debt, but, if possible, to spare something for the poor. Suppose, my brothers, that either through the afflicting hand of God or the criminal neglect of your people unavoidable straits approach; be not afraid of looking poverty in the face, as if it were, in itself considered, a disgraceful evil. For poverty is a very innocent thing, and absolutely free from deserved infamy—except when it is found in scandalous company. But if its forerunner and its associates are pride, laziness, a fondness for good living, a want of economy, and the contracting of debts without a probability of paying them, it deserves detestation and merits contempt; it is inconsistent with virtuous conduct, and must gradually sink the character of any minister. If, on the contrary, it is found closely connected with humility and patience, with diligence, frugality, and integrity—such integrity as impels one, for instance, to wear a thread-bare coat rather than run into debt for a new one; to live on the meanest wholesome food, or to go with half a meal rather than contract a debt which is not likely to be discharged—such penury will never disgrace either the minister himself or the cause of Jesus Christ.

It will not disgrace the minister himself because, in the purest state of Christianity, the most eminent servants of our divine Lord were sometimes distressed with want of both decent apparel and necessary food. It will not disgrace the cause of Jesus Christ for His kingdom, not being of this world but of a spiritual nature, cannot be either adorned by riches or disgraced by poverty. Besides, the ministers of evangelical truth must be poor indeed in order to be in humbler circumstances than Jesus Himself was when proclaiming the glad tidings of His kingdom. It must, however, be acknowledged that so far as a faithful pastor is reduced to the embarrassments of poverty, merely by his people withholding those voluntary supplies which they were well able to have afforded, and to which, in common justice, equally as by the appointment of Christ, He had an undoubted right, the best of causes is disgraced and the offenders are exposed to severe censure.

Were a pastor driven to the painful alternative of either entering into some lawful secular employment or continuing his pastoral relation and stated ministrations in a course of embarrassment by debts which he could not pay, the former would become his duty. This is not only because we ought never to do evil that good may come, but also because it is much more evident that he ought to owe no man anything other than what the Lord ever called him to or qualified him for. But, if necessity does not impel, the following passage seems to have the force of a negative precept respecting the Christian pastor: "No man that warreth entangleth himself with the affairs of this life, that he may please him who hath chosen him to be a soldier." A pastor should be very cautious not only of entering, unnecessarily, into stated secular employment, but also of accepting any trust, though apparently advantageous, in which the preservation and the management of property are confided to his integrity and prudence. For so critically observed is the conduct of a man who has the management of another's pecuniary affairs, and so delicate is a minister's character, that he is in peculiar danger of exposing himself to censure, and of injuring his public usefulness, by such engagements.

6. Take heed, I will venture to add, to your second self in the person of your wife. As it is of high importance for a young minister in a single life to behave with the utmost delicacy in all his intercourse with female friends, treating with peculiar caution those of them who are unmarried, and as it behooves him to pay the most conscientious regard to religious character when choosing a companion for life, so, when in the conjugal state, his tenderest attention is due to the

domestic happiness and the spiritual interest of his wife. This obligation, my brothers, manifestly devolves upon you who are already husbands and fathers. Next after your own soul, therefore, your wife and your children evidently claim the most affectionate, conscientious, and pious care.

Nor can it be reasonably doubted that many a devout and amiable woman has given her hand to a minister of the gospel in preference to a private Christian, though otherwise equally deserving, in sanguine expectation by so doing of enjoying peculiar spiritual advantages in the matrimonial relation. But, alas, there is much reason to apprehend that not a few individuals among those worthy females have often reflected to the following effect: "I have, indeed, married a preacher of the gospel; but I do not find in him the affectionate domestic instructor for either myself or my children. My husband is much esteemed among his religious acquaintances as a respectable Christian character, but his example at home is far from being delightful. He is affable, condescending, and pleasing in the parlors of religious friends, but frequently either trifling and unsavory, or imperious and unsocial in his own family. He prefers the opportunity of being entertained at a plentiful table, and of conversing with the wealthy, the polite, and the sprightly, to the homely fare of his own family, and the company of his wife and children; he often spends his afternoons and evenings away from home until so late an hour that domestic worship is either omitted or performed in a hasty and slovenly manner, with scarcely the appearance of devotion. There is little caring for my soul, or for the management of growing offspring; he seems concerned for hardly anything

more than keeping fair with his people, relative to
which I have often calmly remonstrated and submis-
sively entreated, but all in vain. Surrounded with little
ones, and attended with troubles; destitute of the sympathies, the instructions, the consolations which
might have been expected from the affectionate heart
of a pious husband, connected with the gifts of an
evangelical minister, I pour out my soul to God, and
mourn in secret." Such, there is ground of apprehension, has been the sorrowful soliloquy of many a minister's pious, dutiful, and prudent wife. Take heed, then,
to the best interests of your second self.

To this end, except on extraordinary occasions
when impelled by duty, spend your evenings at home.
Yes, at an early hour in the evening, let your family and
your study receive their demands on your presence in
the lively performance of social and secret devotion.
Thus there will be reason to hope that domestic order
and sociability, the improvement of your own understanding, and communion with God will all be pro-
moted.

Guard, habitually, against every appearance of imprudent intercourse and every indelicate familiarity
with the most virtuous and pious of your female friends.
Be particularly cautious of paying frequent visits to any
single woman who lives alone; otherwise, your conduct
may soon fall under the suspicion of your neighbors,
and also of your wife, so as to become her daily tormentor, even while she believes you innocent of the great
transgression. In cases of this kind, it is not sufficient
that conscience bears witness to the purity of your conduct and the piety of your motives; for in matters of
such a delicate nature there should not be the least

shadow of a ground either to support suspicion or to excite surmise. There is need for us, my brothers, to watch and pray against the greatest sins, even against those to which, perhaps, we never perceive ourselves to be much inclined. For, alas, we have sometimes heard of apparently pious and evangelical ministers falling into such enormous crimes as not only disgrace religion, but degrade humanity!

Of late, I have been much affected with the following reflection: "Though, if not greatly deceived, I have had some degree of experimental acquaintance with Jesus Christ for almost forty years; though I have borne the ministerial character for upwards of twenty-five years; though I have been, perhaps, of some little use in the church of God; and though I have had a greater share of esteem among religious people than I had any reason to expect—yet after all, it is possible for me, in one single hour of temptation, to blast my character, to ruin my public usefulness, and to render my warmest Christian friends ashamed of owning me. Hold Thou me up, O Lord, and I shall be safe!" Ah, brothers, there is little reason for any of us to be high-minded. And, therefore, "Happy is the man that feareth always."

7. Take heed to yourself with regard to the diligent improvement of your talents and opportunities in the whole course of your ministry. It behooves you as a public teacher to spend much of your time in reading and in study. Of this you are convinced, and will act, I trust, agreeably to that conviction. For suitable means must be used not only in your public ministry, in season and out of season, for the good of others, but with a view to the improvement of your own mind in an acquaintance with divine truth. Yes, my Christian friends, it is neces-

sary that your ability to feed the flock with knowledge and understanding may be increased so that your own heart may be deeply tinctured with evangelical principles, that you may be the better prepared for every branch of pastoral duty and for every trying event that may occur. For who can reasonably deny the necessity of diligence in the use of means, adapted, respectively, to promote your own ministerial improvement, and to obtain the great objects of your pastoral office any more than to a rational prospect of success in the management of secular business? Be, then, as careful to improve opportunities of both obtaining and imparting spiritual benefits as the prudent and assiduous tradesman or mechanic is to promote the legitimate designs of his professional calling.

If a minister of the gospel behaves with Christian decorum, possesses tolerable abilities for his work, and, having his heart in it, is habitually industrious, there is reason to conclude that in the common course of providence he shall not labor in vain. As nobody, however, wonders that a merchant or a manufacturer who, having no pleasure in his employment, neglects his affairs, and behaves as if he thought himself above his business, does not succeed but becomes bankrupt, so, if a minister is seldom any further engaged either in the study of truth or in the public exercises of religion than seems necessary to his continuance, with decency, in the pastoral station, there is no reason to wonder that his public devotion is without savor and his preaching is without success. The church of which such a minister is the pastor seems completely warranted to cry in his ears, "Take heed to the ministry which you have received from the Lord! See that you fulfill it."

8. Take heed to yourself respecting the motives by which you are influenced in all your endeavors to obtain useful knowledge. For if you read and study chiefly that you may cut a respectable figure in the pulpit, or to obtain and increase popular applause, the motive is carnal, base, and unworthy of a man of God. Yet, detestable in the sight of Him who searches the heart as that motive is, there will be the greatest necessity for you to guard against it as a besetting evil. It is, perhaps, as hard for a minister habitually to read and study with becoming diligence, without being under this corrupt influence, as it is for a tradesman prudently to manage a lucrative business without seeking the gratification of a covetous disposition. Yet both the minister and the tradesman must either guard against these pernicious evils or be in danger of sinking in final ruin.

Besides, whatever are the motives which principally operate in your private studies, it is highly probable that those very motives will have their influence in the pulpit. If, when secretly studying the Word of God, it was your chief concern to know the divine will, that you might with integrity and benevolence lay it before your people for their benefit, it is likely that the same holy motive will attend you in public service. But if a thirst for popularity or a lust for applause had the principal influence in the choice of your subject, and in your meditations upon it, there will be no reason for surprise if you should be under the same detestable bias when performing your public labor.

Study your discourses, therefore, with a devotional disposition. To this you are bound by the very nature of the case as a Christian minister. For when the Bible is before you it is the Word of God on which you meditate, and the work of God you are preparing to perform. It is reported of Dr. Cotton Mather that in studying and preparing his sermons, he would endeavor to make even that an exercise of devotion for his own soul. Accordingly his way was, at the end of every paragraph, to make a pause, and endeavor to make his own soul feel some holy impression of the truths contained in it. This he thought would be an excellent means of delivering his sermons with life and spirit, and warming the hearts of his people by them; and so he found it.

It is indeed an easy thing for a preacher to make loud professions of regard to the glory of God and the good of immortal souls as the ruling motive in his ministerial conduct; but experience has taught me that it is extremely difficult for any minister to act suitably to such professions. For as that pride which is natural to our species impels the generality of mankind to wish for eminence rather than usefulness in this or the other station, so it is with ministers of the Word. Forty years ago I saw but little need of this caution compared with that conviction of its necessity which I now have. A preacher of the real gospel, I am fully persuaded, may appear exceedingly earnest and very faithful in his public labors, as if his only design were to promote the gospel truth, the happiness of men, and the honor of God, while nevertheless he is more concerned to figure away at the head of a large body of people in the religious world than to advance the genuine interest of Jesus Christ and the felicity of his fellow mortals. What is it but this detestable pride that makes any of us ministers take more pleasure in perceiving our labors to be made useful to the rich, the learned, and the polite than to the poor, the illiterate, and the vulgar? It is, I presume, principally because it adds consequence to our own characters to have wealthy, well-educated, and polished persons in our churches. Jesus, however, in the time of His personal ministry, was far from being influenced by any such motive, and equally far from showing the least predilection for persons of promising dispositions on any such grounds. Witness His behavior to Nicodemus, to the young ruler, and to the nobleman at Capernaum.

I will add, what is it but the same depravity of heart that frequently renders us much more attentive to our wealthy friends than we are to our poor brethren in times of affliction, even though we are well assured that there is little danger of the rich being overlooked in their sorrows? Hoary as I now am in the ministry, and accustomed as I have been to hear conscience cry out against me for this, that, and the other omission of duty, I do not recollect that it ever charged me with neglecting any person in plentiful circumstances when deeply afflicted and requesting my visits. But, alas, I do recollect having frequently heard conscience, with a frowning aspect and an angry tone, either demanding, "Would you be this backward to undergo some little inconvenience in visiting a wealthy patient?" or declaring, "That afflicted brother would not, through mere forgetfulness, have been recently disappointed of your presence, conversation, and prayers had he not been an obscure and a poor man. Had he been less deserving of my compassionate regard, he would have been favored with it." Alas, my brothers, there is reason to fear that few ministers on this ground stand perfectly free from censure at the bar of a tender conscience!

As you should take heed to yourself respecting the

principles on which you act and the ends at which you aim in your preparations for the pulpit, so it behooves you to be still more careful in these respects when you enter on public service. For then you professedly appear as a guilty creature to adore at the feet of the Eternal Majesty, as a minister of the divine Jesus to perform His work, and as the servant of your church to promote the happiness of all its members. Endeavor, therefore, always to enter your pulpit under the force of this conviction: "I am an apostate creature, and am going to worship the omniscient God. I am a wretch who deserves to perish, yet I look to sovereign mercy. I am a sinner called by the gospel, and trust in the great atonement. I am confessedly insufficient for the work on which I am entering, but rely on the aids of grace." This will produce deep solemnity, tempered with devout delight, which mixture of holy awe and sacred pleasure should accompany the Christian, and especially the Christian minister, whenever he approaches the Supreme One.

Remarkable and important is that saying, "Let us have grace whereby we may serve God acceptably, with reverence and godly fear; for our God is a consuming fire." Very observable also is the language of David: "I will go to the altar of God, to God my exceeding joy." May the cumulative import of these passages exert its force on your very soul whenever you take the lead in public worship! Then your graces as a Christian and your gifts as a minister will be exercised at the same time. Your graces being excited, you have communion with God; your gifts being exerted, the people are edified—whereas, were you to enter the pulpit merely to exercise your ministerial talents, though others might be fed by the truths delivered, your own soul would starve. This, I fear, is the case of many who preach the gospel.

But what a figure in the eye of Omniscience must that preacher make who is not habitually desirous of exercising devout affections in the performance of his public work! Like a sign on the high road, he directs others in the way to heaven, but he walks not in it himself. He may prophesy with Balaam or preach with Judas; his learning and knowledge, his natural parts and spiritual gifts may excite admiration and be useful to others; but, being destitute of internal devotion, his heart is not right with God, and he is a wretched creature. Sounding brass or a tinkling cymbal is the image by which he is known in sacred Scripture.

When, however, commencing public service, it is needful to remember that you appear not only as a worshipper of God, but as a minister of Christ. Being such, it is your indispensable duty to preach Christ and not yourself, that is, with sincerity and ardor to aim at displaying the glories of His person and the riches of His grace, the spirituality of His kingdom and the excellence of His government—not your own ingenuity or eloquence, your parts or learning. Guard then, my brothers, against the most pernicious evil; guard, as for your very life, against converting the gospel ministry into a vehicle to exhibit your own excellence, against prostituting the doctrine of Christ crucified to the gratification of your pride or that it may be a pander to your praise. For who can estimate the magnitude of all that guilt which is included in such conduct? Yet I cannot forbear suspecting that many ministers are more or less chargeable with this enormous and horrible evil. Nay, to the commission of this outrage on the honor of

Christ and of grace every minister should consider himself as liable. For so polluted are our hands that, without grace preventing, we defile everything we touch. So depraved are our hearts that we are in danger of committing a robbery on the glory of our divine Lord, even when it is our professed business to exalt it.

When entering on public devotion, you should endeavor to act as becoming your character, under the notion of a guilty creature, in audience with the King Eternal; and as a minister of Christ, whose business it is to display His glory, you are further to consider yourself as the servant of His church. When standing up to address your people, it should ever be with an earnest desire to promote their happiness. They have chosen you to the pastoral office; you have accepted their invitation and are now solemnly ordained to the important service. That mutual agreement and the interesting transactions of this day should operate as a threefold motive to the faithful performance of your public work. Yes, you are bound affectionately to aim at doing them good by laying divine truth before them in such a manner as is adapted to enlighten their minds, affect their hearts, and promote their edification.

Though the occasional exercise of your ministerial talents in other places may be both lawful and commendable, yet, as it is here only that you stand in the pastoral relation, you ought, except in extraordinary cases, to fill this pulpit yourself, and not leave the deacons to procure supplies in a precarious manner while you are serving some other community. It is here as a public teacher that your proper business lies; and it is here, at the usual times of assembling, that your voice must be heard. When the pastor of a church discovers an inclination to avail himself of almost any pretext for being absent from his people in order to serve others, he gives reason for suspicion, whatever his pretenses may be, that either filthy lucre or a lust for popularity has too much place in his heart, and that he accepted the pastoral office rather as an article of convenience than as a matter of duty. It is, indeed, much to be lamented that though dissenting ministers in general justly exclaim against the non-residence and the holding of pluralities which are so common among the clergy, yet the conduct of some pastors among the noncomformists makes near approaches to that of pluralities in our national establishment, and is a violation of pastoral duty.

You should seek with peculiar care to obtain the approbation of conscience in each of your hearers, as appears by the following words: "By manifestations of the truth commending ourselves to every man's conscience in the sight of God." This illustrious passage presents us with a view of Paul in the pulpit, and a very solemn appearance he makes! He has just been adoring in secret at the feet of the Most High; and, fresh from converse with the Most Holy, he is now going to address his fellow sinners. Penetrated with the importance of his office and the solemnity of his present situation, he manifestly feels—he seems to tremble. Nor need we wonder, for the subject on which he is to speak, the object he has in view, and the witness of his conduct are all interesting and solemn to the last degree. Truth, conscience, and God, the most important and impressive thoughts that can enter the human mind, pervade his very soul. Evangelical truth is the subject of his discussion; the approbation of conscience is the object of his desire; and the omniscient Holy One is the witness of his conduct. This example you and I, and every minister of the Word, are bound to imitate. Make it your diligent endeavor, then, to obtain the approbation of conscience from all who hear you, for without deserving that, none of your public labors can be to your honor, or turn to your own account, in the great day of the Lord.

A minister may say things which are profoundly learned and very ingenious, that are uncommonly pretty and extremely pleasing to the generality of his hearers, without aiming to reach their consciences and to impress their hearts either by asserting divine authority or by displaying divine grace. When this is the case, he obtains, it may be, from superficial hearers, the reward which he sought; for he is greatly admired and applauded. But, alas, the unawakened sinner is not alarmed, the hungry soul is not fed, and the Father of mercies is defrauded of that reverence and confidence, of that love and obedience, which a faithful declaration of the gracious and sanctifying truth might have produced. Yes, my brothers, it is much to be suspected that many ministers have recommended themselves to the fancies, the tastes, and the affections of their hearers who never deserved, and who never had, in a serious hour, the approbation of their consciences.

Be ambitious, therefore, to obtain and preserve the suffrage of conscience in your favor, whether admired and honored with verbal applause or not. For it is evident from observation that a preacher who is endued with a competent share of learning and fine parts, a retentive memory and good elocution, may recommend himself to the admiration of great numbers while their consciences, in the hour of solemn reflection, bear testimony against him. As a minister may have all those engaging qualifications while habitually proud and covetous, deceitful and vain, so the conscience never feels itself interested in the fine imagination, the genius, or the learning which a minister displays in his public services. It is worthy of remark, my brothers, that though none of us can command success to our labors were we ever so pious, diligent, and faithful, and though it may not be in our power to obtain the applause of literature, of genius, or of address, yet, in the common course of things, if we are assiduous, benevolent, and upright in our labors, we may secure the approbation of conscience in the generality of our stated hearers; and this is an article of great importance to the tranquility of a minister's own breast.

Now, my young friends, if you keep conscience in view, and if you remember that God Himself is a witness of your latent motives and your public labors, you will not choose an obscure text principally that you may have the honor of explaining it; nor will you select one which has no relation to the subject you mean to discuss in order that your acumen may shine by making it speak what it never thought. The more you keep the approbation of conscience and the presence of God in your eye, the more dependent will you be on divine assistance in all your ministerial addresses. Yes, bearing in mind, on every occasion of this kind, that your business here is to plead for the interests of evangelical truth, under the immediate inspection of Him who is the Truth, you cannot but feel your incapacity and look for assistance to God, whose cause you mean to promote. The more you keep the consciences of men and the presence of God in your view, the more will you be impressed with the importance of your subject, and the more earnest will you be in addressing your hearers; for that minister must have a strange set of passions who does not feel himself roused by such considerations. The more you keep the approbation of conscience and the inspection of God in remembrance, the less will you be disposed to indulge a light and trifling spirit, and the more devotional will you be in the course of your administrations; for the ordinances of God are too sacred to become the vehicles of entertainment, and His presence is too solemn to permit the smile of levity.

Again, keep the consciences of men and the Searcher of hearts in view, and it will afford you much more pleasure to find that persons who have been hearing you left the place bemoaning their apostate state, and very deeply abased before the Most Holy, than to be informed that they greatly admired you as a preacher and loudly applauded your ministerial talents. For a person to depart from public worship in raptures with the minister's abilities is no proof that he has received any spiritual benefit. But if, smitten with a sense of guilt, he cries out, "How shall I escape the wrath to come? God be merciful to me, a sinner!" or if he exclaims, "Who is a God like unto our God? How great is His goodness, and how great is His beauty! What shall I render to the Lord for all His benefits?"—then it looks as if the preacher has commended himself to his conscience, and as if the truth has reached his heart. For language of this kind from a reflecting hearer has a devotional aspect, and gives glory to God. It indicates a soul either as being apprehensive of deserving ruin, or as rejoicing in revealed mercy; as having a good hope through grace, or as revering divine authority. In contrast simply to admire and praise the preacher is quite consistent with reigning depravity and with rooted enmity to God. As it is written, "They sit before thee as My people, and they hear Thy words; with their mouth they show much love, but their heart goeth after their covetousness. And lo, thou art unto them as a very lovely song of one that hath a pleasant voice, and can play well on an instrument; for they hear thy words, but they do them not."

Once more, in proportion as the approbation of conscience and the inspection of God are properly kept in view, the pleasure you have, arising from verbal commendations of professed friends, and the pain of strong opposition from the avowed enemies of evangelical truth will be diminished. For conscience does not often express itself in the language of noisy applause, which, when free from hypocrisy, is commonly the fruit of a weak understanding under the influence of strong passions. Hence it is not uncommon for those who have been the most liberal in praising a minister to be found among the first who entirely desert his ministry. As for unfounded censures and violent opposition, the testimony of a good conscience and the countenance of Scripture are adapted to afford the needful support.

9. Take heed to yourself with regard to that success and those discouragements which may attend your ministry. Should a large degree of apparent success, through the favor of heaven, accompany your labors, there will be the highest necessity to guard against pride and self-esteem. A young man of good ministerial abilities, and honored with great usefulness, is in a delicate situation respecting the prosperity of his own

soul; for through the want of experience and observation, such concurrence of pleasing particulars has proven to be for some very promising characters the innocent occasion of disgrace and ruin. Shining abilities and a blessing upon their labors have rendered them popular. Popularity has intoxicated them with pride. Pride has exposed them to various temptations. Temptations have prevailed, and either precipitated them into some enormous offense, or laid the foundation for a gradual departure from the truth and from the practice of real piety. If the former, their character has been killed as by the stroke of an apoplexy. If the latter, their comfort and usefulness have been destroyed as by a consuming fever, agreeable to that saying, "Pride goeth before destruction, and a haughty spirit before a fall."

Remember, therefore, my brothers, that though it is your indispensable duty to labor and pray for prosperity in your work, yet a season of remarkable success will generally prove to be an hour of peculiar temptation to your own soul. Take heed to yourself at such a time, and watch the secret motions of your own heart. The number of your hearers may increase and your church may flourish, while in your own breast devotional affections and virtuous dispositions are greatly on the decline. Nor need I inform you that every degree of such declension has a tendency to final ruin.

Besides, if there should be an appearance of extensive utility attending your labors (for which I sincerely pray), you may do well to remember the old proverb, "All is not gold that glitters." Many there are who seem to receive the Word with joy but who, in time of temptation, fall away. Many evangelical and popular preachers, I am very suspicious, have greatly overrated the usefulness of their own labors. For the longer I live, the more apprehensive I am that the number of real converts among those who profess the genuine gospel is comparatively very small, according to the import of that alarming declaration, "Many are called, but few are chosen."

On the other hand, should you meet with many and great discouragements, take heed that you do not indulge a desponding temper, as if you had been of no use in the ministerial work. With discouragements you certainly will meet, unless providence were to make your case an exception to the general course of things (which you have no ground to expect). Very painful discouragements, for instance, may sometimes arise from the want of liberty and savor in your own mind when performing public service. This, there is reason to suppose, is not uncommon. I, at least, have had frequent experience of it, and once to such a degree that I began to think very seriously of giving up the ministry, supposing that the Great Shepherd had nothing further for me to do either in the pastoral office or in preaching the Word at large. This exercise of mind, though exceedingly painful for some weeks, was both instructive and useful. Before that well-recollected season, I had frequently talked about the necessity of divine influence to render a minister savory in his own mind, as well as profitable to others, but it was then that I felt it.

Be not discouraged, then, as though some strange thing happened unto you that never befell a real minister of Christ, if a similar trial should occur in the course of your ministry. For it may be to you, as I trust it was to me, of no inconsiderable benefit, because I reckon that whatever curbs our pride, makes us feel our insufficiency, and sends us to the throne of grace is of great profit. Seldom, alas, have I found any remarkable degree of savor and enlargement in public service without experiencing, more or less, self-elation and self-congratulation on that account. Instead of complaining, therefore, that I have no more liberty in my work, or more success attending the performance of it, I have reason to wonder at the condescending kindness of God in that He gives to my extremely imperfect labors the least saving effect, and that He does not frequently leave me to be confounded before all my hearers. Such, brothers, have been the feelings and reasonings of my own mind, and such my confessions before God many a time.

It is not unlikely that, in a course of years, some of your people who had expressed a warm regard for your ministry, and perhaps considered you as their spiritual father, may become, without any just reason, your violent opposers, cast aspersions on your ministerial character, and wish to be rid of you. This, though very trying, is far from an unprecedented case; no, not with regard to much greater men, and far better ministers than any of us. Witness the language of Paul in various parts of his two epistles to the church at Corinth, and his letter to the Galatian churches. Witness also the life of that excellent man, President [Jonathan] Edwards of New England.

Among the dissatisfied, it is probable that some will complain of your ministry being dry, legal, and of an Arminian cast, while others, it may be, will quarrel with it under a supposition that you dwell too much on the

doctrines of divine grace and verge toward
Antinomianism. My own ministry, however, has been
the subject of loud complaint in these opposite ways,
and that at the very same time. Nor have we much reason to wonder at it. For if a minister, to the best of his
ability, should display the glory of sovereign grace in
the election, redemption, and justification of sinners,
he will be sure to offend the pride of the multitudes
who are seeking acceptance with God by their own
obedience. Persons of this character will probably draw
the same inferences from his doctrine, and form the
same objections against it, as those by which the ministry of Paul was opposed. If it is so, they will cry, "Why
does God yet find fault? For who hath resisted His will?
Let us do evil that good may come, and continue in sin
that grace may abound. The law is made void, and personal holiness is quite superfluous."

Does the same preacher insist on the necessity of
that holiness without which no one shall see the Lord,
upon that conformity to the example of Christ, and
upon that spiritual-mindedness without which all pre-
tensions of faith in the Son of God are vain? The covetousness and carnality of others will be disgusted.
They will pronounce him legal, and consider his doctrine as inimical to the prerogatives of sovereign grace,
and this because he maintains that evangelical truths
have a holy influence on all who believe them, or, in
the language of James, that "faith without works is
dead."

Again, you may, it is highly probable, have painful
opportunities of observing that while some of your
people embrace pernicious doctrines, swerve to wide extremes, and are exceedingly desirous of making prose-

lytes to their novel peculiarities, others of them are giddy and flighty, rambling about from one place of worship to another, admiring almost every fresh preacher they hear. They are quite dissatisfied with your ministry, though they hardly know for what. Nor is there any reason to doubt that others among the objects of your pastoral care will administer occasions of grief by formality and lukewarmness in their profession; by their pride, extravagance, or sensuality; by their envy, avarice, or injustice; or, finally, by malevolent attacks, in unfounded charges upon your own character, as in the case of Paul among the Corinthians. You must guard, however, against desponding discouragement when any of these painful particulars should occur to your notice. Nay, should a variety of them appear at the same time, you must not conclude that God has deserted your ministry and entirely forsaken your church. But, while firmly determined to promote the exercise of strict and impartial discipline, and while careful, unless the case is quite peculiar, never to bring the bad conduct of any individual into your public discourses, examine your own ways; humble yourself before God; increase your pastoral exertions; cry mightily to the Father of mercies for assistance; endeavor, as it were, to levy a tax upon these trials so that they may at least afford private advantages to your own souls. And then, leaving your case with God, be of good courage.

I said, endeavor to levy a tax upon your trials. For even malevolent attacks and unfounded charges upon a Christian's character, if his own temper is under proper government, may prove an occasion for promoting his best interests. In such cases, and for this end, it behooves him to examine his heart and ways to see whether he has not contracted the guilt of some greater evil than that which is falsely laid to his charge. If, on impartial inquiry, his conscience attests the affirmative, it will soon appear that he has much less reason to redden with indignation at his accuser's unfounded charge than he has to admire the goodness of God in permitting an arrow to be aimed at his character, which he can easily repel by the impenetrable shield of a good conscience, while greater evils of his heart, or conduct for which he cannot but severely condemn himself, are entirely hidden from his accuser. Besides, the Christian, in such a predicament, may justly say, "Though I am free from the charge alleged, it is not owing to the superior holiness of my heart, but must be ascribed to divine, preserving care."

A Christian, therefore, who in such a conjuncture of circumstances is wisely seeking his own profit, will be disposed to consider the unrighteous allegation as a gracious, providential warning lest at any time he is really overtaken by that very evil with which, at present, he is falsely accused. Little do we know of the spiritual danger to which we are continually exposed, the temptations by which we may be, unawares, powerfully assaulted, or how near we may be to the perpetration of some awful evil from which we have commonly imagined ourselves to be most remote. Neither, on the other hand, is it possible for us thoroughly to understand all the ways and means by which our heavenly Father communicates those hidden provisions of preventing grace which are continually administered for our preservation. But, alas, how seldom it is that any of us have humility and wisdom sufficient thus to improve such an event!

10. Once more, take heed that you pay a habitual regard to divine influence, as that without which you
cannot either enjoy a holy liberty in your work or have
any reason to expect success. We have heard with pleasure that the necessity of such an influence to enlighten, to comfort, and to sanctify the human mind
makes one article in your theological creed, an article,
doubtless, of great importance. For as well might the
material system have sprung out of nonentity without
the almighty fiat as an assemblage of holy qualities
arise in a depraved heart without supernatural agency.
As well might the order, harmony, and beauty of the
visible world be continued without the perpetual exertion of that wisdom, power, and goodness which gave
them birth as the holy qualities of a regenerate soul be
maintained and flourish, independent of the divine
Spirit.

Now, my brothers, as the knowledge of any truth is
no further useful to us than we are influenced by it and
act upon it; as doctrinal sentiments are not beneficial
except in proportion as they become practical principles or produce correspondent feelings and affections
in our own hearts, so you should endeavor to live continually under the operation of that sacred maxim,
"Without Me ye can do nothing." With humility, with
prayer, and with expectation, the assistance of the Holy
Spirit should be daily regarded. In all your private studies, and in all your public administrations, the aids of
that secret Agent should be sought. Consistency of
conduct, peace in your own breast, and success in your
own labors all require it; for, surely, you do not mean
merely to compliment the Holy Spirit by giving His
work a conspicuous place in your creed. Were you

habitually to study and preach your discourses without secret, previous prayer for divine assistance, the criminality of your neglect would equal the inconsistency of your character. If Christianity is the religion of sinners, and adapted to their apostate state, it must provide as well for our depravity by enlightening and sanctifying influence, as for our guilt by atoning blood.

Our Lord, when addressing His disciples relative to the gracious work of the Holy Spirit, says, "He shall glorify Me, for He shall receive of Mine, and shall show it unto you." By this we are led to infer that when a minister sincerely seeks and mercifully obtains divine assistance in preaching the Word, his discourses will have a sweet savor of Christ and His offices, will display His mediatorial glories, and will exhibit His excellent characteristics and condescending relations that are suited to the necessities of miserable sinners. Thus he will feast the mental eye, and excite administration of the Savior's person and undertaking in the believing heart, even though the elocution and manner of the preacher are of an inferior kind. Hence you may learn, my brothers, how to appreciate those discourses which, whether heard from the pulpit or perused from the press, frequently excite admiration of the minister's talents, but are far from raising the same passion to an equal degree by exhibiting the personal and official excellencies of the adorable Jesus.

Nor can you pray over your Bible in a proper manner when meditating on the sacred text without feeling a solemnity in your ministerial employment. That solemnity should always attend you in the pulpit, for a preacher who trifles there not only affronts the understanding of every sensible and serious hearer, but insults the majesty of that divine Presence in which he stands. Guard, therefore, against every appearance of levity in your public work. In all your studies and in all your labors, watch against a spirit of self-sufficiency from which that profane levity often proceeds. Remember that your ability for every spiritual duty, and all your success, must be from God. To Him your eye must be directed, and on His promised aid your expectation of usefulness must be formed. In thus acting the part of a Christian, while you perform the work of a minister for the benefit of others, your own soul will feel itself interested in the doctrines you preach and in the duties you inculcate, in the promises you exhibit and in the reproofs you administer.

I will now, my brothers, for a few minutes direct your attention to another divine precept, and then conclude. Paul, when addressing Titus in the language of apostolic authority, says, "Let no one despise thee." This is a singular and remarkable saying! No one, whether a professed Christian, an unbelieving Jew, or an idolatrous Gentile, should despise him. Observe, however, that it is not said, "Let no one envy, or hate, or persecute thee," but, "Let no one *despise* thee." How, then, was Titus to preserve his character from contempt? By the penal exercise of miraculous powers on those who dared to treat him with indignity? No such expedient is here intimated. By assuming lordly titles, appearing in splendid robes, taking to himself the trappings of state, and causing the vulgar to keep their distance? Nothing less. For that would have been directly contrary to an established law of Christ, and inconsistent with the nature of His kingdom. But, as the apostle in another place plainly intimates, it was by becoming a bright example to the believers in word, in conversation, in charity or love, in spirit, in faith or fidelity, in purity. In other words, by being preeminent among those who adorned the doctrine of God our Savior.

Yes, a minister of the gospel who takes heed to himself—to his Christian character, to his official duties, and to his various relations in life, whether domestic, religious, or civil—is not very likely to be sincerely despised by those who know him. His supposed religious oddities may be treated with contempt, and he may be hated for his conscientious regard for evangelical truth, and for the legislative authority of Jesus Christ; but the manifest respectability of his moral character will find an advocate in the breast of each who knows him, and especially in the hour of serious reflection. For a manner of conduct bearing testimony to the reality of religious principle, to the fear of God, and to the social virtues reigning in his heart will generally secure him from deliberate contempt. Hence it has been observed by an author of eminence in his literary station: "It was pertinent advice that Paul gave to Titus, however oddly it may appear at first: 'Let no one despise thee.' For we may justly say that in ninety-nine cases out of a hundred, if a pastor is despised, he has himself to blame" (Dr. G. Campbell's *Lectures on Ecclesiastical History*).

Yes, and however respectable for literature and science he is, if he entered upon his office chiefly under the influence of secular motives; or if he is habitually trifling and vain, proud or covetous; if, in his general conduct, there is more of the modern fine gentleman than of the primitive pastor, and much more of the man of this world than of the man of God, he deserves, under the pastoral character, to be despised. For the feelings, sympathies, and turn of his heart are neither congenial to those of the Great Shepherd under whom he should serve, and with whom, in order to feed the flock, he must have frequent spiritual intercourse, nor adapted to meet the necessities of any people who know the Chief Pastor's voice. He is a man of the world; and a minister who is not above the world is very likely to be despised by the world.

11. Take heed, then, my brothers, that no one may have any reason to despise you, and that your churches may never, like the church at Colossae, come under the obligation of that precept, "Say to Archippus, 'Take heed to the ministry which thou hast received in the Lord, that thou fulfill it.' " This is an apostolic injunction which, it is to be feared, attaches to many churches respecting their lukewarm and negligent pastors. Nay, what pastor who is daily lamenting over the plague of his own heart, who reflects on the state of religion in what is called the Christian world, who considers the ministerial work and the pastoral office as being both sacred and important, and, finally, who considers that demand of the Supreme Judge, "Give an account of thy stewardship," can forbear to acknowledge the propriety of Dr. Owen's pathetic language when he says, "The Lord help men, and open their eyes before it is too late! For, either the gospel is not true, or there are few who, in a due manner, discharge that ministry which they take upon them."

Take heed, I once more charge you, take heed to yourself. This duty performed, you can scarcely forbear taking heed either to the doctrine you preach or to the

flock over which the Holy Ghost has made you an overseer, to "feed the church of God, which He hath purchased with His own blood." Amen.

The Qualifications Necessary for Teachers of Christianity

by
Dr. John Erskine

"My brethren, be not many masters, knowing that we shall receive the greater condemnation." James 3:1

The words in the original might have been better rendered, "Be not many teachers, knowing that we shall undergo a severer judgment." They were occasioned by certain novices who assumed the office of teachers when they were utterly unqualified for it. The meaning of the words is that the office of a spiritual instructor is attended with great difficulty and danger, and the duties of it are hard to discharge. Let not, therefore, every man rush into that office. Let none undertake it rashly and while destitute of the gifts and graces necessary for so sacred a function, for teachers as well as hearers must appear before the judgment seat of Christ. God will require more from teachers than from others; and their private miscarriages, or unfaithfulness to the duties of their office, will expose them to the severest punishment.

Inattention to this solemn charge, in ministers and candidates for the ministry, is one unhappy source of the low state of religion in the Christian world. If we had more just ideas of the difficulty and importance of the ministerial office, this might prevent our devoting ourselves to it from selfish motives, as it would prevent us from acting a mean and contemptible part when engaged in it. Since, therefore, my reverend fathers and brethren have obliged me to attempt a service for which I am so poorly qualified, permit me to represent some of the qualifications necessary in the spiritual instructor. The subject must greatly suffer by the unskillful hand that manages it; and yet I would hope that my weak endeavors may, by the divine blessing, stir up our remembrance of truths too obvious indeed to be unknown, but which even the best and wisest among us are sometimes apt to forget when a practice corresponding to them becomes our duty.

The principal qualifications necessary in the spiritual instructor are personal religion, soundness in the faith, a good genius improved by a competent measure of true learning, prudence and discretion; and a due mixture of a studious disposition and an active spirit.

1. Personal religion is a necessary qualification in the Christian teacher. God has not, indeed, limited the efficacy of ordinances by the character of the dispenser. Yet the Scriptures warrant us to say that wicked ministers run unsent, and that God generally frowns upon and blasts their labors. When souls are entrusted to the slaves of Satan, we cannot but dread a bad account of them. For what concern will those feel, or what care will they take, about the salvation of others who feel no concern for their own salvation? Ministers are men of God, an expression which surely implies that they are men devoted to His service, conformed to His blessed image, zealous for His honor, animated by His spirit, and breathing after communion and fellowship with

Him. But a man of God living without God in the
world! A man of God whose affections are earthly, sensual, and devilish! A master of Israel who is ignorant of
the new birth! A guide to Zion walking in the paths
that lead to destruction! A soldier of Christ in league
with Satan! These make up a shocking and monstrous
absurdity! "The light of the world" and "the salt of the
earth" are too honorable titles for any under the power
of darkness and corruption. Those must be clean who
bear the vessel of the sanctuary. Their master is holy,
their work is holy, and, therefore, it becomes them to
be holy also. An infinitely wise God would scarcely appoint those to help forward others to Christ who themselves are strangers to Him, or commission those as His
ambassadors, to negotiate a treaty of peace with an
apostate, rebel world, who themselves are obstinately
persisting in treachery and rebellion.

If a bad man desires to be a minister, his ends in desiring it are low, sordid, and mercenary: not to win
souls to Christ, but to gain a comfortable subsistence
for himself and his family; not to secure the substantial
honor of the divine approbation, but to attract the
empty applause of the great or the populace. Hence, if
speaking the truth interferes with his interest or reputation, he would rather risk the salvation of his hearers
than hazard the displeasure of those who can do him a
favor. Having no heart for his work, he is glad to shift it
off, or to perform it in a lazy, careless, unprofitable
manner; and yet he cannot wholly avoid the unpleasant
drudgery of recommending to others what he dislikes
himself, of counterfeiting sentiments he never felt, and
of applauding a behavior the very reverse of his own. He
does not seek the grace of God to assist him in his

labors, and to crown them with success. No wonder, then, that he does no good to souls, since he does not so much as aim at doing it.

How different is the case with those who are fitted to preach the gospel to others by having felt the power of it on their own hearts. They engage in the work of the ministry not seeking their own profit, but the profit of many, so that they may be saved. They take the oversight of the flock not for filthy lucre, but of a ready mind. With eyes divinely enlightened, they contemplate the fervent love for God, the tender compassion for perishing souls, and the infinite hatred of sin which shine so brightly in the example of Jesus, and thus suck in something of these glorious dispositions. Beholding with devout admiration what Christ has done and suffered, to seek and to save that which was lost, they esteem it their highest honor and happiness to contribute, even in the lowest degree, to promote that generous design, though at the expense of everything that unrenewed nature accounts valuable. Their inquiry is not, "How shall I indulge my sloth, raise my fortune, or advance my reputation?" but "How shall I glorify God, advance the interest of the Redeemer's kingdom, and promote the spiritual and eternal welfare of precious and immortal souls?" Having tasted that the Lord is gracious, they are unwilling to eat their spiritual morsels alone, and earnestly wish to have others be partakers of the same grace of life, and, in this respect, not only almost, but altogether such as they are. Having known the terrors of the Lord, they feel a tender compassion for those who have no pity for themselves. Their souls weep for them in secret places, and are grieved at the hardness of their hearts; yea, they travail in birth for them till Christ is formed in them, and long to impart to them some spiritual gift by which they may be edified. I might add that they love all with a pure heart who fervently who love our Lord Jesus in sincerity; and, forgetting little differences of opinion in matters of doubtful disputation, they esteem their persons, value their society, sympathize with them in their distresses, rejoice in their temporal and spiritual prosperity, and, being affectionately desirous of them, are willing to impart to them not the gospel only, but their own souls also, so dear and precious are such in their eyes!

Animated by such a spirit, the pious minister is vigorous and active, diligent and unwearied, in his Master's service. Night and day, his care and vigilance resemble that of the most tender-hearted, affectionate parent. He is careful to find out the necessities of his flock and the most proper methods to supply them, and, having found out these methods, is careful and speedy in applying them. When carnal men cry, "Master, spare thyself," or when the remains of a sluggish and indolent spirit would pull him back, he remembers the dreadful doom of those who hide their talents in a napkin or do the work of the Lord deceitfully. The whole of his time and strength he thinks too little to spend in endeavoring to save even one soul from death. Hence, he stirs up the gift of God that is in him, exerts himself with an unlanguishing vigor, and whatsoever his hand finds to do he does it with all his might. He knows the worth of time too well to trifle it away in vain amusements, in idle visits, in unprofitable studies, or needlessly to immerse himself in secular business, political schemes, or anything else foreign to

his office. Impatient of whatever would divert him from
his work or retard him in it, he counts those hours lost
in which he is not getting good for his own soul, doing
good to the souls of others, or acquiring greater fitness
for his important trust.

For the same reason he keeps as abstracted as possible from the world lest, by engaging too far in its tu-
multuous cares, a worldly spirit kindling in his breast
should gradually consume every devout and benevolent
affection. Such a one was the great apostle to the
Gentiles. Hear from him what were his services: "In
labors more abundant, in journeyings often, in weariness and painfulness, in watchings often, in hunger
and thirst, in fastings often, in cold and nakedness.
Besides these things which are without, that which
cometh upon me daily, the care of all the churches."
Love to Christ set in motion all his springs of action,
and made him fly like a flaming seraph from pole to
pole to proclaim the ineffable glories of the Son of
God, and to offer his inestimable benefits to the sons of
men.[1]

Grace, in lively exercise, makes the teacher honest
and impartial, bold and courageous. These qualifica-

---

[1] Much of this apostolic spirit appeared in some of the first reformers, and has in our own time appeared in the painful and successive labors of the late Mr. David Brainerd, in the conversion of
barbarous Indians to the Christian faith. See his *Journal*, printed at
Philadelphia, 1746, and Mr. Edward's account of his life, printed at
Boston, 1749. It is a pity that the London abridgment of his *Journal*
has omitted a curious account of the difficulties he met with in
Christianizing the Indians, and the methods he used to surmount
these difficulties.

tions he will often have occasion for in the discharge
of his duty. If he strikes at errors or superstitions, which
antiquity has rendered sacred and venerable, many will
count him an enemy to God and religion for telling
them the unwelcome truth, and stamp upon him the
most opprobrious names for paying more regard to the
infallible word of God than to the absurd, unscriptural
traditions of men. If he urges men to costly and self-
denying duties, the covetous and the proud are dis-
obliged. If he reproves particular vices, those notoriously guilty of them are offended. Or if he inflicts
church censures on the openly scandalous and immoral, not only the guilty person, but his friends and
relations take umbrage at it. But none of these things
move him. He will not, through a slavish dread of man,
put his candle under a bushel or withhold the truth in
unrighteousness, but endeavors to keep back from his
hearers nothing profitable, however unpleasant and
distasteful, and to declare to every one of them the
whole counsel of God. He reckons himself a debtor to
the wise and to the unwise, to the bond and to the free,
to young and old, to rich and poor, to friends and enemies, to the meek and to the froward, to those who
have and to those who have not profited by his ministry. Hence, his labors extend to all his people without
exception—not, indeed, in the same measure and degree, but in proportion to their necessities and the
probability of success.

He is no respecter of persons, but warns every man
and teaches every man in all wisdom so that he may
present every man perfect in Christ. The soul of the
meanest is precious in his sight. He enters the cottages
of the poor as willingly as the palaces of the wealthy; he

can esteem holiness, though dressed in rags or lying
on a dunghill. Nor is he biased by the hopes of their favor to cringe and fawn to the great. He scorns to humor
their vices or flatter their weaknesses. If they dare sin,
he dares reprove, however his worldly interest may suffer by it. He uses no flattering words, nor a cloak of
covetousness. Artifice and dissimulation he abhors,
and he will not decline his duty from the fear of exposing himself to hatred or reproach. Though briars and
thorns are with him, and he dwells among scorpions,
he is not afraid of their words, nor dismayed at their
looks, but speaks plainly and straight to the conscience, leaving the result to his great Master. Thus
Christ preached to the Pharisees against covetousness,
hypocrisy, and making void God's law by human traditions. Paul reasoned with Felix of temperance and righteousness. Peter charged his hearers with murdering
the Lord of glory. And John the Baptist told Herod, "It
is not lawful for thee to have thy brother Philip's wife."
The faithful minister deems himself bound to go and
do likewise, and will rather offend man by this boldness than offend God by conniving at sin.

While others walk in craftiness, handle the Word of
God deceitfully, meanly disguise and dissemble their
sentiments, subscribe as true to what they are convinced is false, suit their doctrine to the depraved taste
of their hearers, or express themselves in so ambiguous
a manner that they appear to maintain what inwardly
they disbelieve, he renounces these hidden things of
dishonesty and, by manifestations of the truth, com-
mends himself to every man's conscience in the sight
of God. He is bold in his God to preach the gospel, not
as pleasing to men, but unto God who tries the heart.

The truths of God, whether fashionable or not, he will declare, knowing that if he should please man by concealing them he would not be the servant of Christ. Though errors have long maintained their ground, and are still keenly espoused not only by great but even by good men, he opposes them with a zeal and warmth suited to their importance. He is like Paul, who would not give place by subjection to the judaizing teachers— no, not for an hour—and who even withstood Peter to the face because he was to be blamed. God's Word in his heart is as a burning fire, shut up in his bones; and therefore, cost what it will, he cannot but speak the things which he has seen and heard. His belly is as wine that has no vent, and necessity is laid upon him to speak so that he may be refreshed. He would rather be right in his opinions than be thought so. He will not sacrifice the truth for the reputation of holding it, nor purchase honor at the expense of honesty. With sacred sincerity, what the Lord said that will he speak, though philosophers should call him an enthusiast, the populace declares him a heretic, or the statesman pronounce him mad.

This integrity and uprightness preserves the minister from fainting under a prospect of outward difficulties and a sense of his own weakness. Having put his hand to the plow, he will not draw back. Though he has long labored in vain, and spent his strength for naught, he will not give over laboring, but says in his heart, "It may be that they will consider, though they are a rebellious house." When he considers what men are before their conversion, he sees no cause to despair of the repentance of any, however hardened in their wickedness they may be. He cannot think it much to

wait on his fellow sinners, and bear with their reproaches, injuries, and ingratitude, when he reflects
upon with what patience and long-suffering the great
God has waited upon him. Taught by the divine condescension, he is gentle among his people, even as a
nurse who cherishes her children; and though he
might be bold in Christ to enjoin them that which is
convenient, yet, for love's sake, he rather beseeches
them. And while he cannot but observe much in their
behavior to dampen and discourage him, yet he is willing to see and own anything in it that is good and
commendable, and is prompted by the least favorable
appearances to undertake services the most painful and
difficult.

Grace in lively exercise not only animates the
teacher to his work, but assists him in it and greatly
tends to crown it with success. It does so by disposing
him to give himself to prayer as well as to the ministry
of the Word. Sensible that all his furniture for the ministry, and all his success in it, must come from the
Lord, with humble fervor and confidence he implores
the divine blessing. Yea, he wrestles and makes supplication, and, as a prince, has power with God and pre-
vails. He is a favorite at the court of heaven, and im-
proves all his interest there for his people's good. His
heart's desire and prayer to God for every one of them
is that they might be saved; and "the effectual fervent
prayer of a righteous man availeth much." It opens the
windows of heaven and brings down a blessing till
there is no room to receive. Hence, plentiful outpour-
ings of the Spirit have been often obtained by the
prayers of some of our pious ancestors, whose gifts and
learning were far from being considerable.

Further, personal religion promotes knowledge of the truth and aptness to teach, both of which are indispensably necessary in the spiritual instructor. A sincere devotedness to Christ and a sense of the infinite importance of religion excite him diligently and impartially to inquire what are the genuine doctrines and precepts of Christianity. Hence, with a mind open to conviction, unbiased by prejudice or prepossession, and ready to embrace the truth as soon as sufficient evidence of it shall appear to him, he candidly hears all parties and cheerfully receives religious instruction, whoever is the instrument of conveying it. At the same time, as it is the faith once delivered to the saints (not the established tenets of a party) which he would discover and embrace, he will not blindly follow any human guide, but brings every doctrine to the test of the sacred oracles, and makes these, not the systems of fallible men, the standards of his faith. He seeks for Christianity in the Scriptures by reading them with devout attention, meditating on them day and night, and imploring the illuminations of their divine Inspirer to teach him God's ways and lead him into all truth.

Nor can such petitions fail to receive a gracious answer. For God has promised that if any man will do His will he shall know of the doctrine whether it is of God; this implies that men who have this spirit shall be preserved from fundamental errors. They have an unction from the Holy One whereby they know all things. There is a taste in painting and music which enables some, with great exactness, to perceive the beauties or blemishes of a picture or musical composition. One whose palate is not vitiated knows good food as soon as he tastes it. Good nature points out at once to the

benevolent what is agreeable or disagreeable to the
rules of goodness far more precisely than the brightest
genius does to the sullen and morose. Just so, a holy
soul, when in the lively exercise of grace, without the
trouble of surveying principles and consequences, easily distinguishes between good and evil, and, by an
immediate perception of the beauty or ugliness, sweetness or nauseousness, of such or such actions judges
for itself what is right; for love toward God, heavenly-
mindedness, meekness, humility, and such like graces
display more readily and exactly to one of ordinary capacity what conduct is becoming or unbecoming in a
Christian than the most diligent study and elaborate
reasoning reveal this to a man who has no spiritual
taste, though he may be of the strongest natural abilities. The lips of the righteous know what is acceptable,
for the heart of the righteous teaches his mouth and
adds learning to his lips. Those who are holy, being
transformed by the renewing of their mind, prove what
is that good and perfect and acceptable will of God.
The pleasant harmony there is between the Word of
God and the disposition and relish of the sanctified
brings suitable Scripture rules to their remembrance
on proper occasions, and mightily helps them in judging the true meaning of these rules.

And as piety thus prevents men from mistaking the
duties, so it preserves them from prejudices against the
doctrines of Christianity. The natural man who has
nothing in him but mere unrenewed nature receives
not "the things of the Spirit of God, for they are foolishness unto him; neither can he know them because
they are spiritually discerned." There is a certain glory
and excellency in the gospel scheme of salvation, of

which he has no more idea than a blind man of colors or a deaf man of sounds. No wonder, then, that Christ crucified is to him a stumbling block, and that, being led aside by the error of the wicked, he makes shipwreck of his faith. But the saint, perceiving that so glorious a scheme as the gospel could have none but God for its Author, is fortified by this consideration against the impressions which the subtle reasonings of infidels might otherwise make upon him—just as one who perceives the light and brightness of the sun would be little moved by any attempts to prove that there was nothing but darkness around him.

But, above all, inward piety assists in understanding and explaining experimental religion. Those can best unveil the pangs of new birth and the nature of union and communion with Christ, and describe conversion, progressive sanctification, a life of faith, the struggles of the flesh and spirit, and such like subjects, who can speak of them from their own experience. Those are best suited to speak a word in season to weary souls who can comfort them in their spiritual distresses with those consolations wherewith they themselves have been comforted by God. Their experience of the influence of truths which have been most useful to their own souls leads them to insist much upon these in their public ministrations, and determines them to know nothing in comparison to Christ and Him crucified. On the other hand, some of the most edifying subjects are least relished by a bad man, and can scarcely be managed by him with any advantage. Will he be fit to warn his hearers of the devices of Satan and the deceits of a desperately wicked heart who, being quite a stranger at home, knows nothing of these matters but

from uncertain report? Will not the unconverted minister, when he meets with the discouragements of an
awakened sinner, or the fears and distresses of a doubting, deserted saint, be often at a loss how to deal with
them? And is there not the highest danger lest, on the
one hand, he build up the false hopes of the self-deceiver, or, on the other hand, he makes sad the hearts
of those whom God would not make sad? Surely those
who are animated by the Spirit, who inspired the
Scriptures, bid fairest for explaining them aright, and
applying them to the various necessities of their hearers.

Ministers unconcerned about religion are generally
cold and languid in their addresses to the conscience.
When urging others to repent and believe, they do but
stammer about these things; and their words, not coming from the heart, are not likely to reach it. Even when
the doctrine they preach tends to rouse the secure,
their way of preaching tends to lull them to sleep.[2]
There is something unnatural in endeavoring to excite
in other men's breasts motions we never felt in our
own. No wonder, then, that men behave awkwardly in
attempting it, and that the coldness of the preacher
makes the hearer cold too. But when the faithful minister exhorts out of the abundance of the heart, the
mouth speaks. And the language of the heart has some-

---

[2] Pride, says Mr. Baxter, makes many a man's sermons; and what
pride makes the devil makes. And what sermons the devil will
make, and to what end, we may easily conjecture. Though the
matter is from God, yet if the dress, manner, and end are from
Satan, we have no great reason to expect success. Baxter's *Gildas
Salvianus*, chapter 4, section 2.

thing in it peculiarly lively and persuasive, something of unction not to be equaled by the most labored compositions of others. Unless one's gifts are uncommonly low, a warm concern for souls will animate and enflame his language, dictate to him the most moving and pathetic addresses, and, on some occasions at least, inspire him with a divine and almost irresistible eloquence which, with amazing force, will pierce the conscience, ravish the affections, and strike conviction into the most obdurate offender.

True religion will promote in ministers a pious and exemplary behavior. The best advices lose their weight when the adviser gives us ground to suspect his sincerity, and to taunt him with the proverb, "Physician, cure thyself." Though ministers may not be grossly profligate, if they are more solicitous to promote their own ease, wealth, and grandeur than to advance the glory of God and the good of souls; if they are more diligent to improve their farms than to feed their flock, lovers of pleasures more than lovers of God, and more happy in the company of the libertine than of the serious Christian; if their behavior is light and airy, and their conversation frothy and trifling; if they are always on the popular or fashionable side, and implicitly follow the directions of those who have it in their power to gratify their pride or satiate their avarice, this will greatly lessen our respect for their instructions. But if ministers, by their conduct as well as by their doctrine, hold forth the word of life; if they live what they preach, possess the graces they recommend, and practice the virtues they enforce on others; if they are courteous and affable, kind and condescending, and, while they dare to plead the cause of the God of truth, do it in a man-

ner which may not offend Him as the God of love; if
they can hate a man's vices and yet love his person and
esteem his excellencies, without approving his faults; if
they keep at the widest distance from a sullen morose-
ness and melancholy dejection, and yet are grave and
decent out of the pulpit as well as in it, maintain the
dignity of their character, avoid those liberties which,
though generally deemed innocent, have been guilty of
destroying both the power and form of godliness, and
abridge themselves on proper occasions even of lawful
freedoms, remembering that many things which may
be lawful when practiced by a minister do not edify; if
they are indeed blameless and harmless, the sons of
God without rebuke, shining as lights in the world; if
under the strongest temptations to dissemble, the law
of truth is in their mouth, and no iniquity found in
their lips; if their private behavior breathes a spirit of
genuine undissembled goodness—what a glorious
prospect does this open of the flourishing of religion
under their culture! If all in the ministry did thus walk
with God in truth and equity, might we not expect that
God would honor them by turning many away from iniquity? Might we not hope that so lovely a conduct
would engage others to be followers of them, even as
they are of Christ?

Exemplary holiness, meekness and gentleness, forbearance and patience, candor and moderation, modesty and humility, love for God and for virtue, and a behavior corresponding to these graces must adorn the
teacher's profession, add efficacy to his instructions,
stop the mouth of slander, give freedom and boldness
in reproving vice, gain him the affections of the pious,
command the esteem and reverence of the indifferent,

strike the enemies of religion with awe and dread, restrain the most profligate from many enormities they would otherwise commit, and transform even envy itself into admiration of so amiable a character and a generous desire to copy it.

But, some may inquire, cannot the hypocrite behave well? I grant that he may to a certain degree. But some of the most signal and illustrious evidences of grace in the heart are of so mortifying a nature that the hypocrite will scarcely attempt to counterfeit them: or, if he does, as the part he acts is unnatural and constrained, it is scarcely possible but, when off his guard, something will be done or neglected by him which, though no full evidence of the badness of his heart, may raise such prejudices against him as will render his person contemptible, and his ministry too. Moreover, holy providence often unveils the secret depravity which a splendid profession may, for a while, conceal.

I conclude this heading by observing that if the seeds of godliness are not sown in the heart before we undertake the pastoral office, probably they will never be sown there. True, indeed, a bad minister is not out of the reach of grace; but of all men he has the least reason to expect it. His being engaged in religious services, so far from promoting his cure, tends to harden him in impenitence. And as wicked seamen who continually border on the confines of death by being accustomed to danger learn to despise it, so the most affecting truths, by being familiar to the wicked preacher, lose their efficacy upon him, and he acquires such a habit of talking of the most important and tremendous things, without feeling what he says, that neither the thunders of the law alarm nor the graces of the gospel allure him. To use the words of the judicious Bishop Butler, "Going over the theory of virtue in one's thoughts, talking well, and drawing fine pictures of it—this is so far from necessarily or certainly conducing to form a habit of it, in him who thus employs himself, that it may harden the mind in a contrary course, and, by degrees, render it insensible to all moral considerations. For, from our very faculty of habits, passive impressions, by being repeated, grow weaker. Thoughts, by often passing through the mind, are felt less sensibly."[3]

2. Orthodoxy, or soundness in the faith, is highly necessary in a spiritual instructor. Much more stress is laid upon this in the sacred writings than some seem willing to allow. Timothy is not only instructed what to preach, but commanded to charge some that they teach no other doctrine; to withdraw himself from those who teach otherwise, and who consent not to wholesome words, even the words of our Lord Jesus Christ, and to the doctrine which is according to godliness; to avoid those oppositions of science, falsely so called, in which some professing them have erred concerning the faith; and to hold fast the form of sound words which he had heard from Paul. Titus is advised that a bishop must hold fast the faithful word, as he has been taught and charged to speak the things which become sound doctrine, in doctrine showing uncorruptness, gravity, sincerity, and sound speech that cannot be condemned. But can all this be expected of one whose sentiments are unsound? Or shall we say that these qualifications were necessary in an age when the presence of the

---

[3] Butler's *Analogy*, part I, chapter 5.

apostles might have done much to stop the progress of error, but are unnecessary now? Jude 3 reminds those to whom he wrote, "Beloved, I gave all diligence to write unto you, and exhort you, that ye should contend earnestly for the faith which was once delivered to the saints." Does not this import that the common salvation cannot be secured if fundamental articles of faith are renounced?

I know orthodoxy is a thing everywhere spoken against, and has had the misfortune to be judged and condemned as accessory to crimes which, had men consulted it, they would never have committed. If the name displeases any, we shall give it another. Is it either ridiculous or hurtful to judge of things as they really are? If orthodoxy in this sense has done evil, let its enemies bear witness to the evil; but if good, why do they reproach it? Does superstition, enthusiasm, bigotry, or persecution for conscience' sake flow from just sentiments of religion, and of the proper means to promote it? Or, rather, do they not flow from wrong sentiments of these? Truth and general utility necessarily coincide. The first produces the second. "Observing truth," to use the words of learned Bishop Warburton, "is acting as things really are. He who acts as things really are must gain his end, since all disappointment proceeds from acting as things are not, just as, in reasoning from true or false principles, the conclusion that follows must be necessarily right or wrong. Gaining the end of acting is utility or happiness; disappointment of the end, misery."[4] If, then, as this masterly reasoner has well proven, truth produces utility,

---

[4] Warburton's *Divine Legation*, book 3, section 6.

will it not follow that to despise orthodoxy is to despise happiness?

I would add that, as the end of divine revelation is the glory of God and the holiness and happiness of mankind, it is, in this case, impeaching divine wisdom to say that there is nothing in divine revelation which does not tend in some degree, directly or indirectly, to promote these ends. And, if so, even lesser mistakes in public teachers must be hurtful, as even lesser mistakes will prevent their improving certain truths for the good and wise purposes for which they were revealed. Nevertheless, though a teacher free from error may be wished for, it can scarcely be expected that, in the present state of human nature, such a one should be found; for, as the apostle observes in the verse following our text, "If any man offend not in word, the same is a perfect man." Those, therefore, who entertain just notions of those doctrines which the Holy Spirit uses as the chief means of convincing and converting sinners, and building up saints in the faith, holiness, and comfort, may, notwithstanding their lesser mistakes, be considerably useful in preaching the gospel. But such as have wrong notions of those truths whereby the blessed Spirit ordinarily begins and carries on the life of God in the soul of a man are scarcely fit to be workers together with God in the affair of man's salvation. And those will be likely to corrupt men from the simplicity that is in Christ, and remove them to another gospel, who embrace principles which strike at the vitals and sap the very foundations of religion, principles calculated to flatter the pride or to encourage the sensuality of corrupt nature.

Allow me to adopt the reasoning of a sermon lately

printed in which the importance of right principles in religion is excellently represented. They who hold the good influence of Christian principles to be so inconsiderable as to render the propagation of them of no great importance will be at no loss to give us instances of corrupt and wrong principles having had a great influence on the world. Loud complaints we heard from this quarter of the dreadful effects which superstition and enthusiasm have produced; how they have poisoned the tempers and transformed the manners of men, and have overcome the strongest restraints of law, of reason, and of humanity. Is this, then, the case, that all principles except good ones are supposed to be of such mighty energy? Strange that false religion should do so much and true religion so little. Surely, no impartial inquirer can be of so absurd an opinion. The whole history of mankind shows that religious belief is no inconsiderable principle of action. The mischief such belief has done when misled is indeed a good argument to hope for more from it when rightly directed. These reflections prove not only the importance of Christianity in general, but of just and true sentiments of the particular doctrines contained in it; and, consequently, they prove the importance of an orthodox ministry.

3. A tolerable genius and capacity, with a competent measure of true learning, are requisite to fit for the office of a spiritual instructor. Infidels may wish, as Julian the apostate did, to see learning banished from the Christian church. And men of low education, or of selfish spirits, may think meanly or speak diminutively of a gospel ministry, as if the weakest abilities sufficed to qualify for it. But, as Paul cried out, "Who is sufficient

for these things?" Elihu tells us that scarcely one of a thousand is qualified to deal with the conscience. Jeroboam was blamed for making priests the lowest of the people. And Amos speaks of it as something strange and unusual that he who had not been educated in the schools of the prophets, who was no prophet, neither a prophet's son, but a herdsman and a gatherer of sycamore fruit, should be commissioned by God to prophesy to Israel. However, then, some may speak evil of the things which they know not, we dare engage to prove that a weak, honest man might, with as much propriety and as little inconvenience, be allowed to undertake the office of physician, advocate, or judge, as the office of a minister of Christ; though, doubtless, his good and honest heart, without other qualifications, would be good enough furniture for offices less important and difficult than these. Uncommon talents are necessary to explain obscure passages of Scripture, to resolve intricate cases of conscience, and to defend the truth against gainsayers—services to which ministers have frequent calls.

Nor will a small measure of skill and ability qualify any man to teach the necessary doctrines and duties of religion, to convince the understanding, to interest the affections, to dart irresistible light into the conscience and fix it there, to meet with men's objections and prejudices against religion, to unfold the temptations of Satan and deceits of the heart, and to do all this in a manner becoming the dignity of the pulpit, and yet plain to the dullest capacity. Nothing less than this is the ordinary object of the spiritual instructor. Good sense, expressed so perspicuously, and arranged in such an order as to be easily understood and remembered, is the very soul of composition; and this cannot be expected but from one of a quick invention, a clear head, and a sound judgment, who has gifts as well as grace, a doctrinal and speculative as well as a practical and experimental knowledge, and has acquired a facility of imparting his ideas to others.

And even all this will not go so far as to qualify a man to speak often in public without either a retentive memory or an unusual command of words. Nay, the best natural powers will need to be well cultivated by a liberal education. Without any ability to read the Scripture in the languages in which it was originally written, and some acquaintance with natural and moral philosophy, history, antiquity, the best Greek and Roman authors, and the arts of logic, rhetoric, and criticism, in an age of so much learning as the present, a minister can scarcely fail to be despised; and a despised minister is seldom successful. Besides, on many occasions, the teacher will need all his learning to unfold to him the meaning of difficult passages in sacred writ, especially if, as sometimes happens, his commentaries fail him where he most wants their help. Nor will one wholly ignorant of philosophy, history, and criticism be able to give satisfying answers to the reasonings of infidels founded upon these, to detect their sophistry, to beat them out of their strongholds, and so, if he does not convince their conscience, at least to stop their mouths.

There are some scriptures from which, if they stood in the original as they do in our translations, almost unanswerable objections might be drawn against our holy faith. And what advantage must this give the infidel to triumph over the illiterate teacher! And, indeed, if the hedge of a learned ministry were once removed from these lands, as I am afraid some wish it to be, what could we expect but that ignorance and infidelity, error and heresy, and superstition and enthusiasm should quickly overspread them? Those who, by the blessing of God on their studies, have acquired considerable measures of learning have been the best explainers and defenders of Christianity, and recommended practical religion in the most distinct and persuasive manner. And without a miracle, which we have no ground to expect, illiterate ministers can never equal them.

But above all, one who would teach others to be religious must himself have a clear and distinct notion of religion. We cannot avoid despising the man who is ignorant in his own profession, whatever his knowledge may be of other matters. To say of a physician that he has a good taste in music and poetry, but is grossly ignorant of the nature of diseases and their proper remedies, is giving him the most unfavorable characterization. In like manner, it is a wretchedly poor depiction of a minister of Christ to say of him, "He is a good philosopher, and understands well the Greek and Roman writers, but is little acquainted with the means revealed in Scripture of recovering mankind from the ruins of their apostasy." For, if so, he comes short of the very end of his office, and fails in that in which, above all things, he ought to have excelled. We cannot therefore entertain too low and despicable an opinion of such ignorant presumers as set themselves up as teachers of Christianity, and pretend to show unto others the way of salvation, while their own ideas of it are so dark and confused that they have need to be taught which are the first principles of the oracles of God.

He who would be a scribe, instructed in the kingdom of heaven, able to bring forth out of his treasures things new and old, must understand well the doctrine of man's primitive apostasy from God, with its unhappy effects on the whole human race; the method of recovery through Christ; the work of the Spirit in applying a purchased redemption; the full and free offers of Christ and of salvation through Him, made in the gospel to the very chief of sinners; and the nature of that faith which unites to Christ, of that holiness which makes men meet for the inheritance of saints in light, and which is indeed heaven begun in the soul, and of those various good works of piety or charity by which we are bound to glorify God, to serve Him in our generation, and to prove to ourselves and others the truth and energy of our faith. It is a contradiction to suppose that ministers should be able to represent these important doctrines in a proper light to others if they themselves understand neither what they say nor whereof they affirm. Miserable, therefore, must be the state of the church if left to the care of such unskillful guides! For, if the blind lead the blind, both must fall into the ditch. To prevent so dreadful a calamity, it is required, as an essential qualification of a guide to souls, that he be apt to teach, not a novice, lest, being lifted up with pride, he fall into the condemnation of the devil. Those whose knowledge of divinity is entirely derived from a few modern sermon writers, or books on the deistical controversy, but who have never read and digested into their memories a system of divinity, must be ignorant of many important truths, and can scarcely have any view of that connection of the different parts of religion in which a great deal of its beauty consists.

And will such keep back from their hearers nothing profitable, and teach others what they have never learned themselves? Will they instruct men in the whole of their duty to God, to themselves, and to one another who are unskillful in the word of righteousness, having never studied with care the nature and necessity of these duties, the hindrances in the practice of them, and the methods of removing those hindrances? Or will those who have not thoroughly studied the evidences of Christianity in general, or of particular articles of faith, be ready to give an answer to every man who asks for a reason for the hope that is in them, and thus be able, by sound doctrine, both to exhort and to convince gainsayers?

I conclude this heading by observing that the spiritual minister should be mighty in the Scriptures, able not only to repeat but to explain them, having the Word of God dwelling in him richly in all wisdom and spiritual understanding. It is his duty to declare the whole counsel of God, and to teach men to observe all things whatsoever that Jesus has commanded. But how can he do this without knowing from the sacred oracles what is the counsel of God and what are the commands of Jesus? Any other guide will, in some instances, mislead, or at least prove defective, in his instructions. The Scriptures alone are fully sufficient for doctrine, for reproof, for instruction, and for correction in righteousness; able to make the man of God perfect, thoroughly furnished for every good word and work; able to direct the ministers not only how to live, but how to preach. And he who is little conversant in them will be apt to insist much on things which they rarely mention, and seldom to mention things on

which they chiefly dwell; to lay a great deal of stress on
things on which they lay little stress on, and little stress
on things which they exhibit as of the last importance.
Hence, some discourses on self-examination almost entirely omit, or handle in an overly superficial manner,
some of the plainest, most express, and most frequently
repeated Scripture characteristics of true holiness, on
the one hand, and of counterfeit appearances of it on
the other, as if they had found a better way to distinguish the real Christian from the self-deceiver than
that which the sacred oracles, when treating this subject, have pointed out.[5] Hence, methods have been recommended to preserve the solemnity of ordinances different from—nay, in some instances, contrary to—
those which infinite Wisdom has prescribed. Hence,
some content themselves with recommending holiness
in general without distinctly explaining and enforcing
particular duties, or reproving, as our Lord and His
apostles did, particular sins. Others, in exhorting to
moral virtues, scarcely make any use of the motives to
them that are urged with so divine an eloquence in the
scriptures of truth.[6] And, which is worst of all, some so

---

[5] I know no writer who, in inquiring into this important subject,
has proceeded with such cautious regard to the infallible
touchstone of truth as Mr. Jonathan Edwards of Northampton, in
his judicious treatise concerning religious affections, printed at
Boston, 1746. I scarcely think this age has produced any book on
practical divinity which will so well reward a careful perusal.

[6] "I mean not," says a lively writer, "to exclude morality from
preaching Christ. No, this I testify, that he who neglects the former
shall never be benefited by the latter. Christ profits him nothing.
Religion is the soul's conformity to God in His moral perfections.
So much as a man has of true morality, so much has he of God;

entirely omit the peculiar doctrines of the gospel that
one might hear a long course of sermons from them
without learning that which it was the grand design of
revelation to teach, the way, I mean, in which a fallen
creature may emerge from the ruins of his apostasy.

Hence, instead of rightly dividing the Word of truth,
many confine their sermons to those subjects on which
they find their thoughts flow with the most readiness
and affection, neglecting others of at least equal importance. Some are continually detecting the deceits of
the heart and false resemblances of grace; others are
thundering out the terrors of the law, representing the
dreadful indignation of God against the unconverted,
or arguing the justice of that indignation; and others
content themselves with inviting sinners to accept the
Savior without taking suitable pains, by preaching the

---

and so much as he has of God in this world, so much will he have
of heaven in the next. But then this morality must be baptized in
the name of Christ. Without regard to Christ in principle and in
end, and without entire dependence upon the influences of His
Spirit, the brightest speculations and the strongest arguments, a text
fetched from the Bible and motives brought from heaven, would be
to preach Seneca, rather than Christ. And to urge the duties of
morality upon motives that are not Christian is only to deprive the
lame man of his crutches, and then bid him walk. No man ever
insisted on morality more than St. Paul; but he always Christianized
it. He engrafts the man into faith by Christ, and you quickly find
him budding with every precious grace, and loaded with the fruit of
good works. Never does Paul seem so much in his element as when
he is preaching Christ. How often does he go out of his way to
meet with Him! Here he stretches in his thoughts, and pursues the
glories of the Redeemer till he is almost out of breath." Hobby's
Sermon at Emerson's Ordination, p. 16.

The Qualifications Necessary

duties and sanctions of the law, to convince them of their need of Him. Some seem to forget that to quicken, to warn, to direct, and to encourage true Christians is any part of their work, while others address their audiences as if they were all converted. Some preach continually upon duties, others upon privileges, others upon doubts and temptations. These, and such like defects, would be prevented were Moses and the prophets, Christ and His apostles considered as our patterns in preaching. The deep things of God which He has revealed by His Spirit should be the grand topics of our ministry, as they were of Paul's; and these we should speak, as he did, not in the words which man's wisdom teaches, but which the Holy Ghost teaches, comparing spiritual things with spiritual things.

4. Ministers need to be persons of prudence and conduct, and to know men as well as books. A minister should study himself. He should not only be acquainted with his own spiritual state, but with the particular turn of his genius; for God having distributed among ministers various gifts, and thereby having fitted them to answer different purposes in His service, our usefulness will in a great measure depend upon knowing what our gift is. Thus, some are fittest to inform and convince the judgment by the clear and distinct light in which they represent truth, and the strong and unanswerable arguments with which they support it. Others have a greater talent for touching the conscience or of moving the passions. A minister should study the make and frame of the human mind; for till the springs of human nature are, in a good measure, disclosed to him, and he has learned how far the

bodily passions or a disordered imagination may either
cloud genuine piety or cause a resemblance of it, he
will be often at a loss what judgment to frame of religious experiences. He should know all the avenues to
the soul, and study the different capacities and tempers
of men, so that he may be able, with becoming address,
to suit himself to them all. Physicians consider the age,
constitution, strength, and way of living of their patients, and vary their prescriptions accordingly.
Ministers should, in like manner, be able to adapt
themselves to the different ages, natural dispositions,
genius, temporal circumstances, temptations, errors,
moral characters, and religious inclinations of their
hearers.

No wise prince will employ those to manage affairs
in which honor and the interest of his kingdom are
deeply concerned who have not capacities and accomplishments in some measure adapted to that important
trust; and, as Solomon observes, he who sends a message by the hand of a fool cuts off the feet and drinks in
damage. Can we, then, entertain so low sentiments of
the wisdom of the King of heaven as to think that now,
when extraordinary gifts are ceased, He would ordinarily employ those in the grand but difficult design of advancing His glory and saving precious souls who are
unfit to be employed even about the common affairs of
this life?

The ambassadors of Jesus, then, should be as wise as
serpents as well as harmless as doves. The wisdom that
is from above—which is first pure, then peaceable, gentle, and easy to be entreated, full of mercy and of good
fruits, without partiality and without hypocrisy—should
shine even in their private conversation. They are re-

quired to let no man despise them, and to give no offense in anything, so that the ministry is not blamed. A wicked, ill-natured world is continually watching for their halting, and will gladly improve the least slip or inadvertency to bring a slur upon them. Ministers, therefore, need to shun not only what is sinful, but what is dishonorable or disobliging, and to avoid everything which may justly blast their reputation, and thus lessen their influence and impair their usefulness. If their behavior is low and sordid, ridiculous and affected, rash and imprudent, much hurt is hereby done to religion, and sacred things become contemptible.

They should not indulge the first sallies of a warm imagination, but weigh the more distant consequences of actions lest they mislead the weak and injudicious, provoke the censures of the cautious and severe, and hurt the gospel when they mean to serve it. Where they innocently may, they should accommodate themselves to people's humors, and become all things to all men so that, by an obliging conduct, they may gain them to Christ. They should avoid imprudently intermeddling in controversies of a civil nature, especially among those of their own charge, and saying or doing any thing indiscreet whereby they may prejudice the people against their ministrations. In opposing error and reproving vice, they must know when to keep silent and when to speak, when to come with a rod and when in the spirit of meekness. Likewise, in healing wounded consciences, in reconciling those at variance, in encouraging the disconsolate, in speaking to those on a deathbed, in managing the public business, and in exercising the discipline of the church, all their sagacity, caution, penetration, and judgment are little enough to

choose out the most proper means, and to apply them
with dexterity, so that they may not spoil the best
designs by bad management.

Spiritual instructors need wisdom for rightly managing their public discourses. They should adapt the
choice of their subjects to the particular circumstances
and necessities of their hearers as wise householders,
giving to everyone his portion of meat in due season;
they should compose their sermons so that the lowest
may understand and the most judicious have no cause
to despise them, and so as neither unnecessarily to offend the weak nor give advantage to the maliciously
criticizing. They should imitate their glorious Master,
who patiently bore with the prejudices of His disciples,
and instructed them as they were able to bear it. Much
depends on the timing of things well, and the manner
of doing them; on choosing the most proper seasons
for instruction, and imparting it in an engaging manner; on avoiding offensive phrases and borrowing favorite ones where we honestly can; and on using such
reasonings to confirm the doctrines or to enforce the
duties of religion as we have ground to think, from the
disposition of our hearers or the dealings of providence towards them, will be most apt to strike and work
upon them; for a word fitly spoken is like apples of gold
in pictures of silver. Now, in all this, wisdom is profitable to direct, as no rules can be given to extend to every particular case.

5. A due mixture of a studious disposition and an active spirit is necessary in teachers of Christianity. That
the last of these is so appears, at first sight, from the
time and pains requisite to know the state of our congregations, to catechize, to visit the sick, to administer

private instruction, reproof, or consolation, to prepare young people for the Lord's table, and sometimes to conduct to the Savior the awakened sinner, who is asking the way to Zion with his face set in that direction. The ministry is no idle or easy profession, but requires an almost uninterrupted series of the most painful and laborious services. But ministers of a lazy, indolent disposition will be tempted to hurry over those duties, and will begrudge to spend so much time in them as is really necessary to render them in any degree useful. Nor will ordinary measures of grace suffice to overcome such temptations.

But then a studious disposition is equally necessary. It was not without its use even in the days of inspiration. Solomon found much study a weariness to the flesh, yet was sensible that the advantages of it overbalanced the toil, and tells us that the preacher (meaning himself) sought to find acceptable words, gave good heed, and sought out and set in order many proverbs. Though he excelled all men in understanding, yet he did not turn people off with anything that came first in his mind, but took pains to range his thoughts in a proper method, and to express them in agreeable language, so that his sermons were the fruit of labor and study as well as of inspiration. And he tells what moved him to all these pains: "The words of the wise are as goads, and as nails fastened by the masters of assemblies." That is, "There is like power in words wisely chosen to stir up the slothful to duty as there is in a goad to prick the ox forward. Nor do they only move the affections in a transient way, but stick in the conscience and memory as nails do in a board." Daniel understood from books the number of years whereof the word of the Lord came to Jeremiah the prophet, that he would accomplish seventy years in the desolations of Jerusalem. Paul was brought up at the feet of Gamaliel, and had made considerable proficiency under so eminent a master. And yet, after he had been favored with divine inspiration, he was so far from thinking further study needless that even when in prison, and when he had the near prospect of his approaching martyrdom, he commanded his books and parchments to be sent to him. If this inspired apostle saw occasion for all the learning and knowledge he could attain to by ordinary means, to assist him in instructing mankind, much more must we stand in need of such helps who cannot pretend to his extraordinary gifts. Paul exhorted Timothy to give attendance first to reading, and then to exhortation and doctrine, to instruct himself well before he instructed others. He charged Timothy to meditate on divine things, and give himself wholly to them so that his profiting might appear to all. Though from his childhood he had known the holy Scriptures, was esteemed learned enough to be a minister of Christ, and had extraordinary gifts bestowed upon him, he was warned that reading and meditation were still necessary to fit him to teach and exhort.

Shall we, then, be able, without any reading or meditation at all, to preach the word of life in a way suitable to its majesty and importance? I deny not, indeed, that those whom God has blessed with a ready elocution may preach warmly and accurately without writing their sermons. But even those who have words most at their command will prove to be but a sounding brass and a tinkling cymbal if they do not endeavor, by reading and meditation, to be masters of the subjects on which they preach. Reverence for that God in whose name we speak, regard for the dignity of the pulpit, and concern for the glorious design that brings us there should prevent our rushing into it rashly and unprepared, and serving God and His people with sudden, undigested thoughts that cost us nothing. Ministers are not set apart to their office to trifle away six days of the week, and then go to the pulpit with whatever comes uppermost. Such extemporary performances, though for a little they may please some, seldom do credit to God's ordinances or produce any lasting effects on the hearers. The good matter contained in them is generally despised and overlooked through contempt of the looseness of the method and meanness of the style. Meditations, then, and reading, are necessary branches of a minister's duty; and, consequently, those must be unfit for the pastoral office who are of an unfixed, sauntering disposition, who have no relish for study, know not what it is to meditate, and are never pleased but when with company or abroad.

And now, my dear hearers, let what has been said affect all of you with the deepest concern, that ever the care of souls should have been entrusted to men destitute of these qualifications. Let it excite in you the warmest emotions of gratitude to the Father of mercies for blessing our land in general, and those bounds in particular, with so many able and faithful ministers. Let it procure your prayers for us in the ministry, that the blessed Spirit would more and more qualify us for our difficult work by imparting all needful supplies of gifts and grace, and that, as death is daily thinning our numbers, the Lord of the harvest would, from time to time, repair our breaches by sending forth honest and skilful laborers into His harvest.

Students need scarcely be particularly addressed, since the whole of what has been said was principally designed to warn them not to be too forward and hasty in setting themselves up as teachers. God does not call those to feed the sheep of Christ who have no love for the Shepherd. For all who love not our Lord Jesus are wicked; and unto the wicked God said, "What hast thou to do to declare My statutes, or to take My covenant in thy mouth?" (Psalm 50:16).

How great a trust is committed to the pastor! Hundreds of precious, immortal souls he is bound to watch over, as one who must give an account. And will you be able to give a good account of the souls of others if unable to give a good account of your own? Is it not a most pitiable case to be under a strict and awful charge to affect the minds of your hearers with what never affected your own minds? Presume not, then, to undertake the care of souls without personal holiness or until, by the blessing of God on your education, and your diligent attendance on prayer, reading, and meditation, you have attained a suitable furniture of gifts and graces for the service of the sanctuary. You behold with indignation the quack doctor who will venture to hazard the health and lives of men for a little paltry gain. If such deserve to be accounted murderers of the body, shall not the blood of souls be laid to your charge, if you undertake the care of them while unqualified for it, and if, through your negligence or unskillfulness, they shall eternally perish?

Parents should be well satisfied of the pious disposition of their children, and of the goodness of their genius, before they devote them to the work of the ministry, and should beware of pressing them to undertake the care of souls against their inclination or without it.

Such as are invested with the power of choosing gospel ministers, or in choosing those who are to train up our youth in the various branches of knowledge necessary for the ministry, I would humbly entreat to be wise and faithful in the discharge of so important a trust. Let always the most worthy be preferred. Do all to the glory of God. Esteem the interest of Zion, and of Zion's King, above your chief joy. These are the commands of God, and if you disregard them, sooner or later you shall smart for it. Let not affection for any friend, or fear of disobliging those from whom you expect favors, mislead you to an improper choice.

Patrons, as good Bishop [Gilbert] Burnet has observed in his book *Pastoral Care,* chapters 7 and 10, are bound to pay a sacred regard to the trust vested in them; and if they exercise their legal right, they should first carefully consider what are the qualifications of the person they present to a benefice. Otherwise the souls that may be lost by a bad nomination will be required at their hands by Him who made and purchased these souls, and in whose sight they are of inestimable value. It is all one, with relation to the account they must give at the tribunal of Jesus, whether money, kindred, friendship, or something else was their motive in bestowing a presentation, if regard is not had in the first place to the worth of the person nominated, and his fitness to undertake the care of souls. Did patrons act with a visible regard for true goodness and real merit, and were they never swayed to make a wrong nomination by application and importunity, by ambitious or interested views, or by desire of gratifying a

friend who may have a chaplain to provide for, the
worst grievance in presentations would be removed,
which I take to be this: that many patrons have no
sense of the value of souls, and therefore are indifferent
to whom they entrust them.

Those who are so happy as to be allowed the choice
of a guide to their souls must be charged with the worst
of madness, nay, with the most monstrous and inexcus-
able impiety, if they willingly expose their souls to eternal destruction by committing them to the charge of
those of whose piety and abilities they have no knowledge. Surely, no affair in the whole circle of life calls
for more serious concern and importunate supplication. Let not, then, interest and favor, let not ambition
to be head of a party, let not the solicitations of great
men, on the one hand, or a humor of opposing them,
on the other, determine your conduct. Do not be too
influenced by little showy qualifications, such as a
flowery style, a loud or melodious voice, or a ready delivery. But covet earnestly the best gifts and the most
solid and substantial qualifications, such as piety,
learning, sound principles, and aptness to teach. Seek
advice from faithful and judicious ministers who are
able and willing to serve your best interests, and are
much more competent judges of some of these qualifications than private Christians ordinarily can be.

And let us, my reverend and dear fathers and
brethren, from a genuine regard for the honor of God
and the credit of religion, for the success of the gospel
and the salvation of immortal souls, and as we would
not bring a stain upon our order, and depreciate it in
the eyes of the world, which is often partial enough to
censure the whole clergy for the faults of a few—let us

beware of introducing any into the sacred office but such as we have good evidence are qualified for it by being visibly and, in the judgment of charity, sincere Christians, orthodox as well as learned, having grace as well as gifts. I acknowledge, designing men may counterfeit some of these qualifications with so much artifice as, after the utmost caution we can use, to impose upon us; and in that case, though we commit a mistake, we are guilty of no fault, since such favorable appearances ought to determine us to judge favorably. But if we separate any to the ministry without suitable evidence of their fitness for it, either by personal acquaintance and free, unreserved conversation with them, or by hearing their public performances, and strictly and particularly examining their knowledge of the truth and ability to defend it, or by private inquiries to those on whose skill, integrity, opportunities of information, and cautiousness in recommending we may safely rely—should such afterwards prove incapable of discharging their trust, the blame of their defects will be laid to our charge.

How awful is the warning of Paul to Timothy (1 Timothy 5:22), and in him to all concerned in ordaining others to the pastoral office! "Lay hands suddenly on no man, neither be partaker of other men's sins; keep thyself pure." It is as if he had said, "Though you have no particular reason to suspect a candidate to be unfit for the ministry, be not on that account slight and superficial in trying his qualifications for it, but examine, with the utmost care and exactness, his moral character and aptness to teach. For if, through indolence and carelessness, you neglect to make those inquiries, upon which you might have discovered what

was amiss, or if, through that fear of a man which
brings a snare, or through some other unworthy motive, you so far connive at his known vices or defects as
to grant him ordination, by this conduct you partake
with him not only in the sins he has already committed, but in those also which he shall afterwards commit, while he either teaches or lives badly. And therefore you must answer for all the pernicious consequences of his ordination, in ruining his own soul and
the souls of the flock."

Nay, should other ministers be unwarrantably rash
in this matter, and urge you to concur with them, be
not moved by their entreaties or authority to act contrary to your own judgment, lest you be condemned as
accessory to their guilt. In the verse preceding this caution, ministers are charged not to prefer one before
another, and to do nothing by partiality, that is, not to
determine a cause for or against any person till we hear
what can be said on both sides; not to prefer one before
another where there appears no sufficient reason for
such a preference, and not to be swayed by friendship
or prejudice, to be more favorable to one and more severe to another than we ought to be. And, in the end of
the chapter, to encourage this diligence, the apostle in-
forms us that if we proceed with due deliberation we
shall not lose our labor, but shall ordinarily be able to
form a judgment concerning candidates.

"Some men's sins are open beforehand, going before them to judgment; and some men they (that is,
their sins) follow after. Likewise, also, the good works
of some are manifest beforehand, and they (the good
works) that are otherwise cannot be hidden." The
meaning is that some men's sins are so heinous and

notorious that, their sins going as it were before them to judgment, little or no trial is necessary in order to discover them. And the sins of others follow them to judgment because, though less open, yet they also might, in most cases, by due inquiry, be brought to light. In like manner, the good works of some, and their fitness for ordination, are easily discerned even before they undergo a formal trial; and those good works which are not manifest beforehand, but which, through the modesty or obscure situation of the performer, are little observed, may often, by a diligent search, be discovered.

From this remarkable passage, to which we would do well to take heed, the learned Grotius observes that we ought not only to inquire whether a candidate for ordination is innocent of atrocious crimes, but whether he has done much good, seeing that the pious actions of the eminently pious can seldom be hidden. And, agreeable to this, Paul requires not only that a bishop be blameless, but that he have a good report of those who are outside the church lest he fall into reproach; thus freedom from gross scandals, without certain positive evidences of a pious disposition, is no sufficient warrant for us to ordain anyone. It is criminal to lay hands on a candidate if we have no positive ground to hope that he will preach usefully; and it is equally criminal to do it if we have no positive ground to hope that he will be an example to others in word, in conversation, in charity, in spirit, in faith, and in purity. For the last of these is as really a part of the minister's duty, and as really a means to be used by him for saving souls, as the first. "The things," says Paul to Timothy, "that you have heard from me among many witnesses, the same commit to faithful men who shall be able to teach others also." We must have probable evidence of their faithfulness as well as of their ability to teach. Even deacons are first to be proven, and then to use the office of a deacon. Surely, then, ministers, whose office is much more honorable and important, should not be allowed to exercise it till their fitness for it is well tried. But the vast danger of promiscuous admissions into the ministry has been so well represented in a pamphlet published here three years ago, on occasion of an act and overture of the General Assembly of 1746, that I am sensible I have trespassed on your patience in enlarging so much on this heading.

If any allege that there would not be found a sufficient number of ministers for all our churches if we ordained with such caution, I answer that it is better to hazard this inconvenience than to break an express law of Christ, which, if we are less strict in ordaining, we certainly do. Let us mind our duty, and leave the results to providence. Strictness in admission may, indeed, discourage those who bid fairer for starving or poisoning than for feeding the souls of their flocks. But to discourage such is highly commendable, and a small number of able and faithful pastors is more to be desired than a multitude of raw, ignorant, illiterate novices, incapable either to explain or to defend the religion of Jesus; or of polite apostates from the gospel to philosophy, who think their time more usefully and agreeably spent in studying books of science than in studying their Bibles; or of mercenary hirelings, of as mean and sordid disposition as those we read of in 1 Samuel 2:36, who crouched to the high priest for a piece of silver and a morsel of bread, saying, "Put me, I pray thee, into one of the priest's offices, that I may eat a piece of bread."

May God, in mercy, prevent such low and unhappy men from ever creeping into the sacred function! May a faithful, an able, and a successful ministry ever be the blessing of our land! May the glorious Head of the Church appoint unto every dwelling-place of Mount Zion, and to all her assemblies, pastors according to His own heart, to feed His people with knowledge and understanding! And may He whose words are works say to our church in general, and to this corner of it in particular, "This is My rest forever; here will I dwell; for I have desired it. I will abundantly bless her provision. I will satisfy her poor with bread. I will also clothe her priests with righteousness, and her saints shall shout aloud for joy. There will I make the horn of David to bud. I have ordained a lamp for mine anointed. His enemies will I clothe with shame; but upon himself shall his crown flourish."

Ministers of the Gospel Cautioned against Giving Offense

by
Dr. John Erskine

"Giving no offense in any thing, that the ministry
be not blamed." 2 Corinthians 6:3

These words of the Apostle Paul, which were primarily intended to do justice to his own character, and that of Timothy, his beloved son in the faith, present to the view of gospel ministers in every age a fair and approved pattern which they ought to copy if they wish to prosper in their arduous work. The conduct of these excellent men was, in the main, so circumspect and exemplary that it could give no just cause of offense to Jews, to Gentiles, or to the churches of Christ. They carefully avoided whatever might increase the prejudices of unbelievers against the gospel, or might impair the reputation and success of their ministry, by laying a stumbling block, or occasion of offense, in their brother's way.

I intend, in discoursing on this passage, first to explain the duty of giving no offense, then to inculcate upon myself and my brethren in the ministry the practice of that duty, and, lastly, to conclude with some practical reflections on what may be delivered.

1. I am to explain the duty here recommended to

ministers, giving no offense. To preach and to act so that in fact none shall be offended would indeed be a hard (or rather impossible) task. We cannot govern the sentiments and passions of others; and that can never be our duty which is wholly out of our power. The taste of our hearers is so opposite that what is relished by one set of them will necessarily disgust another. So changeable are the humors of not a few that what yesterday they approved, tomorrow they condemn. The weak and captious will censure our not doing what was either impossible or unfit to be done: not visiting the sick when we were altogether ignorant of their sickness; visiting one person more often than another; preaching a little longer than usual, or a little shorter; insisting often on subjects of general importance, or insisting seldom on subjects of less extensive use; repeating the same sermon from different pulpits; borrowing useful observations from the compositions of others; refusing to spend that time in company which duty requires us to devote to our studies. Nay, they will cite circumstances still more insignificant than these: our parentage, our wealth, our poverty, our dress, our necessary recreations, everything that relates to us, everything we say or do, however innocent. Everything we omit, however needless, may, by one or other, be found fault with. To such trifles, triflers alone can constantly attend. If people will take offense where no shadow of offense has been given, his soul must be groveling, and his time and pains poorly employed, who in such low, inconsiderable matters can entirely guard against it.

Even truth and holiness give offense. If any truth is contrary to generally received opinions, many will be our enemies for telling them that truth. If vice is honestly reproved, the obstinate transgressor will be provoked. But if men take umbrage at us for doing our duty, it becomes us to offend men rather than God. When we hold on steadily in paths of truth and righteousness amidst these unjust reproaches, the testimony of God and of a good conscience will afford us unspeakable support and delight. The faithful minister, though reviled by an ungrateful generation as a troubler of Israel and one who turns the world upside down, is glorious in the eyes of the Lord. Though his character may, for a season, be under a cloud, God will at length bring forth his righteousness as the light, and his judgment as the noon day. It is evident, therefore, that the duty of giving no offense only means giving no just cause for offense by doing anything unbecoming our profession as Christians, or our office as ministers of Christ. But it is proper to descend to particulars.

(1) Our life and conduct should be inoffensive. Our station is elevated and conspicuous, and exposes us to the most strict and critical inspection. Many eyes are upon us, and the same allowances will not be made for our miscarriages as for those of others. Though we could speak with the tongues of men and angels, we shall hardly charm our hearers into a life of piety, and convince them that religion is beautiful, unless we exhibit her beauties in a regular, well-ordered conduct. A dissolute life cannot fail to make us base in the sight of the people. When our practice is manifestly inconsistent with our doctrines, the brightest parts will not protect our character; the finest accomplishments will not screen us from deserved reproach.

Nor is it enough that we are not chargeable with

scandalous wickedness. If we indulge ourselves in practices of a suspicious nature, venture to the utmost
bounds of what is lawful, needlessly frequent the company of scoffers of religion, or, at least, spend more of
our leisure hours with the gay and thoughtless than
with sober, serious Christians; if our conduct betrays a
crafty, political, intriguing spirit; if we manifest no relish for retirement, are often and unnecessarily in the
tavern, seldom in the closet, and reserve little of our
time for reading, meditation, and prayer; if a word
scarcely ever drops from us in ordinary conversation
that can either instruct or edify, we transgress the precept of giving no offense. With whatever force of argument and seeming warmth we recommend from the
pulpit heavenly-mindedness and devotion, humility,
self-denial, weanedness from the world, uprightness
and integrity, the careful improvement of time, and a
tender, circumspect life, few who observe our behavior
will be charitable, or rather will be blind enough, to
fancy us as being in earnest. The judicious will
shrewdly suspect that pleasure, gain, or honor is more
dear to us than God's glory and the salvation of souls.
Good men will be offended; and even bad men, whatever they pretend, will, in their hearts, despise us. We
move in a more exalted sphere than others; and, if we
would shine as lights of the world, we need to avoid every appearance of evil, and to consider well not only
what is just and pure, but what is lovely and of good report. The world expects that we should do honor to our
profession, act up to the dignity of our character, and,
with the great apostle to the Gentiles, magnify our office by acquiring, cultivating, and exercising every accomplishment, gift, and grace that tends to promote

our usefulness in the church of Christ. Many things, abstractly considered, may be lawful which yet are not expedient and do not edify. Duty, indeed, sometimes obliges us to contradict the humors of our people. But it is neither acting a wise nor a good part to contradict them for contradiction's sake. In matters indifferent, we should become all things to all men that we may gain the more, and deny ourselves the use of our lawful liberty when, by indulging it, our brother would be caused to stumble, be offended, or made weak.

(2) We should give no offense by choosing injudiciously the subject of our sermons. When we preach what is the result of mere human reason, or teach as doctrines the commandments of men; when we urge uncertain speculation as warmly as if salvation depended on the belief of them, puzzle our hearers with new schemes unsupported by scripture evidence or, by forced unnatural interpretations, torture the inspired writings to speak our mind; when the things we teach, though possibly true in themselves, yet are not important religious truths, explained and enforced in a Scriptural strain, we practically declare by such conduct that we have no high esteem for divine revelation, and have forgotten our commission as ambassadors of Christ. It would be reckoned arrogant presumption even in the ambassadors of an earthly prince should he exceed his instructions and rely on his own sagacity in adjusting the differences of his sovereign with neighboring states. And can an ambassador commissioned by Him, in whom are hidden all the treasures of wisdom and knowledge, be this unfaithful, without the most daring and impious insolence? He bids fairest to preach with success who preaches in words not of

man's wisdom, but which the Holy Ghost teaches, comparing spiritual things with spiritual things. The blessed Spirit sets His seal only to doctrines stamped with His own authority, and which flow from that sacred fountain, unsullied and pure. The gospel, when mingled with human inventions, loses much of its native luster and, like adulterated milk, affords but scanty and unwholesome nourishment. An itch to say what is curious and uncommon is a dangerous turn of mind in a teacher of Christianity. Common truths are like common blessings, of most use and of truest worth; and that is the best sermon which makes the grace of God sweet, salvation through Christ acceptable, sin ugly and hateful, and holiness amiable to the soul.

If they give just ground of offense who add to the Word of God, they do it also who take away from it. All God's words are right. There is nothing forward or perverse in them. Every doctrine and precept is wisely suited to promote God's glory and man's salvation, and was mercifully revealed for that very purpose. "All Scripture is given by inspiration of God, and is profitable for doctrine, for reproof, for correction, and for instruction in righteousness." Those entertain too high a conceit of their own penetration, and very mean ideas of divine wisdom, who fancy it dangerous to preach what the blessed Spirit judged it proper to reveal. If we would keep back from our people nothing profitable, we must endeavor to declare to them the whole counsel of God. Concealing any part of that form of sound words which our commission directs us to publish is unfaithfulness to God, and injustice to the souls of men. "He that hath My Word, let him speak My Word faithfully" (Jeremiah 23:28). And again, "All the words that I command thee to speak unto them, diminish not a word" (Jeremiah 26:2).

As wise and faithful stewards, we must regard the whole family and give to everyone his proper portion, teaching the young and ignorant in a plain, familiar manner the first principles of the oracles of God, while dispensing strong meat to them of full age who, by reason of use, have their senses exercised to discern both good and evil. The erroneous we must endeavor, by sound reasoning, to convince of their mistakes. We must unfold the strictness, spirituality, and extent of God's law, and display the awful sanctions that enforce it to rouse from their spiritual lethargy the secure and thoughtless, the bold and presumptuous, the proud and self-confident. Awakened souls we must gently allure to Christ by the sweet and free invitation of the gospel; and believers we must exhort by a faithful discharge of every duty to adorn the doctrine of God their Savior in all things.

Perhaps it is one chief occasion of our giving offense by not declaring the whole counsel of God that there are certain subjects peculiarly easy and agreeable to us which, on that account, we are apt to imagine the most important, and to insist upon the most frequently. Lecturing usually on large portions of Scripture might be some remedy to this evil. Occasions would, in that way, soon present themselves of explaining every doctrine and inculcating every duty. Both we and our hearers would grow better acquainted with the lively oracles, and learn to read them more profitably. Besides, short occasional hints which naturally arise in our ordinary course of expounding a gospel or epistle may fall with weight on our hearers before they are aware and force conviction, whereas, when the subject of a sermon is directly leveled against vulgar prejudices or fashionable vices, instantly the alarm is taken, and the mind strengthens itself against evidence. The heart is a fort more easily taken by sap than by storm.

But though we give hints of every truth, our sermons will offend the judicious if we insist most frequently and earnestly on subjects of lesser importance, and more sparingly and coldly on those branches of Christianity which are most frequently introduced and have the greatest stress laid upon them in the sacred writings. Our greatest business is to instruct guilty creatures how they may be recovered from the ruins of their apostasy, serve God acceptably here, and enjoy Him forever hereafter. It is justly offensive if we content ourselves with now and then mentioning, in a slight and overly glib manner, those things which affect the very vitals of our common Christianity.

If Christ and salvation through Him are rarely preached, this will be quite opposite to the apostolic pattern. Let it not be pleaded that these doctrines were more necessary to Jews and heathens than to professed Christians. A little observation may convince us that many of our hearers are Christians only in name, and need to be taught these doctrines more perfectly, or, at least, to have deeper impressions of their truth and importance. Besides, it was not only in addressing infidels that the apostles insisted on such subjects. They did it also in their epistles to the saints and faithful in Jesus, who knew these things and were established in the present truth. A considerable part of many of these epistles immediately relates to the peculiar doctrines of Christianity. And, in the practical part of them, these

peculiar doctrines are often urged as motives even to
social and relative duties. For instance, they are urged
to dissuade from evil speaking, and to recommend
meekness and gentleness (Titus 3:2ff). And in the 8th
verse of that chapter, the apostle, after pronouncing
the doctrine of justification through Christ a faithful
saying, enjoins Titus to affirm it constantly in order to
excite believers to carefulness in maintaining good
works.

But I have a still higher pattern to plead. More of
our Lord's sermons are recorded by the beloved disciple than by the other evangelists; and of these the principal subjects are the dangerous state of the unconverted, and the nature, necessity, and blessed consequences of faith in Christ, of union with Him, and of
the sanctifying influences of His Spirit. The last and
longest of these sermons, though preached to the apostles only, who had long ago professed their dependence on Him as their guide to eternal life, yet chiefly
relates to the mutual love of Christ and His people, and
the safety and comfort that flow from the exercise of
faith in Him. The doctrine of Christ crucified is the instituted means for producing and nourishing the divine life, and should be the center of our sermons, in
reference to and dependence upon which other subjects ought to be considered.

The nature of true religion (as distinguished from
every counterfeit appearance), the genuine workings of
it in the heart, and the fruits of it in the life are subjects
that need to be often explained and inculcated.
Scripture abounds with occasional instructions on
these headings. Psalm 119, our Lord's sermon on the
mount, the epistle of James, and John's first epistle

treat them designedly and at full length. On the one hand, we must inculcate it frequently that however blameless men's outward conduct may appear, yet, if they act barely from self-interested principles, and have no charity and love for God, for Christ, and for their brethren of mankind, they are nothing, have not the spirit of Christ in them, and are none of His: "The end of the commandment is love out of a pure heart, a good conscience, and faith unfeigned." In other words, the end of divine revelation is not gained upon us till we love our duty, see a beauty and excellency in holiness, and esteem it our meat and drink to do the will of our heavenly Father.

On the other hand, we must remind our hearers that, where the tree is good, the fruit also will be good, and that no pretenses to faith or love are well founded which do not justify themselves by a suitable practice. Nor must we content ourselves with general encomiums on holiness and good works. It is necessary minutely to describe the various graces of the Spirit that constitute the Christian temper, and the various duties we owe to God, our neighbors, and ourselves. We do not comply with the precepts of the apostles, and imitate their example in speaking the things that become sound doctrine, unless we inculcate upon our hearers the particular obligations that result from their different ages, stations, and relations (Titus 2:1–2). For vice as well as error is contrary to sound doctrine, according to the glorious gospel of the blessed God (1 Timothy 1:9–11).

Further, we give offense if we do not insist on subjects suited to the spiritual state of our flocks, and to the dispensations of providence towards them. In many discourses, the counsel is good, but not for the time, whereas a well-timed discourse bids fairest to strike and edify. There is also a time to keep silence as well as a time to speak. In many cases, we will instruct and admonish in vain if we do not wait till men's minds are calm, composed, and in proper temper to give us a fair hearing. Paul would not feed with strong meat those who were not able to bear it. On some occasions, an oblique hint will irritate more than a severe, undisguised reproof would do at another season.

It is evident from what has been said that the matter of his sermons must give offense whose ideas of the great truths of Christianity are superficial, confused, and indistinct. Men must have knowledge ere they impart it; and there is one only source whence divine knowledge, without danger of mistake, can be derived, and where it is the duty and interest of the minister of Christ, with the utmost diligence, to dig for it. Let the writings of philosophers, of historians, and of politicians be the study of those whose business it is to unfold the secrets of nature, to transmit to posterity the memorable deeds of heroes, or to give counsel to their sovereign in matters of state. These branches of knowledge are at best ornamental, not essential, to a teacher of Christianity. He may innocently, nay, usefully, amuse himself with them; but he cannot, without sacrilege, devote to them the greatest part of his time. His office is to make known to perishing sinners the sublime, affecting, and comforting truths of the lively oracles, and, for that end, attentively to read them, to meditate on them day and night. And while he does not despise the labors of able and worthy men who have endeavored to illustrate them, he is to secure a better and more effectual help by humbly and fervently imploring the Father of Lights to open his eyes to behold wondrous things out of God's Word. Thus shall he become a scribe instructed into the kingdom of God, and, like a man who is a householder, bring forth out of his treasures things new and old.

(3) When ministers give no offense by the subject of their sermons, they may give a great deal by their manner of handling them, particularly when they do not preach in a manner calculated to inform the judgment. Men are rational creatures, and, if we would address them as such, the understanding should, as the leading power, be first applied to. For this purpose we must clearly open and explain the truth, confirm it by arguments suited to the capacities of our hearers, and do all this in plain, familiar language, which even those in low life may easily understand. Christianity was designed for the peasant as well as the philosopher, and, since the learned and wise comprise a small proportion of most congregations, to preach it in a way in which only they are likely to be the better for it is highly offensive. Philosophy, though from the press it has done religion substantial service, yet when often introduced in the pulpit generally hurts it by usurping the place of what would be more useful, and probably more acceptable too. Scholastic niceties, metaphysical distinctions, and a fine subtle thread of reasoning may indeed sometimes be necessary in answering metaphysical objections against religion; and therefore, on some rare occasions, the use of them in the pulpit may be profitable. But the bulk of audiences are incapable of following a long and intricate train of thought, and therefore will be confounded by it, not instructed and

convinced. While some may applaud such sermons as deep and rational, the more wise will despise them as idle and injudicious. This, however, is no apology for any who verge to the opposite extreme, slighting order and exactness in their compositions, and who instead of keeping close to a subject entertain their hearers with confused, incoherent discourses, empty of sentiment, but full of insipid repetitions and impertinent, rambling excursions.

I say nothing of those whose long perplexed periods, occasioned by unnecessary epithets and expletives, parentheses and digressions, render their sermons at once tedious and obscure. This unhappiness of style is remarkable in some who stand in the first rank of genius and penetration, who, exerting thought more intensely than others, had little attention to spare for expression. Their fault is more voluntary, and therefore more offensive, who by a false affectation of the elegant or the sublime, soar aloft above the comprehension of the hearers. Bombastic descriptions, glittering flowers of eloquence, and luxuriant flights of wit had better be left to the heroes of romance. Sermons composed in such a style may indeed entertain and amuse, but they lack perspicuity, the very first and fundamental excellency of speech. Even the justest metaphors, when too much crowded, enervate a discourse; they darken instead of illustrate the sense, and, to use the words of another, resemble the windows in old cathedrals, in which the painting keeps out the light. I acknowledge the best sentiments, if conveyed in mean and low images, and clothed in a rustic and slovenly dress, provoke laughter in some and occasion uneasiness in others; but we need not run into a finical nicety of style in order to avoid a sordid negligence.

Still more offensive than these is an obscurity affected for its own sake. It must offend every honest man if, to conceal unpopular opinions and put on an air of orthodoxy, we use expressions which may be interpreted with equal ease to various, and even contrary purposes. Paul's words are emarkable in 1 Corinthians 14:8–9: "If the trumpet give an uncertain sound, who shall prepare himself for the battle? So likewise ye, except ye utter by the tongue words easy to be understood, how shall it be known what is spoken? For ye shall speak to the air." If this is a good argument against preaching in an unknown tongue, it is equally good against everything else that disguises instead of unfolding our sentiments of Christianity. The apostles used great plainness of speech; and it is an apostolic injunction, "If any man speak, let him speak as the oracles of God." Let his style be plain and clear like that of the sacred writings, not dark and ambiguous like the oracles of the heathen.[1]

After all, informing the judgment, though the first part of our work, is far from the whole of it. Sermons will do little service if they are not also calculated to command a reverend attention, to strike the conscience, and to warn and affect the heart. We speak as ministers of God; therefore it becomes us to speak with dignity and boldness, not fearing the face of man.

---

[1] It was justly observed of the council of Trent: "We know the skill and craft of these men; scarcely at any time do they speak something plainly or simply. And while other men speak so that men may understand, these wish nothing more than not to be understood." Too many Protestants have imitated them in this.

Favor should not bribe, nor frowns nor dangers affright us, from delivering our Master's message. I do
not mean to vindicate pride nor passion. A proper
decorum should be observed, especially in administering reproof. It is not fit to say to a king, "You are
wicked," or to princes, "You are ungodly." Persons in
public positions must be treated with a deference suited
to their station; and even the meanest must not be in-
sulted. Courage, however, and faithfulness are by no
means inconsistent with meekness and discretion; and
if the greatest dare grossly and openly to transgress, the
minister of Christ should dare to reprove.

Besides the meanness of some in conniving at fashionable vices, there are others whose thoughtless, unconcerned gesture and pronunciation greatly diminish
the dignity of their pulpit performances, and make
them be received with indifference, perhaps indignation, instead of respect. A light and merry air, or an an-
tic, jovial carriage in executing the weighty commission with which God has entrusted us, is contrary to the
rules of decency, and cannot fail to prejudice the hearers. It is impossible to be too grave and serious in addresses on the success of which the happiness of immortal souls in so great a measure depends.

But though our language is plain and elegant, our
method accurate, and our manner grave and solemn,
yet, if our discourses are flat and lifeless, they will seldom warm the heart. Mr. Melmoth has observed that in
Archbishop Tillotson's sermons a pathetic, animated
address is often wanting, even on occasions when naturally we would have expected it. Abundance of spirit,
however, appears in some of his discourses, especially
in exposing the absurdities and impieties of the church

of Rome. And it might have been remarked with equal justice that numerous volumes of sermons published in England since that time, while inferior to the Archbishop's in important sentiments well arrangd, and in many genuine beauties of style, resemble them only in that languid manner of which Melmoth complains. Alas, my brethren, dull and pointless arrows are ill-suited to pierce the consciences of hardened sinners. Soft and drowsy harangues, instead of rousing a secure generation, will rather increase their spiritual lethargy; and a cold preacher will soon have a cold audience. Jesus has entrusted us with the concerns of His people, a people dearly bought and greatly beloved; we have to do with souls that must be happy or miserable forever; we address them in the name of God upon matters of infinite importance; and is it not an indignity to Him, whose ambassadors we are, to execute our commission coolly and as if half asleep? Will it not tempt others to slight our message if, by our manner of delivering it, we appear to slight ourselves? When our own hearts are most impressed with the inestimable worth of immortal souls; when out of the abundance of the heart the mouth speaks; when our sentiments, style, voice, and gesture reveal how much we are in earnest— then we are most likely to touch the hearts of our hearers, and make them feel the force of what we say.

I have said so much on preaching since there are more directions and exhortations in Scripture related to it than are related to any other branch of our office. I must barely hint at the remaining particulars lest I encroach too far on your time and patience.

(4) We may give offense not only by an improper manner of preaching, but by a neglect or undue perfor-

mance of the other public offices of our station. In leading the devotions of the church, we give offense when either the matter, expression, or manner is unsuitable; when we are long and tedious; when we mingle our own passions and prejudices in our addresses to God; when we introduce disputable matters, in which many sincere Christians cannot join with us; when we do not adapt our prayers to the particular circumstances and necessities of our people; when we hurry over our prayers carelessly; when we manifest no becoming seriousness and solemnity of spirit, no realizing sense of the value of the blessings for which we plead; and when we seem to forget that Jesus is the way, the truth, and the life, through whom alone our guilty race can obtain access to God and acceptance with Him.

It is just cause of offense, and, did vital piety flourish, would be offensive to our people that the Lord's Supper is so seldom dispensed. And as our manner of dispensing that ordinance is one chief hindrance of its frequency, it is worthy of our inquiry how far that also is blamable. Undoubtedly we give offense if for trifling, unwarrantable causes we put off administrating it, or if we usurp the prerogative of Christ as sole Lawgiver of the church by making the terms of Christian communion either wider or narrower than He has made them.

And this leads me to observe that, as the discipline of the church is in part committed to us, we give offense if we exercise it with respect of persons and, through a mistaken tenderness for any, or a fear of incurring their displeasure, allow them to live without due censure in the open practice of scandalous crimes instead of rebuking them with authority so that others also may fear. At the same time, we give offense if we claim a right to judge those who are outside the church. It is an offense against common sense to expel men from a society to which they never seemed to belong, and to debar them from privileges to which they never had, or pretended to have, any title.

Probably some might be offended, and none greatly edified, should I say much on our conduct in judicatures. Of this subject much has been said from the pulpit, and on occasions too where no purpose of edification could be gained by saying anything. This much, however, I hope may be said without impropriety on such an occasion. To act a juggling, unsteady part, and, due to connections of any kind, to vary from our professed principles; to sneak, cringe, and prostitute our consciences either to the humors of the great or to the prejudices of the populace; to behave with insolence to men who are our superiors in age and experience; to listen with avidity to one side of the question while we deny a fair and full hearing to the other; to silence sober reasoning by raillery, by dark, malicious innuendoes, by bitter, satirical invectives, or by noisy cries for a vote; to treat one another with harshness and severity for different sentiments and different conduct in matters of doubtful disputation—these cannot fail to offend every cool and impartial observer. Nor can it, I think, be disputed that we give offense if we examine slightly the opinions, dispositions, and abilities of those we recommend to important offices, and solemnly attest that men have qualifications which either we know that they lack, or at best they do not know that they have.

In ordaining to the ministry we act in the name of

Christ, and therefore give offense if we act against His authority or without it. Genius, learning, prudence, and aptness to teach are all necessary parts of furniture for a minister; and, in ordinary cases, without some measure of them none ought to be set apart to that honorable service. But the most eminent gifts and abilities, when grace does not direct the proper use of them, may too probably qualify men to be plagues instead of blessings to the church of God. Jesus would not commit His sheep to Peter till he had answered satisfyingly the question, "Lovest thou Me?" He who knows all things knew the love of His disciple, and therefore thus inquired, chiefly for our sakes, that in committing to others the ministry of reconciliation we should follow his steps. They who have seen Christ's beauty, tasted His love, and felt the pleasures and advantages of religion are peculiarly qualified by their Christian experience to recommend them to others with dignity and freedom. Singular activity is requisite in the many labors, and singular fortitude and firmness of mind in the many difficulties and afflictions, to which faithful ministers are exposed. Now, love and love alone will reconcile to these, nay, render them a delight. We are untender, therefore, and unkind to the feeble flock of Christ if we commit them to men who, for all we know or care, bear them no affection, and probably, instead of feeding and defending them, may poison them, or expose them to be devoured. None will presume thus to plead before Christ in the great day of account: "It is true, we entrusted our souls, dear in Thy sight, and for whom Thou didst shed Thy precious blood, to one whose conduct seemed to reveal that his natural enmity to Thee remained unsubdued. But he was an agreeable companion, a man of strong natural powers, and an accomplished orator." If such a plea would be absurd, must not that conduct be absurd which requires it? We are not indeed to seek, for we cannot obtain an absolute certainty, that those we ordain are lovers of Jesus. It is God's prerogative to search the heart, and the judgment we form on the most probable evidence may prove wrong. But it is enough to warrant our act if there is a profession of real religion, and an outward conduct in some measure agreeable to that profession. Without a doubt, different sentiments of a candidate, and different opportunities of knowing him thoroughly, may justify some in bearing a part in his ordination when it would be in others presumptuous wickedness.

There is one thing more in our ordinations which, I think, merits our serious attention, and that is the act of solemnly giving to one, in the name of Jesus, the charge of a congregation unwilling to submit to him, and among whom there is no probability of his usefulness.[2] Upon what principles this can be vindicated, I am yet to learn. The state must no doubt determine

---

[2] The zeal of Passius, canon of Valencia, outran his knowledge when he maintained in the Council of Trent that it was a devilish, pestilent invention of late heretics, destructive of faith and of the church of God, to ascribe to any claim of right the voice or consent allowed the people in the choice of their pastors, which was a mere favor, revocable at pleasure. Yet he certainly argued consistently in insisting that those passages should be expunged from the pontifical which seem to suppose such consent necessary; particularly where the bishop says, in ordaining a presbyter, "It is not an error from the practice of the fathers, when in order to choose who will lead to the altar, counselors and people, it is necessary, and easy to obediently deliver, whom they approve and supply ordination."

what shall be the established religion, and who shall be entitled to the legal benefice for teaching it, but no government ought, and our government does not attempt, to impose upon any either a religion or an instructor in religion. It is still more difficult to conceive why a conscientious scruple to bear a part in an ordination, the form of which seems to assert a falsehood, should exclude a man otherwise qualified from serving God in the gospel of His Son. I have seen no act of Parliament or constitution of the church of Scotland that enjoins this. Sure I am, it is not enjoined by Christian forbearance and love.

(5) We give offense by the neglect or undue performance of the more private duties of our calling. If we pay no regard to the souls of our charge, unless in the pulpit and in our immediate preparation for it; if we seem indifferent to how we stand in the esteem and affection of our people, or to what is the success of our labors; if we do not use every proper method for conveying and cherishing religious impressions, for preventing backsliding, and for recovering those who have fallen from their spiritual decays; if we neglect to warn the unruly, to comfort those who mourn, to visit the afflicted, and to catechize the young and ignorant when we have any probable prospect that these services may be useful; or if we manage our visits to the sick so incautiously that bystanders are encouraged to put off thoughts of repentance to their last moments, and thereby sustain a hurt which any good done to the dying will seldom balance, we greatly fail in our duty, and are guilty of giving offense.

2. I now proceed briefly to enforce the exhortation of giving no offense. The text itself suggests a powerful

argument: if we give offense, the ministry will be blamed. The people of God will justly be angry with us, and will condemn our faulty conduct. Nay, possibly, all our future ministrations will, in their eyes, become hateful or contemptible; and thus a fair prospect of usefulness will be unhappily blasted. Though a man could speak like an oracle, little regard will be paid to what he says when his credit has sunk.

Nor is this the worst; the ungodly do not confine their censures to the weak or worthless minister, but, as though one clergyman stood representative of all, take occasion from his licentiousness or imprudence to traduce ministers in general as being fools or knaves. In every place there are subtle emissaries of Satan who incessantly watch for our halting, and take a handle from the least misbehavior of which we are guilty to reflect on the most innocent of our brethren. The enemies of Jesus are fond of everything that can expose our order; and if our conduct is profligate, or our pulpit compositions despicable, that affords them the wished-for pretext to gratify their malice. The cry is, "They are all alike." Nay, it is well if the sacred office itself is not aspersed, and the wisdom of God who instituted it arraigned. Thus, when we depart out of the way, it causes many to stumble at the law, and to abhor the offering of the Lord. Jesus Himself is crucified afresh, and His holy religion reproached through our faults, unjustly imputed to them. We are ambassadors for Christ, and, by our ill management of that trust, disgrace is reflected on Him in whose name we act, the cause of God suffers, the hearts of the godly are grieved, the wicked are hardened in their wickedness, and precious souls eternally perish.

"Woe to the world because of offenses. It must needs be that offenses come, but woe to the man (and double woe to the minister) by whom they come. It were better for him that a millstone were hanged about his neck, and he cast into the depths of the sea." Though his heavenly Master, who invested him with so honorable an office, is present and observes his conduct, he dares to be indolent in His service, and basely to betray His interest. He commits the most direct and horrible perjury by violating the solemn engagements he came under to take heed to the flock of which he was ordained an overseer. He feels no remorse for offending the Sovereign of Zion by a neglect of duty and a breach of trust which, in his own servant, or in the servant of an earthly sovereign, would have appeared to him infamous and detestable. But possibly, when death is about to seal the eyes of his body, the eyes of his soul may be opened to perceive things as they really are.

After having spent his life in doing the work of the Lord deceitfully, and pursuing the honors, riches, and pleasures of this world, not the glory of God and the salvation of souls, I think I see him receive the awful summons, "Give an account of your stewardship, for you must be no longer a steward." He feels himself about to be dragged to a state of misery, eternal and intolerable. Conscience awakens from its fatal slumber and, by the most cruel and unsupportable reproaches, avenges his contempt of its old and long-forgotten remonstrances. His wonted arts of stilling this inward tormentor now lose their power. Fearfulness and trembling come upon him, and horror overwhelms him. Hell is naked before him, and destruction without a covering. And God, justly provoked, laughs at his calamity, and mocks when his fear comes.

Yet, possibly, another, equally unfaithful, may have no bonds in his death, and leave this world as he lived in it, thoughtless of God and duty, and regardless of eternity. But if dying does not, surely death shall put an end to his peace. See him appearing before the tribunal of a now–inexorable Judge. Behold his countenance changed, his thoughts troubling him, the joints of his loins loosed, and his knees smiting one against another, when, lo, a voice more dreadful than thunder thus accosts him: "Wicked and slothful servant, what hadst thou to do to declare My statutes, or that thou shouldst take My covenant in thy mouth, seeing thou hatest instruction, and castest My words behind thee?" Mark a numerous flock ruined by his negligence or bad example. Listen to them calling for vengeance. The cry of their blood enters into the ears of the Lord of Sabaoth, and the irreversible doom is pronounced: "Take him, bind him hand and foot, cast him into utter darkness; there shall be weeping, and wailing, and gnashing of teeth."

Turn away from this shocking scene, and observe on the right hand of the Son of Man a faithful pastor. Possibly his dying words were words of triumph and transport: "This is my rejoicing, the testimony of my conscience, that in simplicity and godly sincerity, not with fleshly wisdom, but by the grace of God, I have had my conversation in the world. I have fought the good fight, I have finished my course, I have kept the faith. Henceforth is laid up for me a crown of righteousness, which the Lord, the righteous Judge, shall give me at that day; and not to me only but to all them also that love His appearing." But with what superior joy does he lift up his head when he rests from his labors, when his warfare is accomplished, and when the day of his complete redemption dawns! He walked with God in peace and equity, and turned many away from iniquity. These he now presents to the great Shepherd of the sheep, saying, "Behold me, and the children Thou hast given me." He is their rejoicing, and they also are his rejoicing in the day of the Lord Jesus. Joyful to both was the sound of the gospel, but more joyful now is the final sentence: "Well done, good and faithful servant. Thou hast been faithful over a few things, I will make thee ruler over many things; enter thou into the joy of thy Lord."

If, therefore, we have any zeal for the glory of God, if any interest in the Redeemer's kingdom, if any tender concern for the salvation of our hearers, and if, in the great day of the Lord, we would not be found among them who offend, and work iniquity, and who after having prophesied in Christ's name hear Him pronounce against us the dreadful sentence, "Depart from me, I know you not," let us take heed to ourselves and to our doctrine, and walk circumspectly, not as fools, but as wise, giving no offense in anything that the ministry be not blamed.

It is now time to hasten to a conclusion. If it is our duty to give no offense, how difficult then is our office! What superior accomplishments, natural and acquired, what exalted improvements in vital piety, what continual aids of the Holy Spirit are requisite to preserve from giving offense in anything, as we are exposed to such a variety of temptations and snares! The best of us have cause, with grief and self-abasement, to acknowledge that in many things we daily offend. Let us not, however, sink into slothfulness and despair. God's grace will be sufficient for us if we implore it, and He will perfect strength in our weakness. "Say not, O humble servant of Christ, 'I am a child'; for thou shalt go to all that God shall send thee; and whatsoever He commandeth thee, thou shalt speak."

What he has done for many others may greatly encourage our prayers and endeavors. We have heard with our ears, our fathers have told us, what burning and shining lights have gone before us in the work of the Lord. We have heard of their holy, exemplary lives; their strict discipline, both in their own families and in the church of God; the gravity, nay, dignity, of their appearance; their animated, penetrating sermons, and their edifying manner in familiar discourse. May a double portion of their excellent spirit rest upon us who come after them! And when, from time to time, our fathers are stripped of their priestly robes, may the sons of the prophets who stand up in their room even exceed them in knowledge of divine things, in piety, in wisdom, in diligence, and in success, so that thus our holy religion may descend uncorrupted to distant ages, and that the people who shall be created may praise the Lord.

I have been exhorting myself and my reverend fathers and brethren not to give offense. It is equally necessary to exhort you, our hearers, not to be hasty in taking it. Be tender, my friends, of our reputation. If anything is insinuated to our disadvantage, be not rash and easy in believing it. If the charge is not supported by sufficient evidence, regard it not. Against an elder, receive not an accusation unless it comes by two or three witnesses. By wounding our good name, you ren-

der our ministry despicable and unsuccessful; and
nothing can be more pleasing to Satan, or hurtful to
your own eternal interests. Judge not our cause till you
have given it fair, impartial hearing. Pass no sentence
against us till you know we have done what is alleged,
and till you also know we had no good reason for doing
it. And since God instructs you by men of like passion
and infirmities as yourselves, do not expect from them
angelic perfection. Make candid allowances for those
errors and frailties that are incident to the wisest and
best of men. Throw over them the veil of charity. Do
not form a judgment of our general character from one
unguarded word or action. God has threatened that
those shall be cut off who watch for iniquity, who make
a man an offender for a word, and who lay a snare for
him who reproves in the gate. You expect we should
give no offense by the neglect of our duty; and we, with
the same justice, expect that you should give no offense
by the neglect of yours. And offense you give us if you
do not attend our ministerial instructions, implore the
blessing of God upon them, and actually improve by
them. If many professed Christians spent no more time
in censuring ministers than in praying for them, the
ministry in this land would be less blamed than it is at
present, and probably less blameworthy too. Meantime,
what is amiss in our conduct will be no excuse for despising the message we bring in the name of Jesus, and
persisting in impenitence and unbelief.

If an inoffensive ministry is this important, how
careful should patrons be to present and parishes, still
enjoying the important privilege of election, to call
none to the pastoral office who may be in danger of
giving offense by their weak abilities, unsound princi-

ples, or dissolute lives! And how foolish and criminal a part do candidates act who hastily rush into the sacred function ere they have laid in the necessary furniture for discharging it honorably! Is there not cause to fear that not only their character, but religion in general, may suffer for the reproach of their youth?

Upon the whole, would we give no offense as men, as Christians, as ministers of Christ? Let us search out the sins and infirmities to which we are chiefly liable so that we may guard against these with peculiar care. In order to discover our weak side, let us duly regard the opinion others entertain of us. Let us not interpret friendly admonition as a disparagement and affront, but thankfully receive it as a mark of unfeigned affection. Say, with David, "Let the righteous smite me, it shall be a kindness; and let him reprove me, it shall be as excellent oil which shall not break my head." We are often blind to our own failings; and happy are we if we can engage some wise and good man who tenderly regards our welfare to point them out. But if we find none this faithful and honest, let us wisely improve the accusations of enemies, and learn from them those blemishes and defects to which, without help of such ill-natured monitors, we might have remained strangers.

May we all, whether in public or private stations, be blameless and harmless, the sons of God without rebuke, shining as lights in the world, maintaining always consciences void of offense toward God and towards man. And may the Lord our God be with us, as He was with our fathers. Let Him not leave us nor forsake us, so that we may incline our hearts to Him, to walk in all His ways, and to keep His holy commandments forever.

Appendix

[The preceding sermon having been first preached at an ordination, the charges then delivered to the minister and congregation are here added.]

Charge to the Minister

Though giving the usual charge would have better become one or another of our venerable fathers, yet, since the place where I stand requires it, suffer me, reverend sir, to be your monitor. Providence has called you to an honorable, but at the same time a difficult office. Gifts are necessary to capacitate you for it; grace, to animate you to discharge it faithfully. A small measure of gifts and low attainments in grace will poorly answer these important purposes. If you would be a vessel unto honor, sanctified and meet for the Master's use, and prepared unto every good work, covet earnestly the best gifts: the gift of knowledge, the gift of utterance, the gift of prudence. Lift up your heart to the Father of lights in humble, fervent supplication that He would plentifully pour out upon you these and all other good and perfect gifts. And as they are not now imparted miraculously, but acquired through the blessing of God in the use of means, join to your prayers diligent application to study. Meditate on divine things; give yourself wholly to them so that your profiting might appear unto all. Those of the most extensive knowledge know only in part, and need to learn the way of God more perfectly.

Give attendance to reading. Make a wise choice of the books you read. Study those most which most tend to increase in you the dispositions and abilities proper for your office. There is one book, or rather a collection of books, which, without an appearance of arrogance, I may venture to recommend as of all others the best. I need not say that I mean the Bible. Make that your chief study; for, if rightly understood and improved, it is able to make the man of God perfect, thoroughly furnished unto every good word and work. Apollos's character was that of "an eloquent man, and mighty in the Scriptures." It is to be wished that both branches of that character were found in every minister; yet the last is by much the most valuable. If we are well acquainted with the doctrines of the gospel and the arguments that support them, and understand the duties of the Christian life, the motives that enforce them, the hindrances of their practice, and the best methods of removing these hindrances, we may, by manifestation of the truth, commend ourselves to men's consciences in the sight of God—though to those who are enamored with the enticing words of man's wisdom, and who regard sound and show more than substance, our bodily presence may appear weak and our speech contemptible.

Be equally diligent to improve in every holy disposition. Your public work will be much affected by the frame of your spirit. If you decline in religion, your flock will fare the worse; but the better Christian you are, the more useful minister you are likely to be. Seek, therefore, above all things, to grow in grace, especially in that grace of love: love for God, love for Christ, and love for precious souls. For this purpose, live a life of faith on the Son of God. Abide in Him, and constantly depend upon Him for all needful supplies of divine influence. Then will you feel your Master's work to be a

delight, not a burden, and will vigorously exert your
abilities for the glory of God and the welfare of man.
Your sermons will be serious and your prayers fervent;
your private conversation will naturally turn to subjects
good for the use of edifying, and your life, as well as
your doctrine, will point out the path to the heavenly
mansions.

With pure and upright intentions, dedicate yourself
to the service of God in the gospel of His Son. Take the
oversight of the flock, not by constraint, but willingly;
not for filthy lucre, but of a ready mind. To use the
words of another on a similar occasion, "You would
better be the offscouring of all flesh than preach to
gain the vain applause of your fellow worms. You would
better beg your bread than enter upon the ministry as a
trade to live by. However those may live who act from no
higher principle, it will be dreadful to die for them,
and more dreadful for them to appear before their
Judge." Expect, therefore, your reward from God only.
Resolve, in divine strength, at no time to use flattering
words or a cloak of covetousness, neither of man to
seek glory, but ever to speak and act not as pleasing to
men but to God who tries the heart.

Be diligent and faithful in the actual discharge of
your office. Take heed that you fulfill the ministry you
have received from the Lord. The longest life quickly
hastens to a period; your time for service swiftly flies
away, and will soon be irrecoverably past and gone.
Work, therefore, the work of Him who sent you while it
is day. "The night cometh, when no man can work."
Make full proof of your ministry. Do not think that performing one branch of duty will atone for neglecting
another, but, insofar as time and strength permit, at-

tend upon each in its proper season.

Allot the greatest portion of your time to those parts of your work, public or private, that are most essential and important. Preach the Word, reprove, rebuke, and exhort, with all long-suffering. Study your sermons well, and beware of offering to God and His people that which costs you nothing. Endeavor to be thoroughly acquainted with the circumstances and dispositions of your hearers, their prejudices against religion, and the rocks in which their souls are in the greatest hazard of being shipwrecked. Suit your discourses to their various necessities. "Study to show thyself approved unto God, a workman that needeth not to be ashamed, rightly dividing the Word of truth." Seek out and set in order acceptable words; and when about to prepare for the pulpit, beg the direction of the Spirit in choosing a subject, His assistance in composing and delivering your sermon, and His blessing to render it effectual. Arrows thus fetched from heaven bid fairest to reach the cases of your hearers, and to pierce their hearts.

Take heed to yourself, as well as to your doctrine. Let your life testify that you believe what you preach. Be wise as a serpent and harmless as a dove. "Watch and pray, that ye enter not into temptation." Flee youthful lusts; be a pattern to believers in words, in conversation, in charity, in spirit, in faith, and in purity. Win the affections of all by an obliging, courteous behavior, and, by preserving a suitable dignity of character, secure their esteem. An affable, condescending manner has often recommended a bad cause; and sourness and ill nature have raised unconquerable prejudices against many a good one. "The wrath of man worketh not the righteousness of God." The servant of the Lord must not strive, but be gentle to all men, patient, in meekness instructing those who oppose themselves, if God, peradventure, will give them repentance to the acknowledgment of the truth. But though meekness should temper your zeal, remember that zeal in return should enliven your meekness. You enter into the ministry on a day in which iniquity abounds and the love of many waxes cold. The peculiar doctrines of Christianity are run down and opposed, and a tender, circumspect behavior is ridiculed by many who value themselves as standards of genius or politeness. In such a day, exert your courage to stem that torrent of infidelity and vice which threatens to break in upon us and destroy everything valuable. Contend earnestly for the faith once delivered to the saints. Be not ashamed of Christ's words and ways in an adulterous and perverse generation, lest the Son of Man be ashamed of you when He comes in the glory of His Father with the holy angels.

These things, my dear brother, are no easy task. I hope you have often counted the cost, and with deep concern lamented your insufficiency. But know for your encouragement that through Christ strengthening you, you may do all things. He has said to His ministers, "Lo, I am with you always, even to the end of the world." And "faithful is He who hath promised, who also will do it."

If your labors should not be crowned with the desired success, be not weary in well-doing; for in due season you shall reap if you faint not. Though Israel should not be gathered, yet, if faithful in your work, you shall receive a glorious recompense. Besides, success may come when you expect it least. Be instant, therefore, in season and out of season. He who observes the wind shall not reap. "In the morning sow thy seed, and in the evening withhold not thine hand; for thou knowest not whether shall prosper, either this or that, or whether they both shall be alike good."

Charge to the People

I shall now conclude with a short address to the people of this congregation.

Be thankful, my brethren, for a gospel ministry. Let the infidel and profane account it a burden, not a blessing to society; but admire the goodness of God in an institution so wisely calculated to promote your best interest. Were it not for public teaching, ignorance and vice should soon grow to so prodigious a height that not even the form of religion would remain. Receive with becoming affection him who is this day ordained your pastor. Consider the dignity of the office with which he is invested, and entertain him with suitable respect. Ministers are men of God; they minister in His name and by His appointment. See, then, that your pastor is with you without fear, because he works the work of the Lord. Esteem him highly in love, for his work's sake. Ministers would labor with better success if they lived more in the hearts of their people. Add not, therefore, to your pastor's difficulties by an undutiful carriage. Rather, assist and strengthen him to bear up under them. Put the best construction on his words and actions which they can possibly bear; do not treat him rudely; and do not vent your spleen against him, though in his doctrine or life lesser blemishes should appear. Curb such an insolent, intemperate zeal by reflecting on the apostle's direction: "Rebuke not an elder, but entreat him as a father." Contempt cast upon

faithful ministers, and injuries done to them, Christ
will resent as done to Himself.

Forsake not the assembling of yourselves together,
as the manner of some is. Withdraw not from ordinances dispensed by your pastor, though his sentiments in lesser matters should differ from yours. I say
"in lesser matters" for if an angel may be lawfully accursed, surely a minister may be lawfully deserted who
preaches another gospel, who lays another foundation
for the hopes of guilty sinners than God has laid. But
bring not against him unjustly so heavy a charge.
Remember, in this imperfect state lesser mistakes are
unavoidable, and will not vindicate your separating
from him. And where a case is not extremely clear, you
owe considerable deference to his judgment, as he has
greater leisure than most of you for studying, and
greater advantages for understanding the sacred oracles. Let, therefore, your pastor ever find you humble
and teachable, swift to hear, slow to speak, slow to
wrath. Do not come to church with a captious, quarrel-
some disposition. With what heart can ministers
preach when hearers are eager to pick up something
with which to find fault? Act a worthier part. Laying
aside all malice, and guile, and hypocrisy, and envying,
and evil speaking, hearken with meekness to that engrafted Word which is able to save your souls; like the
noble Bereans, receive the instructions of your teachers
with all readiness of mind. Do not yield them, however,
an implicit faith, but search the Scriptures daily
whether these things are so. Insofar as they stand the
test of that infallible touchstone, regard them not as
the words of a man, but as they are in truth the word of
the living God.

See that you reject not Christ when, by His ministers, He speaks to you from heaven. When He calls, do not refuse; when He stretches forth His hand, do not disregard it. "Be doers of the Word and not hearers only, deceiving your own souls." While you have the light, walk in the light, lest darkness come upon you. It is but for a little while that ministers can be useful; ere long they must cease to preach, and you to hear. Those servants of God who now show you the way of salvation must, in a while, resign their places, and the eye that now sees them must see them no more. Comply, then, with their wholesome counsels while yet you enjoy them, lest you mourn at the last, and say, "How have I hated instruction, and my soul despised reproof! I have not obeyed the voice of my teachers, nor inclined my ear to them who instructed me."

Second the labors of your minister by private endeavors, suitable to your several stations, for the good of souls. Train up your children in the way they should go, and encourage any serious impressions made upon them. When discipline is exercised against open offenders, show that the honor of God and the happiness of precious souls lie nearer your hearts than the ease and reputation of any man. The efficacy of church censures will much depend on your conduct towards those who fall under them. Have no company with such so that they may be ashamed; and if they will not hear the church, let them be to you as heathen men and publicans.

And when you are allowed the nearest access to a throne of grace, and feel your hearts to be in the most devout and heavenly frame, wrestle and make supplication for your minister, that his own soul may prosper and be in health, that the presence of God may accompany him in all his administrations, and that, when he plants and waters, God Himself may give the increase.

May his doctrine drop as the rain, and his speech distill as the dew. And may the soul of every one of you be like a watered garden, and like a spring of water whose water fails not.

Difficulties of the Pastoral Office

by
Dr. John Erskine

"Who is sufficient for these things?" 2 Corinthians 2:10

These are the words of Paul, the great apostle to the Gentiles, and they express his lively apprehensions of the dignity of the gospel, the importance of its success, and the difficulty of preaching it aright. And if he, who was not a whit behind the very chief of the apostles, felt so deep a sense of his insufficiency for that arduous work, surely it would be presumption in any ordinary gospel minister to deem himself sufficient. I have therefore made choice of these words to correct the mistakes of such who account the labors of our office easy and inconsiderable, and to excite your prayers that, seeing that we are of ourselves insufficient for them, our sufficiency may be of God. For this purpose, let us first take a survey of the numerous and important duties of the pastoral office, and then consider the temptations from within, and opposition from without, which may probably arise to divert us from the due discharge of them.

I shall briefly survey some of the many and important duties of the pastoral office. And I begin with public preaching, the duty to which my text immediately relates, and on which the Scripture insists most and lays the greatest stress. When this and other ministerial

185

duties interfere, this, as the most important and most extensively useful, should be preferred.

Christ crucified and salvation through Him, the law as a schoolmaster to bring men to Christ, and exhorting the disciples of Jesus to adorn His doctrine by the conscientious performance of every duty ought to be the chief subjects of our sermons. A comprehensive knowledge of Christian faith and practice, and an ability to read and understand the Scriptures in the languages in which they were originally written, are highly important if we would be ready scribes, instructed unto the kingdom of heaven, and, like unto a man who is a householder, able to bring out of our treasures things new and old. Inspiration and miraculous gifts have now ceased; and therefore much time must be spent in reading and meditation in order to attain such knowledge. And yet our utmost diligence and application poorly qualify us for rightly expounding the sacred oracles unless, through divine teachings, we imbibe the sentiment and spirit of their inspired penmen. Nay, the union of speculative and experimental knowledge, though necessary, is not sufficient to qualify for preaching usefully. Knowledge is one thing; a faculty of imparting it to others, and of improving it for their benefit, is quite another.

Great skill is requisite to explain the sublime mysteries of our holy faith, to unfold their mutual connections and dependencies, and so to demonstrate their certainty, so that the sincere lover of truth may be convinced and even the captious silenced. Great penetration is required to search the secret folds of the understanding and heart, to trace the various sources of error and vice, and, when we have detected them, neither, by overlooking the reasonings of infidels and profligates, to give them a handle for boasting that they are unanswerable, nor by mentioning them without necessity, or weakly answering them, so as to betray the cause we mean to defend.

Our task, however, would be comparatively easy were men lovers of truth and holiness, and sincerely disposed to hearken to the voice of sober reason rather than to the clamorous demands of headstrong appetites. But many are the very reverse of this. Corrupt affections are fully ascendant over them. The gospel is an enemy to these corrupt affections, and therefore they are enemies of the gospel. Our business is to persuade such to hate and renounce what is their chief delight; to engage them in a course of life to which they are strongly averse; nay, to prevail with them to accuse, judge, and condemn themselves. The advocate pleads with success because he pleads against those for whom the judge has no particular affection, and with whom he is in no way connected. But often the minister pleads against that which is dearer to the judge than a right hand or a right eye. And what justice can be expected when the judge is also the party, and the cause in which men are to pass sentence is their own?

Add to all this that the genius, spiritual condition, and outward circumstances of our hearers are various, and that a manner of address proper for some would be very improper for others. The secure must be alarmed, the ignorant enlightened, the wounded in spirit led to the Physician of souls, the tempted fortified against temptation, the doubting resolved, the weak strengthened, the backslider reclaimed, and the mourner in Zion comforted. Even those truths which are the com-

mon nourishment of all must be differently dressed,
and seasoned ministers are debtors to the wise and to
the unwise, to the young and to the old, to the bond
and to the free. But how difficult is it to discharge that
debt and, as wise and faithful stewards, to distribute to
everyone his portion of food in due season! Little pains
may serve to display criticism and literature on subjects
which do not need them, or without occasion to
plunge so deeply in abstract, philosophical speculations that the bulk of an audience shall lose sight of us.
But it is incomparably more difficult to compose a
popular discourse in a style that is plain, elegant, ner-
vous, grave, and animated; neither bombastic nor groveling; neither scrupulously exact nor sordidly negligent. Humble prayers and much preparation are necessary for that edifying strain of preaching where the sentiments natively flow from the subject, and are all solid,
useful, and calculated to strike; where every heading,
and everything said by way of enlargement, is arranged
in its proper order; and where the turn of thought and
expression is scriptural and devout, natural and unaffected, sweet and insinuating, tender and affectionate. I
say nothing of committing a discourse to memory, and
of pronouncing it with suitable warmth, solemnity, and
distinctness. Hardly can it be hoped that so many different excellencies should be found united in one
preacher. It would be well if none put in trust with the
gospel lacked the most essential qualifications. But
even in these we are often greatly defective. Nor is this
any cause of wonder. The door to the sacred office is
opened ere the judgment is ripe, ere opinions are sufficiently formed, and ere the fire and the thoughtless-
ness of youth have fully evaporated. Our scheme of

divinity has not acquired a proper degree of consistency, a small proportion of time having been employed in studying it, and that not always in the wisest manner. Hence, we have shallow, superficial views of the doctrines and duties in which we should instruct others; and, wanting distinct, extensive ideas of a subject, we content ourselves to skim over the surface of it, disguising poor, insipid thoughts with the charms of expression and pronunciation.

I hope you are now convinced that if preaching was our only work, it would be no easy task to preach with that dignity which becomes discourses spoken in the name of God, and on subjects of the highest importance. It is equally difficult to lead the devotions of a numerous congregation, and in their name as well as our own to plead and wrestle with God for the blessings suited to their respective necessities. I will pass over dispensing the sacraments, and the other public duties of our office.

But our services are not confined to the pulpit, or to closet preparation for it. It is one important branch of our work to instruct and catechize the young and ignorant in the first principles of religion, seeing that without this knowledge the heart cannot be good. If childhood and youth are left to their natural ignorance and vanity, manhood and old age will be generally unprofitable; and sermons, however excellent, will prove to be of little service because they cannot be understood without the previous knowledge of these first principles of religion. Christ has therefore solemnly enjoined us to feed His lambs. We are bound to nourish up children in the words of faith and of sound doctrine; and experience shows that plain and short questions and answers are the most effectual way of gradually instilling religious instruction into tender minds. We must feed them with milk and not with strong meat, which as yet they are unable to bear. Do not discourage them at their first outset by obliging them to learn a multitude of words they in no degree understand; but we must adapt ourselves to the weakness of their capacity, beginning with the history of the Bible, the more necessary articles of our holy faith, and the plainer and more general precepts of Christian morals. Haughty looks or an angry tone may increase their aversion to what is serious, and make them eager to get rid of us; but an insinuating and agreeable manner may gain their esteem and affection, and make religion appear to them venerable and lovely. Familiar comparisons, examples from history, and appeals to conscience must often illustrate and enforce these instructions. To impress all on their minds, tedious as it may seem, at one time the same sentiments, and even words, must be repeated over and over again; and at other times the same sentiments must be presented in various points of light so that the young learner may not mistake our meaning or remain unaffected.

Would we teach knowledge, and make them to understand doctrine who are weaned from the milk and drawn from the breast? Precept must be upon precept, line upon line, here a little and there a little (Isaiah 28:9–10). To do all this requires prudence, gravity, condescension, meekness, and patience. Perhaps, all things weighed, it is more difficult to catechize than to preach well. It might greatly promote the interest of religion if men of eminent piety and abilities were set apart to give themselves wholly to this important work, for which the other duties of ministers leave them too little or no leisure. Meantime, inability to do what could be wished does not excuse us from doing what we can. Rather, next to public preaching, there is no method in which we can be so eminently and extensively useful.

Parochial visitation, if managed in a way easy to plan (I will not say easy to execute), would be equally useful. But a formal visit once a year, with a short prayer and a few general advices, is, I am afraid, a bodily exercise which profiteth little. It is a weariness to the flesh, of small service to the great ends of our office, unless as it affords some opportunity to gain the affection of those entrusted to our care; and this it will hardly do if we do not carry our connection and intercourse with them beyond these formalities, gladly lending them our friendly aid when it may in any way advance their spiritual welfare, and, in such cases, not overlooking even the meanest and poorest of our people. Displaying a pure, disinterested affection, a sincere desire to oblige, and a good stock of discretion, candor, and charity encourages them to unbosom to us their spiritual joys and griefs, to ask our counsel in their perplexities, and freely to impart to us their doubts and objections against religion. Thus we may learn their various circumstances, and instruct, exhort, reprove, and comfort them accordingly.

Sermons, like arrows shot at a venture, seldom hit the mark when we do not know the character of our hearers; and, in many instances, our knowledge of their character must be imperfect if we contract no familiarity with them. Yet this, however desirable, is next to impossible in a numerous charge, or in a charge almost continually shifting its inhabitants. Though this may be one cause why religion seldom flourishes in large cities, yet ministers ought not to be blamed for not doing what they have no strength or leisure to do. Public duties, which at once promote the good of many, are to be preferred to private duties, which promote the good of a few families or individuals. Much good, however, might be done even by civil visits, could we learn the art of being grave without affectation and cheerful without levity; never leave a company without dropping something to render them wiser or better.

There are, however, circumstances in which our visits are peculiarly seasonable. Sometimes, when families are favored with signal mercies and deliverances, our advice may restrain their joy within proper bounds, remind them of the precarious nature of temporal comforts, and excite a thankful sense and a suitable improvement of God's goodness. But our visits are most likely to be acceptable, and, if wisely improved, useful too, when God brings upon a family afflictive providences, or when the Lord makes the heart soft and the Almighty troubles it. The mind is then the more susceptible of serious impressions, and hearkens with avidity to what, in the day of prosperity, was despised. Yet so various are the outward troubles and inward distresses of mankind that almost every day we meet with cases wholly new to us, and which we are quite at a loss how to manage. So opposite, too, are the opinions and tempers of people in distress that what is best calculated to strike one does not make the least impression on another, and what is necessary to arouse one from security would sink another into despair.

Security, however, is the more common and dangerous extreme, and too great indulgence has worse consequences than too great severity. They therefore mistake it greatly who send for ministers on a deathbed only to speak to them the language of comfort, and to pray for mercy to their souls. Promising pardon to those who do not feel their spiritual maladies is saying, "Peace, peace," when there is no peace. But men love to be flattered and deceived; and therefore, one's being much sent for by people of all characters to visit the sick is a sign that he has no great talent of rousing their consciences. After all, where the concerns of the soul have been neglected to a deathbed, it is to be feared that such visits are often more pernicious to the healthy than profitable to the diseased. We ought not, however, to neglect them, because diseases which wear the most threatening aspect may not prove mortal; because the call of the gospel extends to every living man; and because this, when prudently managed, is a proper opportunity to warn bystanders not to defer the work of conversion to so unfit a season.

Reconciling differences is a work highly suitable to the character of ambassadors of the Prince of Peace. Not that it becomes them to be judges and dividers in matters of property, but when unhappy differences arise between Christian friends, the pastor of a church should do his best to quickly cement them. I say quickly, for divisions, like diseases, when neglected in their first beginnings, become incurable; and evil-minded people who delight in sowing tares, or in watering them where already sown, will not be wanting to insinuate that such an affront or such a neglect is insupportable. So we cannot be too speedy in fortifying the parties at variance against these malicious artifices, provided we have gotten a firm hold of their esteem and confidence, and fully convinced them that we mean our advice for their mutual benefit.

To conduct our friendly offices with success, we must beware of displaying partiality by listening too favorably to one side of the question. When a superior is in the wrong, we must not diminish the respect due to his station by saying so too bluntly in the presence of his inferior, but rather take him aside and endeavor privately to convince him of his fault. Nor, when parties are together, ought we to suffer them to debate the cause of their differences. This would generally tend to widen the breach, and to embitter and chafe their spirits more than before. We should rather advise them to behave themselves as the disciples of Jesus, by forgetting and forgiving what is past.

In private reproof, what zeal for God, and what tender compassion for perishing souls, is needful to overcome that aversion every good-natured man must feel to tell another he has done amiss, and which every wise man must feel to offend or to distress those whose friendship he values! What skill is needed to temper severity with mildness, and to proportion our censures to the degree of the fault, and to the character and circumstances of the offender! What prudence is needed to seize the most proper season, and to choose the fittest manner of administering this bitter medicine! What presence of mind is needed to detect the weakness of those pretenses by which the reproved would vindicate his conduct! Though we should argue weakly from the pulpit, we are in no danger of immediate, open contradiction; but when we reprove in private, pride is immediately at work to spy out any fallacy in our reasoning, and to raise specious doubts and objections by which, if we cannot resolve them, our labor is lost and our rashness despised. In private endeavors to reclaim infidels, or those who err in the fundamental articles of the faith, the difficulties are much the same, save that misguided conscience joins pride in making headway against us, and thus renders our success more improbable. Readiness of thought, as well as extent of knowledge, is necessary to refute the sophistical cavils of subtle adversaries, and to offer such arguments in support of truth as shall leave no room for reply.

I shall not say much on the discipline and government of the church. In many entangled, perplexing cases that come before us, it is hard to know what measures ought to be preferred. But it is much harder to conduct ourselves with such prudence and moderation as to retain the esteem of those who differ from us, and yet with such integrity as to preserve the approbation of our own consciences.

There is another duty, incumbent on ministers as such, more difficult than any I have yet mentioned, and that is to show themselves to be patterns of good works (Titus 2:7), and to be examples to others in word, in conversation, in charity, in spirit, in faith, and in purity (1 Timothy 4:12). Setting a good example is not only a moral duty incumbent on them in common with others, but seems to be given to them in charge as a part of their sacred office, and an instituted means for saving souls. Hence Paul enjoins Timothy in 1 Timothy 4:16, "Take heed to thyself and to thy doctrine; for in doing this thou shalt both save thyself, and them that hear thee." A holy, exemplary behavior gives a force and energy to sermons which learning, genius, and eloquence could never have procured. When a minister's life proves that he is in earnest, his admonitions strike with authority on the conscience and sink deep into the heart, while the strongest reasonings against sin have little effect if hearers can apply the bitter proverb, "Physician, heal thyself."

Ministers, as guides to their flock, should not only cautiously avoid what is in itself unlawful, but what, if practiced by others, would prove to them a probable occasion of stumbling. Many things have no intrinsic evil, and yet are so near the confines of vice that uncommon prudence is necessary to indulge in them without being defiled. As such prudence is extremely rare, ministers, ere they give any practice the sanction of their example, need to examine not only what is safe for them in particular, but what is safe for that flock of Christ to which they ought to be patterns and guides. When traveling alone, we may choose the shortest and most convenient road, though it is somewhat slippery and dangerous, provided we are conscious and have prudence enough to guard against those dangers. But he must be a merciless and unfaithful guide who, knowing that a number of weak, thoughtless children would follow his footsteps, should choose a path safe for himself, but in which it was morally certain that the greatest part of his followers would stumble and fall. This adds considerably to the difficulties of our office, not only as all restraints are in their own nature burdensome, but as it is often hard to resist the importunity of those who traduce our caution as being overly righteous.

I have presented to you a rude and imperfect draft of the duties of our function to convince you that the of-

fice of a bishop, though a good work, is a difficult one.
Justly did the pious [Robert] Leighton observe that
even the best would have cause to faint and give over in
it were not our Lord the chief Shepherd, were not all
our sufficiency laid up in His rich fullness, and all our
insufficiency covered in His gracious acceptance.

I shall now complete the argument by considering
the temptations and opposition which may probably
arise to divert us from the right discharge of the duties
of our office. Ministers, though bound to exemplary
holiness, are men of like passions and infirmities with
others, and equally exposed to be seduced by Satan, the
world, and the flesh. The devil assaults the shepherd so
that he may make easier prey of the sheep; and he has
many faithful agents who enter fully into his malicious
views and lay snares for ministers so that, having them
to quote as their patterns, they may excuse their own licentiousness and silence their reprovers. Is a minister
at some form of entertainment? Then they entice him
to excessive mirth, to do as others, and not to affront
men at religion by stiffness and singularity. If they succeed, though openly they may applaud, yet secretly they
despise and ridicule him for acting so much out of
character. That degree of solitude and retirement
which happily secures others from many temptations is
impossible for a minister who takes heed to the flock
over which the Holy Ghost has made him overseer. His
duty obliges him to converse with men of all stations
and characters: with the infidel, the licentious, and the
debauched person as well as the sober, the virtuous,
and the pious. And he often sees what it is improper for
him to imitate.

One heaps favors upon him to pave the way for demands with which, without doing violence to the religious principle, he cannot comply. Another would intimidate him from doing his duty by threatening the loss of his friendship; and, rather than suffer for well-doing, he may be in danger of purchasing ease and prosperity at the expense of honor and conscience. If he dares to defend the truth and importance of those doctrines which are the peculiar glory of our holy religion, the persecution of tongues is what he cannot avoid. No personal virtue will atone for so unpardonable a crime. No evidence of learning, prudence, or moderation will shelter him from the odious name of "bigot" and "enthusiast" which some, who affect to be valued for their candor and charity, so very liberally bestow. And there are many who cannot bear to be despised and laughed at, even when sensible that the ridicule is ill-founded. In every place, briars and thorns are with us, and we dwell among scorpions. Nay, even good men, through the remaining darkness in their understandings and corruptions in their hearts, may greatly hinder us in our Master's work; and by an excessive deference to them, we may be betrayed to forego our own judgment, and to act a part which will be bitterness to us in the latter end. Surely, then, we need to take heed to our steps, and to watch and pray that we do not enter into temptation.

But our chief danger arises from indwelling corruption. Our office obliges us to preach and pray on many occasions when our frames are dull and languid. Hence there is a danger lest we grow accustomed to speak of God, Christ, and eternity without feeling the importance of what we speak and realizing our own concern in it. If we fall into such a habit, the most

striking truths, preached by ourselves or others, make
no impression upon us; and that quick and powerful
Word which ought to recover us from deadness and formality loses its power and energy. Thus we go on from
evil to worse, have no relish for our work, do as little in
it as we possibly can, and do that little without spirit.
We will draw nigh to God with the mouth, and honor-
ing Him with the lip, while the heart is far from Him.

Ministers ought to be men of superior knowledge.
But too often superior knowledge produces contempt
for others, and puffs up with pride and self-conceit.
Pride inclines us stiffly to maintain an error we have
once asserted, even in spite of the clearest evidence
against it; to compose sermons with a view to our own
honor rather than the glory of God and edification of
souls; and hence to make an idle show of learning, genius, or eloquence which, though it pleases the ear,
neither enlightens the understanding nor affects the
heart. Flattery greatly strengthens this self-conceit.
When that intoxicating poison is artfully conveyed, few
are entirely protected against it. Though persons applaud us who are not competent judges, or whose heart
is at variance with their lips, self-conceit regards their
praise as sincere and well-founded.

If we escape this rock, the opposite extreme of discouragement may have a fatal influence. Some,
through too close application to study, contract unhappy disorders in their blood and spirits; and Satan
takes advantage of this to raise a world of darkness and
confusion in their minds so that they are pressed out of
measure, and ready to sink under their burden. God
may write bitter things against us, and cause us to possess the iniquities of our youth. Possibly, some special

opportunity of serving God was afforded us and neglected; or, like Solomon, we may have forsaken Him
after He has spoken to us twice. By this the Comforter,
who should comfort our souls, is provoked to withdraw
and to leave us, for a long season, in a languishing
frame. Thus, we go mourning without the sun, our feet
lame, our knees feeble, our hands hanging down.
Performing any difficult duty appears impossible, and
even the grasshopper is a burden.

After a series of years spent in vigorous endeavors to
promote the cause of truth and holiness, ignorance,
profanity, and contempt of the gospel too often continue to prevail. From the pulpit, and in private, too, we
address our hearers in the warmest manner. But we
preach, pray, watch, and labor in vain. He who was unclean is unclean still, and he who was filthy is filthy
still. We are ready to say, "Why exert ourselves thus to
no purpose? Why cultivate a soil which, after our utmost care, remains barren?" Hence ministers, after
laudable diligence in the first years of their ministry,
are in danger of overly sparing themselves, and in doing little in the duties of their office, save what decency
and character constrain them to do. The temptations
gain additional force when those among whom we
have faithfully labored fail in due gratitude and respect,
and display an eagerness to pick faults in our sermons
or private behavior. Though we act with the purest intentions, everything is taken by a wrong handle, and
sure to displease. This froward, censorious spirit our
Lord beautifully describes in Luke 7:31–35. Conscious
that we merit better treatment, we sometimes peevishly
take offense at the public; and, when we find they are
resolved to blame even without cause, we become less

concerned to avoid just cause of censure.

As we grow older, aversion to fatigue and love of ease grow upon us, and often lead us to neglect or delay our duty when some motive stronger than indolence does not push us on to the discharge of it. Nay, indolence, feeble and languishing as it seems, often triumphs over the more violent passions; and, as it restrains bad men from much wickedness, so it hinders the servants of Christ from doing a deal of good which they might and ought to have done. It puts off till tomorrow what had better been dispatched today. To study a subject to the bottom, and to compose with exactness, is so fatiguing that if we have a certain readiness of expression, we are apt to get rid of it, and to venture into the pulpit with little preparation. It is hard to resist this bias; to prosecute studies which, though necessary, are perhaps unpleasant; to allow a suitable portion of time to every different duty; and resolutely to employ our precious hours to the best advantage. And when indolence, by long habit, has acquired force, overcoming it is next to impossible.

Judge, my brethren, from the whole of what has been said, if the work of the ministry is so light and easy as many, through ignorance and inadvertence, are apt to imagine. It is an honorable service, but it is also a laborious and arduous one—and no man, by his own strength, is sufficient for it. How vain, then, and presumptuous are such who, depending on their natural abilities, hastily thrust themselves into the sacred office without spending suitable time in preparatory studies, and without any eye to Christ to assist, to accept, and to prosper their labors! What can be expected but that, being unlearned and unstable, they should wrest the

Scripture to the destruction of themselves and others?
Even men of the most distinguished talents and purest
zeal, when they survey the extent and importance of
their charge, and the strict account they must one day
give of their stewardship, have cause, with Moses, exceedingly to quake and fear, and with David to plead,
"Enter not, O Lord, into judgment with Thy servant; for
in Thy sight no living flesh shall be justified." How
dreadful, then, is it to engage in such a work without
delight in it, fitness for it, or regard to its great end and
design!

I do not know if any student of divinity or young
preachers are now hearing me. If there are, I hope they
will receive what I have said with meekness and candor.
As a sincere friend, I would warn them of rocks, some
of which I myself have found dangerous. If my heart de-
ceives me not, my ends in entering into the ministry
were pure and disinterested. I have seen no cause to repent of my choice of a profession. I am not ashamed of
the gospel of Christ, "for it is the power of God unto
salvation to everyone that believeth." I esteem it my
honor and happiness to preach the unsearchable
riches of Christ. But I lament that I entered on the sacred function ere I had spent one fourth of the time in
reading, in meditation, and in devotional exercises
which would have been necessary in any tolerable degree to qualify me for it. I have made some feeble efforts
to supply these defects. But, besides the public duties of
my office and a variety of unavoidable avocations, indolence of temper, employing too much time in studies
or labors less important, and other culpable causes,
partly formerly hinted at, partly needless or improper to
be mentioned, have been considerable bars in the way

of my success. You who now enjoy the golden season of youth, be careful to improve it to better purposes. The advantages you now have for acquiring gifts and grace may never return in any future period.

And now, you have heard the duties I owe to this numerous congregation, and the difficulties I have to surmount in the faithful discharge of them. I say "to this congregation" as I have neither leisure nor inclination to do the office of a bishop in another diocese, when there are souls in my own more than enough for my care. The charge of all the souls in this large and populous city is a yoke which the most vigorous minister in it would be unable to bear. And as one minister cannot inspect every family, so no one family can reasonably desire the inspection of every minister. It is ordinarily fit that people should apply to those ministers in whose district they dwell, and to whose immediate inspection providence has entrusted them. In this way, few, if any, will be wholly overlooked. But if we pursue no regular plan but leave it to chance or to personal attachments to determine our work, multitudes who most need our assistance will enjoy the least of it, and others will engross a greater proportion of our time than ought to be allowed them. I therefore hope my many friends and acquaintances in other congregations of this city will forgive me for preferring a greater to a lesser good, and for employing my labors where, through the blessing of God, I think they bid fairest to be useful.

If my relationship to this congregation forbids me, in ordinary cases, to alienate them from my ministerial services, much more does my relationship to the Church in general forbid me needlessly to trifle away my time, or to employ it in a way foreign to my office. God has given me a charge, to meditate on divine things and give myself wholly to them; and friends and innocent recreations must not claim those hours which ought to be consecrated to God and His people. I would say to friends and I would say to innocent recreations, as Nehemiah to Sanballat, "I am doing a great work, so that I cannot come down; why should the work cease whilst I leave it, and come down to you?" (Nehemiah 6:3). If the apostles thought it unreasonable to leave the Word of God in order to redress the abuses committed in administering the alms of the church, shall we leave it for causes of a less worthy nature? Doubtless, it becomes us to employ what time we can spare from the duties we owe to our souls, to our families, and to our congregations in studies or labors that may tend to the general benefit of the church of God. This would afford us abundant work, though we were fixed in the smallest and most inconsiderable charges. But though such services are often expected from ministers in this great city, and though it must be owned that our situation procures some peculiar advantages for engaging in them, yet we must be singularly frugal of our time if we would redeem any considerable proportion of it for those desirable ends.

But it is now time, briefly, to address my dear Christian friends and brethren in this congregation, of which the spiritual oversight, through the providence of God, is committed to me. When I think on the many great and good men who have formerly filled this pulpit, and cast an eye on my own unworthiness and insufficiency, I cannot but tremble that one so poorly qualified is now called to the same work. When I review my defects and miscarriages when exercising the sacred office in two charges that were comparatively easy, and in the last of which I had the aid of a faithful and affectionate fellow laborer, I am ready to say, "If I have run with the footmen and they have wearied me, how shall I run with the chariots? And if in the day of prosperity, wherein I trusted, my heart fainted, what shall I do in the dwellings of Jordan?" I am called to enter upon labors, and to encounter difficulties hitherto unknown to me. My task is increased, but my vigor is not. I am with you in weakness, in fear, and in much trembling, lest I shall not find you such as I would, and lest I shall be found unto you such as you would not. Struck with the disproportion between my strength of this important charge, I must beg your candor and indulgence; and yet, weak as I am, and feeble as my endeavors are, they may tend to our mutual salvation through your prayers and the supply of the Spirit of Christ.

I beseech you, therefore, brethren, for the Lord Jesus Christ's sake, and for the love of the Spirit, that you strive together with me in your prayers to God for me that I may be delivered from them who do not believe; that my ministerial services in this city may be accepted by the saints and that to you in particular I may come with joy by the will of God, and may be refreshed with you (Romans 15:30–32). Send up your warmest addresses to the Father of Lights, from whom comes every good and perfect gift, that His grace may be sufficient for me, and His strength perfected in my weakness; that in my closet He would enable me to incline my ear to wisdom, and to apply my heart to understanding—yea, to cry after knowledge, and lift up my voice for understanding—to seek her as silver, and to search for her as for hidden treasures; that in the pulpit, and in the more private duties of my office, He would touch my cold heart and faltering lips with a live coal from His altar, and give me the tongue of the learned, to speak words in season to every soul; that the law of truth may be in my mouth, and no iniquity found in my lips; that I may walk with God in peace and equity, and turn many away from iniquity.

Brethren, pray for us, that the Word of the Lord may have free course and be glorified, and that we may be delivered from wicked and unreasonable men; for all men do not have faith (2 Thessalonians 3:1–2). Pray always, with all prayer and supplication in the Spirit; and watch thereto, with all perseverance and supplication for all saints; and for me, that utterance may be given unto me, that I may open my mouth boldly, to make known the mystery of the gospel (Ephesians 6:18–19).

Moreover, as for me, God forbid that I should sin against the Lord in ceasing to pray for you; but I will teach you, through divine strength, the good and the right way. For my friends' and brethren's sake, I will now say, "Peace be within you; and because of the house of the Lord our God, I will seek your good."

I conclude with the prayer of the psalmist: "Hide Thy face from my sins, and blot out all mine iniquities. Create in me a clean heart, O God, and renew a right spirit within me. Cast me not away from Thy presence, and take not Thy Holy Spirit from me. Restore unto me the joy of Thy salvation, and uphold me with Thy free Spirit. Then will I teach transgressors Thy ways, and sinners shall be converted unto Thee. O Lord, open Thou my lips, and my mouth shall show forth Thy praise" (Psalm 51:9–13, 15).

Rules for the Preacher's Conduct

by
Dr. Isaac Watts

When true religion falls under a general and remarkable decay, it is time for all who are concerned to awaken and arouse themselves to fresh vigor and activity in their several posts of service. If the interests of piety and virtue are things fit to be encouraged and maintained in the world, if the kingdom of the blessed God among men is worthy to be supported, surely it is a necessary and becoming zeal for everyone who has the honor to be a minister of this kingdom to take alarm at the appearance of such danger; and each of us should inquire, "What can I do to strengthen the things that remain and are ready to die, as well as to recover what is lost?" Let my brethren therefore in the ministry forgive me if I presume at this season to set before them a plain and serious exhortation.

What I have to say on this subject shall be contained under four general headings.

1. Take heed to your own personal religion, as being absolutely necessary to the right discharge of the ministerial office.

2. Take heed to your private studies and preparation for public service.

3. Take heed to your public labors and actual ministrations in the church.

4. Take heed to your conversation in the world, and

especially among the flock of Christ over whom you preside.

1. Take heed to your personal religion, especially to the work of God in your own heart, as absolutely necessary to the right discharge of the ministerial work. Surely, there is the highest obligation on a preacher of the gospel to believe and practice what he preaches. He is under the most powerful and sacred engagements to be a Christian himself who goes forth to persuade the world to become Christians. A minister of Christ who is not a hearty believer in Christ, and a sincere follower of Him, is a most shameful and inconsistent character, and forbids in practice what he recommends in words and sentences.

But it is not enough for a minister to have a common degree of piety and virtue equal to the rest of Christians; he should transcend and surpass others. The leaders and officers under the army of the blessed Jesus should be more expert in the Christian exercises, and more advanced in the holy warfare, than their fellow soldiers are supposed to be. 2 Corinthians 6:4: "In all things approving ourselves as the ministers of God, in much patience," and so forth. And, I may add, in much of every Christian grace. A small and low degree of it is not sufficient for a minister; see therefore that you not only practice every part and instance of piety and virtue that you preach to others, but abound therein, and be eminent beyond and above the rest, as your station in the church is more exalted and as your character demands.

Now, since your helps in the way to heaven, both to the knowledge and practice of duty, are much greater than what others enjoy, and your obstacles and imped-iments are in some instances less than theirs, it will be a shameful thing in you, as it is a matter of shame to any of us, to sink below the character of other Chris-tians in the practice of our holy religion, or even if we do not excel most of them—since our obligations to it, as well as our advantages for it, are so much greater than those of others.

Take heed, therefore, to your own practical and vital religion, as to the reality and clear, undoubted evidence of it in your conscience. Give double diligence to make your calling and election sure. See to it, with earnest so-licitude, that you are not mistaken in so necessary and important a concern, for a minister who preaches up the religion of Christ and yet has no evidence of it in his own heart will lie under vast discouragements in his work; and if he is not a real Christian himself, he will justly fall under double damnation.

Call your own soul often to account; examine the temper, the frame, and the motions of your heart with all holy severity, so that the evidences of your faith in Jesus, of your repentance for sin, and of your conver-sion to God are many and fair, strong and unquestion-able, and so that you may walk on with courage and joy-ful hope toward heaven, and lead the flock of Christ there with holy assurance and joy.

Take heed to your own religion, as to the liveliness and power of it. Let it not be a sleepy thing in your bo-som, but sprightly and active, and always awake. Keep your own soul near to God, and in the way in which you first came near to Him, that is, by the mediation of Jesus Christ. Let no distance and estrangement grow between God and you, between Christ and you.

Maintain much converse with God by prayer, by reading His Word, by holy meditation, by heavenly-mindedness, and by universal holiness in the frame and temper of your own spirit. Converse with God and with your own soul in the duties of secret religion, and walk always in the world as under the eye of God. Every leader of the flock of God should act as Moses did; he should live as seeing Him who is invisible.

Take heed to your personal religion, as to the growth and increase of it. Let it be ever advancing. Be tenderly sensible of every wandering affection toward vanity, every deviation from God and your duty, every rising sin, every degree of growing distance from God. Watch and pray much, and converse much with God, as one of His ministering angels in flesh and blood; grow daily in conformity to God and your blessed Savior, who is the first minister of His Father's kingdom, and the fairest image of His Father.

Such a conduct will have several happy influences towards the fulfilling of your ministry, and will render you more fit for every part of your public ministrations.

Hereby you will improve in your acquaintance with divine things and the spiritual parts of religion, so that you may better teach the people both truth and duty. Those who are much with God may expect and hope that He will teach them the secret of His covenant and the ways of His mercy by communications of divine light to their spirits. "The secret of the Lord is with them that fear Him, and He will show them His covenant." Luther used to say that he sometimes got more knowledge from a short time of prayer than by the study and labor of many hours.

Hereby you will be more fit to speak to the great God

at all times, as a son with holy confidence in Him as your Father, and you will be better prepared to pray with and for your people. You will have a habitual readiness for the work, and increase in the gift of prayer. You will obtain a treasure and fluency of sacred language, suited to address God on all occasions.

Hereby you will be kept near to the Spring of all grace, to the Fountain of strength and comfort in your work; you will be ever deriving fresh anointings, fresh influences, daily lights and powers, to enable you to go through all the difficulties and labors of your sacred office.

Hereby, when you come among men in your sacred ministrations, you will appear, speak, and act like a man who has come from being with God. You will be like Moses, with a luster upon his face when he had conversed with God; like a minister of the court of heaven employed in a divine office; like a messenger of grace who has just been with God and received instructions from Him. And the world will take cognizance of you, as they did of the apostles, that they were men who had been with Jesus.

This will better furnish you for serious converse with the souls and consciences of men, by giving you experimental acquaintances with the things of religion as they are translated in the heart. You will learn more of the springs of sin and holiness, the workings of nature and grace, the deceitfulness of sin, the subtlety of temptation, and the holy skill of counter-working the snares of sin, the devices of Satan, and all their designs to ruin the souls of men. You will speak with more divine compassion to wretched and perishing mortals, with more life and power to stupid sinners, with more sweetness and comfort to awakened consciences, and with more awful language and influence to backsliding Christians.

You will hereby learn to preach more powerfully in all respects for the salvation of men, and talk more feelingly on every sacred subject, when the power, sense, and life of godliness are kept up in your own spirit. Then, on some special occasions, it may not be improper to borrow the language of David the prophet and of St. Paul and St. John, two great apostles, though it may be best in public to speak in the plural number: "We have believed, therefore we have spoken; what we have heard and learned from Christ, we have declared unto you; what we have seen and felt, we are bold to speak. Attend, and we will tell you what God has done for our souls." You may then at proper seasons convince, direct, and comfort others by the same words of light and power, of precept and promise, of joy and of hope, which have convinced, directed, and comforted you. A word coming from the heart will sooner reach the heart.

2. Take heed to your own private studies. These private studies are of various kinds, whether you consider them in general, as necessary to furnish the mind with knowledge for the office of the sacred ministry, or in particular, as necessary to prepare discourses for the pulpit.

Those general studies may be just mentioned in this place which furnish the mind with knowledge for the work of a minister; for though it is known that you have passed through the several stages of studies in your younger years, and have made a good improvement in them, yet a review of many of them will be found needful, and an increase in some (so far as leisure permits) may be proper and useful, even through the whole course of life.

But among all these inquiries and studies, and these various improvements of the mind, let us take heed that none of them carry our thoughts away too far from our chief and glorious design, which is the ministry of the gospel of Christ. Let none of them entrench upon those hours which should be devoted to our study of the Bible or preparations for the pulpit; and whenever we find our inclination too much attached to any particular human science, let us set a guard upon ourselves lest it rob us of our more divine studies and our best improvement. A minister should remember that he, with all his studies, is consecrated to the service of the sanctuary. Let everything be done therefore with a view to our great end; let all the rest of our knowledge be like lines drawn from the vast circumference of universal nature, pointing to that divine center, God and religion; and let us pursue every course of study with a design to gain better qualifications thereby for our sacred work.

I come to speak of those particular studies which are preparatory for the public work of the pulpit. And here, when you retire to compose a sermon, let your great end be ever kept in view, which is to say something for the honor of God, for the glory of Christ, and for the salvation of the souls of men. For this purpose, a few rules may perhaps be of some service.

One great and general rule is to ask advice of heaven by prayer about every part of your preparatory studies; seek the direction and assistance of the Spirit of God for inclining your thoughts to proper subjects, for guiding you to proper Scriptures, and for framing your whole sermon, as to both the matter and the manner, so that it may attain the divine and sacred ends proposed. But I do not insist at length upon this here, because prayer for aids and counsels from heaven belongs to every part of your work, in the closet, in the pulpit, and in your daily conversation.

The particular rules for your preparatory work may be such as these:

RULE 1. In choosing your texts or themes of discourse, seek such as are more suited to do good to souls, according to the present wants, dangers, and circumstances of the people; whether for the instruction of the ignorant, for the conviction of the stupid and senseless, for the melting and softening of the obstinate, for the conversion of the wicked, for the edification of converts, for the comfort of the timorous and mournful, for gentle admonition of backsliders, or for more severe reproof. Some acquaintance with the general case and character of your hearers is needful for this end.

RULE 2. In handling the text, divide, explain, illustrate, prove, convince, infer, and apply in such a manner as to do real service to men, and honor to our Lord Jesus Christ. Do not say within yourself, "How much or how elegantly can I talk upon such a text?" but "What can I say most usefully to those who hear me, for the instruction of their minds, for the conviction of their consciences, and for the persuasion of their hearts?" Do not be fond of displaying your learned criticisms in clearing up terms or phrases of a text, where scholars alone can be edified by them; nor spend the precious moments of the congregation in making them hear you explain what is clear enough already, and has no need of explanation, or in proving that which is so obvious that it needs no proof. This is little better than trifling with God and man.

Do not think, "How can I make a sermon soonest and easiest?" but "How can I make the most profitable sermon for my hearers?" Not, "What fine things can I say, either in a way of criticism or philosophy or in a way of oratory and harangue?" but "What powerful words can I speak to impress the consciences of them who hear with a lasting sense of moral, divine, and eternal things?" Judge wisely what to leave out as well as what to speak. Let not your chief design be to work up a sheet, or to hold out for an hour, but to save a soul.

RULE 3. In speaking of the great things of God and religion, remember that you are a minister of Christ and the gospel, sent to publish to men what God has revealed by His prophets and apostles, and by His Son Jesus; you are not a heathen philosopher, to teach the people merely what the light of reason can search out. You are not to stand up here as a professor of ancient or modern philosophy, nor as an usher in the school of Plato, Seneca, or Locke, but as a teacher in the school of Christ, as a preacher of the New Testament. You are not a Jewish priest, to instruct men in the precise niceties of ancient Judaism, legal rights and ceremonies; but you are a Christian minister. Let Christianity, therefore, run through all your compositions, and spread its glories over them.

It is granted, indeed, that reasoning from the light of nature has a considerable use in the ministry of the gospel. It is by the principles of natural religion, and by reasoning from them on the wonderful events of prophecy and miracles, that we ourselves must learn the truth of the Christian religion; and we must teach the people to build their faith in the gospel on just and rational grounds. This may, perhaps, at some time or other, require a few whole discourses on some of the principal themes of natural religion in order to introduce and display the religion of Jesus; but such occasions will seldom arise in the course of your ministry.

It is granted also that it is very useful labor, sometimes, in a sermon to show how far the light of nature and reason will carry us on in the search of duty and happiness, and then to manifest how happily the light of Scripture supplies the deficiency of it, so that the people may know how greatly they are indebted to the peculiar favor of God for the book of divine revelation.

If you speak of the duties which men owe to God or to one another, even those which are found out by reason and natural conscience, show how the gospel of Christ has advanced and refined everything that nature and reason teach us. Enforce these duties by motives of Christianity as well as by philosophical arguments drawn from the nature of things; stir your listeners up to the practice of them by the examples of Christ and His apostles, by that heaven and that hell which are revealed to the world by Jesus Christ our Savior; impress them on the heart by the constraining influence of the mercy of God and the dying love of our Lord Jesus Christ, by His glorious appearance to judge the living and the dead, and by our blessed hope of attending Him on that day. These are the appointed arguments of our holy religion, and may expect more divine success.

When you have occasion to represent what need

there is of diligence and labor in the duties of holiness, show also what aids are promised in the gospel to humble souls who are sensible of their own frailty to resist temptation, or to discharge religious and moral duties, and what influences of the Holy Spirit may be expected by those who seek Him. Let them know that Christ is exalted to send forth this Spirit, to bestow repentance and sanctification as well as forgiveness; for without Him we can do nothing.

If you would raise the hearts of your hearers to a just and high esteem of this gospel of grace, and impress them with an awful sense of the divine importance and worth of it, be not afraid to lay human nature low, and to represent it in its ruins by the fall of the first Adam. It is the vain exaltation of ruined nature that makes the gospel so much despised in our age. Labor therefore to make them see and feel the deplorable state of mankind as described in Scripture; that by one man sin entered into the world, and death by sin, and a sentence of death has passed upon all men, for all have sinned. Let them hear and know that Jews and Gentiles are all under sin; that there is none righteous, no, not one; that every mouth may be stopped, and all the world may appear guilty before God. Let them know that it is not in man who walks to direct his steps; that we are not sufficient of ourselves to think any good thing; that we are without strength, alienated from the life of God through the ignorance and darkness of our understanding, and are by nature children of disobedience and children of wrath; that we are unable to recover ourselves out of these depths of wretchedness without the condescensions of divine grace, and that the gospel of Christ is introduced as the only sovereign remedy and relief under all this desolation of nature, this over-whelming distress; neither is there salvation in any other, for there is no other name under heaven given among men whereby we must be saved. And they who willfully and obstinately reject this message of divine love must perish without remedy and without hope; for there remains no more sacrifice for sin, but a certain fearful expectation of vengeance.

These were the sacred weapons with which those were armed to whom our exalted Savior gave commission to travel through the dominions of Satan, which were spread over the heathen countries, and raise up a kingdom for Himself among them. It was with principles, rules, and motives derived from the gospel that they were sent to attack the reigning vices of mankind, to reform profligate nations, and to turn them from dumb idols to serve the living God. And though St. Paul was a man of learning above the rest, yet he was not sent to preach the enticing words of man's wisdom, nor to talk as the disputers of the age and the philosophers did in their schools, but his business was to preach Christ crucified. Though this doctrine of the cross, and the Son of God suspended on it, was a stumbling block to the Jews, and the Greeks counted it foolishness, yet to them who were called, both Jews and Greeks, this doctrine was the power of God, and the wisdom of God for the salvation of men. And therefore St. Paul determined to know nothing among them in comparison to the doctrine of Christ and Him crucified. These were the weapons of his warfare which were mighty, through God, to the pulling down of the strongholds of sin and Satan in the hearts of men, and brought every thought into captivity to the obedience of Christ. It was by the ministrations of this gospel that the fornicators were made chaste and holy, and idolaters became worshippers of the God of heaven; that thieves learned honest labor, and the covetous were taught to seek treasures in heaven; that the drunkards grew out of love with their cups, and renounced all intemperance; that the revilers governed their tongues, and spoke well of their neighbors, and the cruel extortioners and oppressors learned to practice compassion and charity. These vilest of sinners, these children of hell, were made heirs of the kingdom of heaven, being washed, being sanctified, being justified in the name of the Lord Jesus, and by the Spirit of our God.

Had you all the refined science of Plato or Socrates, all the skill in morals that ever was attained by Zeno, Seneca, or Epitcetus; were you furnished with all the flowing oratory of Cicero, or the thunder of Demosthenes; were all these talents and excellencies united in one man, and you were the person so richly endowed; and could you employ them all in every sermon you preach—yet you could have no reasonable hope to convert and save one soul in Great Britain, where the gospel is published, while you lay aside the glorious gospel of Christ and leave it entirely out of your discourses.

Let me proceed yet further and say, had you the fullest acquaintance that ever man acquired with all the principles and duties of natural religion, both in its regard to God and to your fellow creatures; had you the skill and tongue of an angel to range all these in their fairest order, to place them in the fullest light, and to pronounce and represent the whole law of God with such force and splendor to a British audience as was done to the Israelites at Mt. Sinai, you might, perhaps, lay the consciences of men under deep conviction, for by the law is knowledge of sin. But I am fully persuaded that you would never reconcile one soul to God; you would never change the heart of one sinner, bring him into the favor of God, nor fit him for the joys of heaven, without this blessed gospel which is committed to your hands.

The great and glorious God is jealous of His own authority, and of the honor of His Son Jesus. He will not condescend to bless any other methods for obtaining so divine an end than what He Himself has prescribed; nor will His Holy Spirit, whose office it is to glorify Christ, stoop to confer with any other sort of means for the saving of sinners, where the name and offices of His Son, the only appointed Savior, are known, but are despised and neglected. It is the gospel alone that is the power of God unto salvation. If the prophets will not stand in His counsel, nor cause the people to hear His words, they will never be able to turn Israel from the iniquity of their ways, nor the evil of their doings.

Was it not the special design of these doctrines of Christ, when they were first graciously communicated to the world, to reform the vices of mankind which reason could not reform, and to restore the world to piety and virtue, for which the powers of reason appeared too feeble and impotent? The nations of the earth had made long and fruitless inquiries into what the light of nature and philosophy would do to bring wandering, degenerate man back again to his Maker; fruitless and long essays, indeed, when after some thousands of years the world, which had forgotten its Maker and His laws, still ran further from God, and plunged itself into all abominable impieties and corrupt practices! Now if the all-wise God saw the gospel of Christ to be so fit and happy an instrument for the recovery of wretched man to religion and morality; if He furnished His apostles with these doctrines for this very purpose, and pronounced a blessing upon them as His own appointment—why should we not suppose that this gospel is still as fit, in its own nature, for the same purpose as it was at first? And why may we not hope that the same heavenly blessing, in a great measure, will remain upon it for these purposes to the end of the world?

Shall I inquire yet further? Is this a day when we should leave the particular articles of the religion of Christ out of our ministrations, when the truth of them is boldly called into question, and denied by such multitudes who dwell among us? Is this a proper time for us to forget the name of Christ in our public labors, when the witty talents and reasonings of men join together and labor hard to cast out His sacred name with contempt and scorn? Is it so seasonable a practice in this age to neglect these evangelical themes, and to preach up virtue without the special principles and motives with which Christ has furnished us, when there are such numbers among us who are fond of heathenism, who are endeavoring to introduce it again into a Christian country and spread the poison of infidelity through a nation called by His name? If this is our practice, our hearers will begin to think, indeed, that infidels may have some reason on their side, and that the glorious doctrines of the gospel of Christ are not so necessary as our fathers thought them, while they find no mention of them in the pulpit, no use of them in our discourses from week to week and from month to month, and yet we profess to preach for the salvation of souls. Will this be our glory, to imitate the heathen philosophers and to drop the gospel of the Son of God, to be complimented by unbelievers as men of superior sense, and as deep reasoners, while we abandon the faith of Jesus and starve the souls of our hearers by neglecting to distribute to them this bread of life which came down from heaven? Oh, let us who are His ministers remember the last words of our departing Lord: "Go, preach the gospel to every nation; he that believeth and is baptized shall be saved; and he that believeth not shall be damned. And, lo, I am with you always, even to the end of the world." Let us fulfill the command, let us publish the threatening with a promise, and let us wait for the attendant blessing.

Forgive me, my dear brother and friend, and you my beloved and honored brethren in the ministry, forgive me, if I have indulged too much vehemence in this part of my discourse, or if I have given too great a freedom to passionate language on this important subject. I doubt not but your own consciences bear me witness that this elevated voice is not the voice of reproof, but of friendly warning; and I persuade myself that you will join with me in this sentiment, that if ever we are so happy as to reform the lives of our hearers, to convert their hearts to God, and to train them up for heaven, it must be done by the principles of the gospel of Christ. On the occasion of such urgent advice, therefore, I assure myself that you will forgive these warm emotions of spirit. Can there be any more just cause or season to exert fervor and zeal than while we are pleading for the name, honor, and kingdom of our Lord Jesus? Let Him live, let Him reign forever on His throne of glory. Let

Him live upon our lips, and reign in all our ministrations; let Him live in the hearts of all our hearers; let Him live and reign through Great Britain, and through all the nations, till iniquity is subdued, till the kingdom of Satan is destroyed, and till the whole world has become willing subjects to the scepter of His grace.

RULE 4. In addressing your discourses to your hearers, remember to distinguish the different characteristics of saints and sinners: the converted and the unconverted, the sincere Christian and the formal professor, the stupid and the awakened, the diligent and the backsliding, the fearful or humble soul, the obstinate and presumptuous; and at various seasons introduce a word for each of them. Thus you will divide the Word of God aright, and give to everyone his portion.

The general way of speaking to all persons in one view, and under one character, as though all your hearers were certainly true Christians and converted already, and wanted only a little further reformation of heart and life, is too common in the world—but I think it is a dangerous way of preaching. It has a powerful and unhappy tendency to lull unregenerate sinners asleep into security, to flatter and deceive them with dreams of happiness, and to make their consciences easy without a real conversion of the heart to God.

Let your hearers know that there is a vast and unspeakable difference between a saint and a sinner, one in Christ and one out of Christ; between one whose heart is in the state of corrupt nature or unrenewed, and one who is in a state of grace, and renewed to faith and holiness; between one who is only born of the flesh, and is a child of wrath, and one who is born again, or born of the Spirit, and has become a child of

God, a member of Christ, and an heir of heaven. Let them know that this distinction is great and necessary, a most real change, and of infinite importance; and however it has been derided by men, it is glorious in the eyes of God, and will be made to appear so at the last day in the eyes of men and angels. That little treatise written by the learned Mr. John Jennings, concerning "Preaching Christ and Experimental Preaching" [chapter 2 of this book], has many valuable hints relating to these last two particulars of my exhortation.

RULE 5. Lead your hearers wisely into the knowledge of the truth, and teach them to build their faith upon solid ground. Let them first know why they are Christians, so that they may be firmly established in the belief and profession of the religion of Christ; that they may be guarded against all the assaults of temptation and infidelity in this evil day, and may be able to render a reason for the hope that is in them. Furnish them with arguments in opposition to the rude cavils and blasphemies which are frequently thrown out into the world against the name and the doctrines of the holy Jesus.

Then let the great, the most important, and the most necessary articles of our religion be set before your hearers in their fairest light. Convey them into the understanding of those of meanest capacity by condescending sometimes to plain and familiar methods of speech; prove these important doctrines and duties to them by all proper reasons and arguments. But as to the introducing of controversies into the pulpit, be neither fond of it nor frequent in it. In your common course of preaching avoid disputes, especially about things of less importance, without an apparent call of

providence. Religious controversies, frequently introduced without real necessity, have an unhappy tendency to hurt the spirit of true godliness, in the hearts
of both preachers and hearers.

And beware of laying too much stress on the peculiar notions, terms, and phrases of the little sects and
parties in Christianity; take heed that you do not make
your hearers bigots and uncharitable while you endeavor to make them knowing Christians. Establish
them in all the chief and most important articles of the
gospel of Christ without endeavoring to render those
who differ from you odious in the sight of your hearers.
Whenever you are constrained to declare your disapprobation of particular opinions, keep up and manifest
your love to the persons of those who espouse them,
and especially if they are persons of virtue and piety.

RULE 6. Do not content yourself to compose a sermon of mere doctrinal truths and articles of belief, but
into every sermon (if possible) bring something practical. It is true, knowledge is the foundation of practice—
the head must be furnished with a degree of knowledge
or the heart cannot be good—but take heed that dry
speculations and mere schemes of orthodoxy do not
take up too large a part of your compositions. And be
sure to impress it frequently on your hearers that holiness is the great end of all knowledge, and of much
more value than the sublimest speculations; nor is
there any doctrine but what requires some correspondent practice of piety or virtue.

And among the practical parts of Christianity,
sometimes make it your business to insist on those subjects which are inward and spiritual, and which go by
the name of "experimental religion." Now and then

take some themes as these: the first awakenings of the
conscience of a sinner by some special and awful providence, by some particular passage in the Word of God,
in pious writings or public sermons; the inward terrors
of mind, and fears of the wrath of God, which sometimes accompany such awakenings; the temptations
which arise to divert the mind from them, and to
soothe the sinner in the course of his iniquities; the
inward conflicts of the spirit in these seasons, and the
methods of relief under such temptations; the arguments that may fix the heart and will for God against
all the enticements and opposition of the world; the
labors of the conscience fluctuating between hope and
fear; the rising and working of indwelling sin in the
heart; the subtle excesses framed by the flesh for the
indulgence of it; the peace of God derived from the
gospel, allaying the inward terrors of the soul under a
sense of guilt; the victories obtained over strong corruptions and powerful temptations by faith in unseen
things, by repeated addresses to God in prayer, and by
trusting in Jesus, the great Mediator, who is made of
God to us wisdom and righteousness, sanctification
and redemption.

While you are teaching on these subjects, give me
leave to put you again in mind that it will sometimes
have a very happy influence on the minds of hearers to
speak what you have learned from your own experiences, though there is no need to tell them publicly it
is your own. You may inform them what you have borrowed from your own observation, and from the experiences of Christians, ancient or modern, who have
passed through the same trials, who have wrestled with
the same corruptions of nature, who have grappled

with the same difficulties and at last have been made conquerors over the same temptations. As face answers face in the glass, so the heart of one man answers to another; and the workings of the different principles of flesh and spirit, corrupt nature and renewing grace, have a great deal of resemblance in the hearts of different persons who have passed through them. This sort of instruction, drawn from just and solid experience, will animate and encourage the young Christian who begins to shake off the slavery of sin and to set his face toward heaven. This will make it appear that religion is no impracticable thing. It will establish and comfort the professors of the gospel, and excite them with new vigor to proceed in the way of holiness; it will raise a steadfast courage and hope, and will generally obtain a most happy effect upon the souls of the hearers, beyond all that you can say to them from principles of mere reasoning and dry speculation, and especially where you have the concurrent experience of scriptural examples.

RULE 7. Whether you are discoursing on doctrine or duty, take great care that you impose nothing on your hearers, as either a matter of faith or practice, but what your Lord and Master, Christ Jesus, has imposed. But in this state of frailty and imperfection, dangers attend us on either hand. As we must take heed that we do not add the fancies of men to our divine religion, so we should take equal care that we do not curtail the appointments of Christ. With a sacred vigilance and zeal we should maintain the plain, express, and necessary articles that we find evidently written in the word of God, and suffer none of them to be lost through our default. The world has been so long imposed upon by

these shameful additions of men to the gospel of Christ
that they seem now to be resolved to bear them no
longer; but they are unhappily running into another
extreme. Because several sects and parties of Christians
have tacked on so many false and unbecoming ornaments to Christianity, they resolve to deliver her from
these disguises; but while they are paring off all this
foreign trumpery, they too often cut her to the quick,
and sometimes let out her life-blood (if I may so express
it) and maim her of her very limbs and vital parts.
Because so many irrational notions and follies have
been mixed up with the Christian scheme, it is now a
fashionable humor of the age to renounce almost everything that reason does not discover, and to reduce
Christianity itself to little more than the light of nature
and the dictates of reason. And under this sort of influence, there are some who are believers of the Bible and
the divine mission of Christ, and dare not renounce
the gospel itself, yet they interpret some of the peculiar
and express doctrines of it into so poor, so narrow, and
so jejune a meaning that they suffer but little to remain
beyond the articles of natural religion. This leads some
of the learned and polite men of the age to explain
away the sacrifice and atonement made for our sins by
the death of Christ, and to bereave our religion of the
ordinary aids of the Holy Spirit, though these truths are
plainly and expressly revealed, are frequently repeated
in the New Testament, and are two of the chief glories
of the blessed gospel, as well as, perhaps, two of the
chief uses of those sacred names of the Son and the
Holy Spirit, into which we are baptized.

It is this very humor that persuades some persons to
reduce the injury and mischief that we have sustained

by the sin and fall of Adam to so slight a bruise, and so inconsiderable a wound, that only a small matter of grace is needful for our recovery; and accordingly they impoverish the rich and admirable remedy of the gospel to a very culpable degree, supposing no more to be necessary for the restoration of man than those few ingredients which, in their opinion, make up the whole composition. Hence it comes to pass that the doctrine of regeneration, or an entire change of corrupt nature by a principle of divine grace, is almost lost out of their Christianity.

RULE 8. Remember that you have to do with the understanding, reason, and memory of man, with the heart and conscience, with the will and affections; and therefore you must use every method of speech which may be most proper to engage and employ each of these faculties or powers of human nature on the side of religion, and in the interest of God and the gospel.

Your first business is with the understanding, to make even the lower parts of your audience know what you mean. Endeavor, therefore, to find out all the clearest and most easy forms of speech to convey divine truths into the minds of men. Seek to obtain a perspicuous style and a clear and distinct manner of speaking, so that you may effectually impress the understanding while you pronounce the words, and that you may so exactly imprint on the mind of the hearers the same ideas which you yourself have conceived that they may never mistake your meaning. This talent is sooner attained in your younger years by having some judicious friend hear or read over your discourses and inform you where perspicuity is wanting in your language, and where the hearers may be in danger of mistaking your sense; for want of this, some young preachers have fixed themselves in such an obscure way of writing and talking as has much prevented their hearers from obtaining distinct ideas of their discourse. And if a man gets such an unhappy habit, he will be sometimes talking to the aïr, and will make the people stare at him as though he were speaking some unknown language.

Remember next that you have to do with the reasoning powers of man in preaching the gospel of Christ; for though this gospel is revealed from heaven, and could never have been discovered by all the efforts of human reason, yet the reason of man must judge the several things relating to it. It is reason that must determine whether the evidence of its heavenly origin is clear and strong; it is reason that must judge whether such a doctrine or such a duty is contained in the gospel, or may be justly deduced from it; it is the work of human reason to compare one Scripture with another, and to find out the true sense of any particular text by this means. Reason also must give its sentence whether a doctrine which is pretended to be contained in Scripture is contrary to the eternal and unchangeable relations and reasons of things; and, if so, then reason may pronounce that this doctrine is not from God, nor can be given us by divine revelation. Reason, therefore, has its office and proper province, even in matters of revelation; yet it must always be confessed that some propositions may be revealed to us from heaven which may be so far superior to the limits and sphere of our reasoning powers in the present state that human reason ought not to reject them simply because it cannot fully understand them nor clearly and perfectly reconcile them, unless it plainly sees a natural

absurdity in them, a real impossibility, or a plain inconsistency with other parts of divine revelation.

And in your representation of things to the reason
and understanding of men, it would sometimes be of
special advantage to have some power over the fancy or
imagination. This would help us to paint our themes in
their proper colors, whether of the alluring or the forbidding kind; and now and then we should make use of
both, in order to impress the idea on the soul with
happier force and success.

When you would describe any of the personal or social virtues of life, so as to enforce their practice, set
yourself to display the beauties and excellencies of
them in their own agreeable and lovely forms and colors. But do not content yourself with this alone; this is
not sufficient to allure the degenerate and sensual
mind of man to practice them. Few persons are of so
happy a disposition, and so refined a genius, as to be
wrought upon by the mere aspect of such inviting qualities. Endeavor, therefore, to illustrate the virtues by
their contrary vices, and set forth these moral mischiefs, in both their deformities and their dangerous
consequences, before the eyes of your hearers. Think it
not enough to represent to them the shining excellencies of humility and benevolence, of justice, veracity,
gratitude, and temperance; but produce to sight the vile
features of pride, envy, malice, spite, knavery, falsehood,
revenge, sensuality, luxury, and the rest of that cursed
train, in their proper places and seasons. Make it evident how contrary they are both to the law of God and
the gospel of Christ; describe them in all their several
forms, shapes, and appearances; strip them of their
false pretenses and disguises; show how they insinuate

and exert themselves in different occurrences of life and different constitutions; and pursue them so narrowly, as it were, with a hue and cry, and with such exact descriptions that if any of these vices are indulged by your hearers, they may be found out by strict self-examination, that the consciences of the guilty may be laid under conviction of sin and be set in the way of repentance and reformation.

Whenever any vice has found the way into our bosoms and makes its nest there, its proper and evil features and characters ought to be marked out by the preacher with great accuracy so that it may be discovered to our consciences, in order to cause its destruction; for these wretched hearts of ours are naturally so fond of all their own inmates that they are too ready to hide their ill qualities from our own sight and conviction, and thus they cover and save them from the sentence of mortification and death which is pronounced against every sin in the Word of God. Let the preacher and the hearer both remember that sin must be pursued to the death, or else there is no life for the soul. Only the Christian who, by the Spirit, mortifies the sinful deeds of the body has the promise of salvation and life.

Think farther that you should take some care also to engage the memory, and to make it serve the purposes of religion. Let your reasonings be ever so forcible and convincing, let your language be ever so clear and intelligible, yet, if the whole discourse glides over the ear in a smooth and delightful stream, and if nothing is fixed on the memory, the sermon is in great danger of being lost and fruitless.

Now, to avoid this danger, I would recommend to

you a clear and distinct method; and let this method appear to the hearers by the division of your discourses into several plain and distinct particulars so that the whole may not be a mere loose harangue without evident members and discernible rests and pauses. Whatsoever proper and natural divisions belong to your subject, mark them out by their numbers: 1st, 2nd, 3rd, and so on. This will afford you time to breathe in the delivery of your discourses, and will give hearers a short season for the recollection of the particulars which have been mentioned before.

But in this matter take care always to maintain a happy medium, so as never to arise to such a number of particulars as may make your sermon look like a tree full of branches in the winter without the beautiful, profitable appearance of leaves and fruit.

Cast the scheme of your discourse into some distinct, general headings and lesser subdivisions in your first sketches and rudiments of it; this will greatly assist you in the amplification. This will help to preserve a just method throughout, and secure you from repeating the same thoughts too often; this will enable you to commit your sermon to your own memory the better, so that you may deliver it with ease; and it will greatly assist the understanding as well as the memory of all who hear you. It will furnish them with matter and method for an easy recollection at home, for meditation in their devout retirement, and for religious conference or rehearsal after the public worship is ended.

Consider again that your business is with the consciences, wills, and affections of men. A mere conviction of the reason and judgment by the strongest arguments is hardly sufficient, in matters of piety and virtue, to command the will into obedience, because the appetites of the flesh and the interests of this world are engaged on the opposite side. It is a very common case with the sons and daughters of Adam to see and know their proper duty, and to have their reasons that enforce it fresh in their memory; and yet the powerful efforts of the flesh and the world withhold the will from the practice, forbid its holy resolutions for God and heaven, or keep them always feeble, doubtful, and wavering. The God of nature therefore has furnished mankind with those powers which we call "passions" or "affections of the heart" in order to excite the will, with superior vigor and activity, to avoid the evil and pursue the good. Upon this account the preacher must learn to address the passions in a proper manner; and I cannot but think it a very imperfect characteristic of a Christian preacher that he reasons well upon every subject and talks clearly upon his text if he has nothing of the pathos in his ministrations, no talent at all to strike the passions of the heart.

Awaken your spirit, therefore, in your compositions; contrive all lively, forcible, and penetrating forms of speech to make your words powerful and impressive on the hearts of your hearers when light is first let into the mind. Practice all the awful and solemn ways of address to the conscience, all the soft and tender influences on the heart. Try all methods to rouse and awaken the cold, the stupid, the sleepy race of sinners. Learn all the language of holy jealousy and terror to affright the presumptuous; all the compassionate and encouraging manners of speaking, to comfort, encourage, and direct the awakened, the penitent, the willing, and the humble; all the winning and engaging modes of discourse and expostulation to constrain the hearer of every character to attend. Seek this happy skill of reigning and triumphing over the hearts of an assembly; persuade them with power to love and practice all the important duties of godliness in opposition to the flesh and the world; endeavor to kindle the soul to zeal in the holy warfare, and to make it bravely victorious over all the enemies of its salvation.

But in all these efforts of sacred oratory, remember still that you are a minister of the gospel of Christ; and as your style must not affect the pomp and magnificence of the theater, so neither should you borrow your expressions or your metaphors from the coarsest occupations, or any of the mean and uncleanly occurences in life. Do not swell the sound of your periods with ambitious or pedantic phrases; do not dress your serious discourses to the people in too glittery an array, with an affectation of gaudy and flaunting ornaments, nor ever descend to so low a degree of familiarity and meanness as to sink your language below the dignity of your subject or your office.

RULE 9. As the art of reasoning and the happy skill of persuasion are both necessary to be used in framing your discourses, so both of them may be borrowed, in a good measure, from the holy Scriptures. The Word of God will furnish you with a rich variety of forms, to both prove and persuade. Clear instruction, convincing argument, and pathetic address to the heart may be all drawn from the sacred writers. Many fine strokes of true logic and rhetoric are scattered through that divine book, the Bible. Words of force and elegance to charm and allure the soul, glitter and sparkle like golden ore in some particular parts of it. You may find there noble examples of the awful and compassionate style, and inimitable patterns of the terrible and tender. Shall I therefore take the freedom once again to call upon you to remember that you are a minister of the Word of God, a professor and preacher of the Bible, and not a mere philosopher upon the foot of reason, nor an orator in a heathen school?

And as for bright, warm, and pathetic language to strike the imagination or to affect the heart, to kindle the divine passions or to melt the soul, none of the heathen orators can better furnish you than the moving expostulations of the ancient prophets, the tender and sprightly odes of holy David, or the affectionate part of the letters of St. Paul, which even his enemies in the church of Corinth confessed to be powerful. The eastern writers, among whom we number the Jews, were particularly famous for lively oratory, bright images, and bold, animated figures of speech. Could I have heard Isaiah or Jeremiah pronouncing some of their sermons, or attended St. Paul in some of his pathetic strains of preaching, I would never mourn a want of acquaintance with Tully or Demosthenes.

A preacher whose mind is well stored and enriched with the divine sense and sentiments, the reasoning and language of Scripture (and especially if these are wrought in his heart by Christian experience), supposing his other talents are equal to those of his brethren, will always have a considerable advantage over them in composing such discourses as shall be most popular and most useful in Christian assemblies; and he may better expect the presence and blessing of God to make His Word triumph over the souls of men, and will generally speak to their hearts with more power for their eternal salvation. Show me one sinner turned to God and holiness by the labors of a preacher who is generally entertaining the audience with a long and weighty chain of reasoning from the principles of nature, and teaching virtue in the language of heathen philosophy, and I think I may undertake to show you ten who have been convinced and converted, and have become holy persons and lively Christians, by an attendance upon a spiritual, affectionate, and experimental ministry. The whole assembly hangs attentively upon the lips of a man who speaks to the heart as well as to the understanding, and who can enforce his exhortations from a manifold experience of the success of them. They delight to hear the preacher whose plain and powerful address to the conscience, and whose frequent methods of reasoning in the pulpit, have been drawn from what they themselves have read in Scripture concerning God and man, sin and duty, our misery and divine mercy, death, resurrection, judgment, heaven and hell. They attend with holy reverence and affection on such a minister whose frequent argument, in points of both doctrine and practice, is "Thus saith the Lord."

RULE 10. Be not slothful or negligent in your weekly preparation for the pulpit. Take due time for it; begin so early in the week that you may have time enough before you to furnish your preparation well; and always allow for accidental occurences, either from indisposition of the body, from interruptions by company, or from unforeseen business or trouble, so that you may not be reduced to the necessity of hurrying over your work in haste at the end of the week, and serving God and the souls of men with poor, cold, and careless performances. Remember that awful word, though spoken on another occasion: "Cursed be he that doeth the work of the Lord deceitfully." Manage so as to leave the Saturday evening, or at least the Lord's Day morning entire, for the review and correction of your discourse, and for your own spiritual improvement by the sermon which you have prepared for the people.

If it should happen that the mere providence of God, without any neglect of yours, has hindered you from making so good a preparation as you designed, you may, with courage and hope of divine assistance, venture into the assembly with more slender and imperfect furniture; but if your conscience tells you that your preparations are very slight, and if the neglect is your own, you have less reason to expect aid from above without great humiliation for your negligence. And what if God should forsake you so far in the pulpit as to expose you to public shame, and thus punish you for your carelessness in the midst of the congregation!

Study your matter well by meditation and reading, and comparing Scriptures together, till you have gotten it completely within your grasp and survey. Then, if you should happen to be so situated in preaching that you could not refresh your memory by the inspection of your paper every minute, yet you will not be exposed to hurry and confusion; a ready thought will suggest something pertinent to your purpose. Let your preparation be usually so perfect that you may be able to fill up the time allotted for the discourse with solid sense and proper language, even if your natural spirits should happen to be heavy and indisposed at the hour of preaching, and if your mind should have no new thoughts arising in the delivery of your discourse.

Labor carefully in the formation of your sermons in

your younger years. A habit of thinking and speaking well, procured by the studies of youth, will make the labor of your middle age easy when, perhaps, you will have much less time and leisure.

3. Take heed to your public labors and ministrations in the church, which may be done by attending to the following particulars:
(1) Apply yourself to your work with pious delight, not as a toil or task which you wish were done and ended, but as a matter of inward pleasure to your own soul. Enter the pulpit with solemnity of holy joy so that you have an opportunity to speak for the honor of God and the salvation of men. Then you will not preach or pray with sloth or laziness, with coldness or indifference. We are not usually slothful and indifferent in the pursuit of our joys or the relish of our chosen pleasures. Stir up yourself to the work with sacred vigor so that the assembly may feel what you speak; but if you deliver the most solemn and lively compositions like a man who is half asleep, it will be no wonder if your hearers slumber. A dull preacher makes a drowsy church.
(2) Endeavor to get your heart into a temper of divine love, zealous for the laws of God, affected with the grace of Christ, and compassionate for the souls of men. Engage in public work with this temper. Let your frame of spirit be holy with regard to your own inward devotion, near to God and delighting in Him; and let it be zealous for the name of Christ and the increase of His kingdom. Oh, pity perishing sinners when you are sent to invite them to be reconciled to God! Let not self be the subject or the end of your preaching, but Christ

and the salvation of souls. "We preach not ourselves,"
said the apostle, "but Christ Jesus the Lord, and ourselves as your servants for Jesus' sake." Speak as a dying
preacher to dying hearers, with the utmost compassion
for the ignorant, the tempted, the foolish, and the obstinate; for all these are in danger of eternal death.
Attend to your work with the utmost desire to save souls
from hell, and to enlarge the kingdom of Christ your
Lord.

Go into the public assembly with a design (if God
pleases) to strike and persuade some souls there into
repentance, faith, holiness, and salvation! Go to open
blind eyes, to unstop deaf ears, to make the lame walk,
to make the foolish wise, to raise those who are dead in
trespasses and sins to a heavenly and divine life, and to
bring guilty rebels to return to the love and obedience
of their Maker by Jesus Christ, the great Reconciler, so
that they may be pardoned and saved! Go to diffuse the
savor of the name of Christ and His gospel through a
whole assembly, and to allure souls to partake of grace
and glory!

(3) Go forth in the strength of Christ, for these
glorious strengths are above your own strength, and
transcend all the powers of the brightest preachers! "Be
strong in the grace which is in Christ Jesus." Without
Him we can do nothing. Go with a design to work
wonders of salvation on sinful creatures, but in the
strength of Jesus, who has all power given to Him in
heaven and earth, and has promised to be with His
ministers to the end of the world! Pray earnestly for the
promised aids of the Spirit; plead with God, who has
sent you forth in the service of the gospel of His Son,
that you may not return empty, but bring in a fair har-

vest of converts to heaven. It is the Lord of the harvest who alone can give this divine success to the laborers. "He that planteth is nothing, and he that watereth is nothing; but all our hope is in God, who giveth the increase."

(4) Get the substance of the sermon that you have prepared for the pulpit so wrought in your head and heart, by review and meditation, that you may have it at command, and speak to your hearers with freedom—not as if you were reading or repeating your lessons to them, but as a man sent to teach and persuade them to faith and holiness. Deliver your discourses to the people like a man who is talking to them in good earnest about their most important concerns and their everlasting welfare; like a messenger sent from heaven who would fain save sinners from hell and allure souls to God and happiness. Do not indulge that lazy way of reading over your prepared paper as a schoolboy does an oration out of Livy or Cicero, who has no concern in the things he speaks; but let all the warmest zeal for God and compassion for perishing men animate your voice and countenance, and let the people see and feel, as well as hear, that you are speaking to them about things of infinite moment, and in which your own eternal interest lies as well as theirs.

(5) If you pray and hope for the assistance of the Spirit of God in every part of your work, do not resolve always to confine yourself precisely to the mere words and sentences which you have written down in your private preparations. Far be it from me to encourage a preacher to venture into public work without due preparation by study, or without a regular composition of his discourse. We must not serve God with what costs

us nothing. All our wisest thoughts and cares are due to the sacred service of the temple; but what I mean is that we should not impose upon ourselves just such a number of precomposed words and lines to be delivered in the hour without daring to speak a warm sentiment that comes fresh upon the mind. Why may you not hope for some lively turns of thought, some new pious sentiments, which may strike light, heat, and life into the understandings and the hearts of those who hear you? In the zeal of your ministrations, why may you not expect some bright, warm, and pathetic forms of argument and persuasion to offer themselves to your lips for the more powerful conviction of sinners, and for the encouragement and comfort of humble Christians?

Have you not often found such an enlargement of thought, such a variety of sentiment and freedom of speech, in common conversation upon an important subject, beyond what you were apprised of beforehand? And why should you forbid yourself this natural advantage in the pulpit, and in the fervor of sacred ministrations, where also you have more reason to hope for divine assistance?

(6) Here would be a proper place to interpose a few directions concerning elocution, and the whole manner of delivery of your discourse to the people, which includes a voice, gesture, and behavior suited to the subject and design of every part of the sermon; but the rules that are necessary for this part of our work are much better derived from books written on this subject, from an observation of the best preachers in order to imitate them, and from an avoidance of that which we find offensive when we ourselves are hearers.

If I had a design to go through the whole of the

ministerial office, I should here also find a proper place to speak of the manner of your performance of public prayer, of your direction of that part of worship which is called psalmody, and of your ministration of the ordinance of baptism and the Lord's Supper; but this would require more time, and my chief design was to put you in mind of a few useful things which relate to preaching.

(7) Be very solicitous about the success of your labors in the pulpit. Water the seed sown, not only with public but with secret prayer. Plead with God importunately, that He would not suffer you to labor in vain. Do not be like that foolish bird, the ostrich, which lays her eggs in the dust and leaves them there, regardless of whether they come to life or not. God has not given her understanding. But let not this folly be your character or practice. Labor, watch, and pray that your sermons and the fruit of your studies may become words of divine life to souls.

It is an observation of pious Mr. [Richard] Baxter, which I have read somewhere in his works, that he has never known any considerable success from the brightest and noblest talents, nor the most excellent kind of preaching, and that even where the preachers themselves have been truly religious, if they have not had a solicitous concern for the success of their ministrations. Let the awful and important thought of souls being saved by my preaching, or left to perish and be condemned to hell by my negligence—I say, let this awful and tremendous thought dwell ever upon your spirit. We are made watchmen to the house of Israel, as Ezekiel was; and if we give no warning of approaching danger, the souls of multitudes may perish through our neglect, but the blood of souls will be terribly required at our hands.

4. Take heed to your whole conversation in the world; let that be managed not only as becomes a professor of Christianity, but as becomes a minister of the gospel of Christ. Now, among other rules which may render your conduct agreeable to your character, I entreat you to take these few into your thoughts:

RULE 1. Let it be blameless and inoffensive. Be vigilant and temperate in all things, not only as a soldier in Christ, but as an under-leader of part of His army. Be temperate, and abstain sometimes even from lawful delights, so that you may make the work of self-denial easy, and that you may bear hardship as becomes a soldier. But always be watchful lest you are too entangled with the affairs of this life, that you may better please Him who has chosen you for an officer in His battalions, and that you may not be easily surprised into the snares of sin. Guard against a love of pleasure, a sensual temper, an indulgence of appetite, an excessive relish of wine or dainties; these carnalize the soul, and give occasion to the world to reproach us all too justly.

RULE 2. Let your conduct be exemplary in all the duties of holiness and virtue, in all the instances of worship and piety toward God, and in those of justice, honor, and hearty benevolence towards men. Be forward and ready to engage in every good word and work so that you may be a pattern and a leader of the flock, and that you may be able to address the people committed to your care in the language of the blessed apostle: "Be ye followers of me, even as I also am of Christ." "Brethren, be followers together of me, and mark them which walk so, as ye have us for an example; for our conversation is in heaven." "Those things, which ye have both learned and received, and heard and seen in me, do you practice, and the God of peace shall be with you."

RULE 3. Let your conduct be grave and manly, yet pleasant and engaging. Let it be grave, manly, and venerable. Remember your station in the church so that you do not sink into levity and vain trifling, that you do not indulge any ridiculous humors or childish follies below the dignity of your character. Keep up the honor of your office among men by a remarkable sanctity of manners, by a decent and manly deportment. Remember that our station does not permit any of us to play the buffoon; nor will it be any glory to us to excel in farce and comedy. Let others obtain the honor of being good jesters, and of having it in their power to spread a laugh round the company when they please; but let it be our ambition to act on the stage of life as men who are devoted to the service of the God of heaven, to the real benefit of mankind on earth, and to their eternal interest.

Yet there is no need that your behavior should have anything stiff or haughty, anything sullen or gloomy in it. There is an art of pleasing in conversation that will maintain the honor of a superior office without a morose silence, without an affected stiffness, and without a haughty superiority. A pleasant story may proceed without offense from a minister's lips, but he should never aim at the title of a man of mirth, nor abound in such tales as carry no useful instruction in them, no lessons of piety, wisdom, or virtue.

Let a cheerful freedom, a generous friendship, and

an innocent pleasure generally appear on your countenance, and let your speech be ever kind and affectionate. Do not put on any forbidding airs, nor let the humblest soul be afraid to speak to you. Let your whole carriage be civil and affable; let your address to men be usually open and free, such as may allure persons to be open and free with you in the important concerns of their souls. Seek, as far as possible, to obtain all your pious designs by soft and gentle methods of persuasion.

If you are ever called to the unpleasing and painful work of reproof, this may be done effectually, upon some occasions, without speaking a word. When vicious, unclean, or unbecoming speeches arise in public conversation, a sudden silence, with assumed gravity, will often be a sensible and sufficient reproof. Or where words of admonition may not be proper because of the company, sometimes a sudden departure may be the best way to acquaint them with your disapprobation.

But there are cases wherein such a tacit rebuke is not sufficient to represent your character and your office. Sometimes it is necessary for a minister to bear a public and express witness against shocking immorality, or against vile and impious discourse. Yet, in general, it must be said that if a reproof can be given in secret, it is best and most likely to prevail upon the offender, because it less irritates his passions, nor awakens his pride to vindicate himself and to despise all reproof.

Whenever providence calls you to this work, make it appear to the transgressor that you do it with regret and pain; let him see that you are not giving vent to your own wrath, but seeking his interest and welfare, and that were it not for the honor of God and for his good, you would gladly excuse yourself from the ungrateful task; that it is a work in which your spirit takes no delight. If the case and circumstances require some speeches that are awful and severe, let it appear still that your love and pity are the prevailing passions, and that even your anger has something divine and holy in it, as being raised and pointed against the sin rather than against the sinner.

Study to make the whole of your carriage and discourse among men so engaging as may invite strangers to love you, and allure them to love religion for your sake.

RULE 4. In order to attain the same end, let your conversation be attended with much self-denial and meekness; avoid the character of humorist, nor be unreasonably fond of little things, nor peevish for the want of them. Suppress rising passion early. If you are providentially led into argument and dispute, whether on themes of belief or practice, be very watchful lest you run into fierce contention, into angry and noisy debate. Guard against every word that savors of malice or bitter strife; watch against the first stirrings of sudden wrath or resentment; bear with patience the contradiction of others, and forbear to return railing for railing. A minister must be gentle, and not apt to strive, but meekly instructing gainsayers.

He should never be ready either to give or take offense, but he should teach his people to neglect and bury resentment, to be deaf to reproaches, and to forgive injuries by his own example, even as God has forgiven all of us. Let us imitate His divine pattern, who

cancels and forgives our infinite offenses for the sake
of Christ. "A bishop must not be a brawler or striker,"
but such as the apostle was, "gentle among the people,
even as a nurse cherishes her children." And, being affectionately desirous of their welfare, we should be willing to impart not only the gospel of God to them, but
anything that is dear to us for the salvation of their
souls.

Never suffer any differences, if possible, to arise between you and any of the people who are committed to
your care, or attend on your ministrations; this will en-
danger the success of your best labors among them.
And, for this reason, though you visit families with
freedom, yet avoid all unnecessary inquiries into their
domestic affairs by a prying curiosity. The pleasure of
such secrets will never pay for the danger that attends
them, and your own business is sufficient for you.

Avoid entering into any of the little private and personal quarrels that may arise among them, unless providence gives you an evident call to become peacemaker.
But even in this blessed work there is some danger of
disobliging one side or the other; for though both
sides are often to blame, yet each supposes himself so
much in the right that your softest and most candid in-
timation of their being culpable, even in little things,
will sometimes awaken the jealousy of one or both parties against you. This will tend to abate their esteem of
you, and give a coldness to their attention on your sacred services. We need to be wise as serpents, in this
case, and harmless as doves.

RULE 5. Let your conduct be as fruitful and edifying
as your station and opportunities will allow. Wherever
you come, use your utmost endeavors that the world

may be the better for you. If it is the duty of every Christian, much more is it the indispensable duty of a minister of Christ to take heed that no corrupt communication proceed out of his mouth but that which is good for edification, that it may minister grace to the hearers.

In your private visits to the members of your flock, or to the houses of those who attend on your ministry, depart not without putting in, if possible, some word for God and religion, for Christ and His gospel. Take occasion from common occurrences that arise to artfully and insensibly introduce some discourse of things sacred. Let it be done with prudence and holy skill so that the company may be led into it ere they are aware. The ingenious Mr. Norris's little *Discourse on Religious Conversation* and Mr. Matthew Henry's *Sermon on Friendly Visits* have many excellent and valuable hints in them for our use.

It is to be confessed that the best of ministers and Christians sometimes fall into such company that it is hardly possible to speak a word for God and the gospel among them. Try then whether you cannot lead the discourse to some useful theme in matters of science, art, and ingenuity, or to rules of prudence, morality, or human conduct. There is a time for keeping silence and restraining our lips as with a bridle, even from everything that is piously good, while some sort of wicked men stand before us. The best men are sometimes dumb with silence, and dare not speak of God or religion lest they should cast their pearls before swine and give their holy things to dogs, and lest they should provoke the unclean or the envious animals to foam out their impurities, or to turn again and rend them. But I doubt this caution has been carried much farther by our own cowardice and carnality of spirit than David practiced it, or than Jesus Christ meant it, in the seventh chapter of Matthew. Let us take heed that we do not abuse this prudent caution to manifest neglect of our duty, and to withhold our lips from the things of God where providence gives us fair opportunity to speak of them.

Now and then take occasion to speak a kind and religious word to the children of the household; put them in mind of avoiding some childish folly, or of practicing some duty that belongs to their age. Let your memory be well furnished with the words of Scripture, suited to the several ages of mankind, as well as to the various occasions of life, so that out of the abundance of the heart your mouth may speak to the advantage of all who hear you, and particularly to the younger parts of mankind, who are the hopes of the next generation. Make the lambs of the flock love you and hear your voice with delight, that they may grow up under your instruction to fill up the room of their fathers when they are called away to heaven; nor let servants be utterly neglected where providence may afford you an opportunity to speak a word to their souls.

He who has the happy talent of parlor-preaching has sometimes done more for Christ and souls in the space of a few minutes than by the labor of many hours and days in the usual course of preaching in the pulpit. Our character should be all of a piece, and we should help forward the success of our public ministrations by our private addresses to the hearts and consciences of men, where providence favors us with just occasions.

In order to promote this work of particular watchfulness over the flock of Christ, where He has made you a shepherd and overseer, it is useful to keep a catalogue of their names, and now and then review them with a pastoral eye and affection. This will awaken and incline you to lift up proper petitions for each of them, so far as you are acquainted with their circumstances in body or mind. This will excite you to give thanks to God on account of those who walk as becomes the gospel, and who have either begun or proceeded and increased in the Christian life and temper by your ministry; you will observe the names of the negligent and backsliding Christians, to mourn over them and admonish them; you will be put in mind how to dispose of your time in Christian visits, and learn the better to fulfill your whole ministry among them.

5. The things which I have spoken hitherto have been a display of the best methods I can think of for the execution of the sacred office of the ministry; and so far as they are conformable to the Word of God, we may venture to say that these are your duties, my dear brothers, and these are ours. It remains now to be considered, in what manner shall we enforce them on our own consciences, and on yours? What solemn obtestations shall I use to press these momentous concerns on all our hearts? What pathetic language shall I choose, what words of awful efficacy and divine fervor, which may first melt our spirits into softness, and then imprint these duties upon them with lasting power? We exhort and charge you, we exhort and charge ourselves, by all that is serious and sacred, by all that is important and everlasting, by all the solemn transactions between God and man which are past, and by all the more

solemn and awful scenes which are yet to come; by all
things in our holy religion which are dreadful and
tremendous, and by all things in this gospel which are
glorious and amiable, heavenly and divine. We charge
you by all that is written in this book of God, according
to which we shall be judged in the last day, by all the infinite and astonishing glories and terrors of an invisible world and an unseen eternity; we charge and exhort
you, we exhort and charge ourselves, that we all take
heed to the ministry which we have received of the
Lord Jesus, that we fulfill it.

We charge you, and we charge ourselves, by the de-
caying interest of religion and the withering state of
Christianity at this day, that we do not increase this
general and lamentable decay, this growing and dreadful apostasy, by our slothful and careless management
of the trust which is committed to us. It is a divine interest indeed, but declining; it is a heavenly cause, but
among us it is sinking and dying. Oh, let us stir up our
hearts, and all that is within us, and strive mightily in
prayer and in preaching to revive the work of God, and
beg earnestly that God, by a fresh and abundant infu-
sion of His Spirit, would revive His work among us.
Revive Thine own work, O Lord, in the midst of these
years of sin and degeneracy; do not let us labor in vain!
Where is Thy zeal, O Lord, and Thy strength, the
sounding of Thy compassions and Thy mercies? Are
they restrained? Oh, let us rouse our souls with all holy
fervor to fulfill our ministry, for it will be a dreadful reproach upon us, and a burden too heavy for us to bear,
if we let the cause of Christ and godliness die under our
hands for want of a lively zeal, and of pious fervor and
faithfulness in our ministrations!

We entreat, we exhort and charge you, and we charge ourselves, by the solemn and awful circumstances of a dying bed, and the thoughts of conscience in that important hour when we shall enter into the world of spirits, that we take heed to the ministry which we have received. Surely that hour is hastening upon us when our heads will lie upon a dying pillow. When a few more mornings and evenings have visited our windows, the shadows of a long night will begin to spread themselves over us; in that gloomy hour, conscience will review the behavior of the days that are past, will take account of the conduct of our whole lives, and will particularly examine our labors and cares in our sacred office. Oh, may we ever dread the thoughts of making bitter work for repentance in that hour, and of treasuring up terrors for a deathbed by a careless and useless ministry!

We exhort and charge you, and we charge ourselves, by our gathering together before the throne of our Lord Jesus Christ, and the solemn account we must there give of the ministry with which He has entrusted us, that we prepare, by our present zeal and labor, to render that most awful scene peaceful to our souls, and the result of it joyful and happy. Let us look forward to that illustrious and tremendous appearance, when our Lord shall come with ten thousand of His holy angels to inquire into the conduct of men, and particularly of the ministers of His kingdom here on earth. Let us remember that we shall be examined, in the light of the flames of that day, as to what have we done with His gospel which He gave us to preach. What we have done with His promise of rich salvation, which He sent us to offer in His name? What has become of the souls committed to our care! Oh, that we may give up our account with joy and not with grief, to the Judge of the living and the dead in that glorious, that dreadful and decisive hour!

We charge and warn you, my dear brothers, and warn and charge ourselves, by all the terrors written in this divine book, and by all the indignation and vengeance of God, which we are sent to display before a sinful world—by all the torments and agonies of hell which we are commissioned to pronounce against impenitent sinners, in order to persuade men to turn to God and receive and obey the gospel—that we take heed to our ministry and that we fulfill it. This vengeance and these terrors will fall upon our souls, and that with intolerable weight, with double and immortal anguish, if we have trifled with these terrible solemnities and made no use of these awful scenes to awaken men to lay hold of the offered grace of the gospel. Knowing, therefore, the terrors of the Lord, let us persuade men; for we must all stand before the judgment seat of Christ, to receive according to our works.

In the last place, we entreat, we exhort and charge you, by all the joys of paradise and the blessings of an eternal heaven, which are our hope and support under all our labors, and which, in the name of Christ, we offer to sinful, perishing men, and invite them to partake thereof. Can we speak of such joys and glories with a sleepy heart and indolent language? Can we invite sinners, who are running headlong into hell, to return and partake of these felicities, and not be excited to the warmest forms of address and the most lively and engaging methods of persuasion? What scenes of brightness and delight can animate the lips and language of an orator, if the glories and the joys of the Christian's heaven and our immortal hopes cannot do it? We charge and entreat you, therefore, and we charge ourselves, by the shining recompenses which are promised to faithful ministers, that we keep this glory ever in view, and awaken our dying zeal in our sacred work.

Directions to the Student and the Pastor

by
Rev. John Mason

Part 1: The Student

He who devotes himself to the work of the sacred ministry should be continually intent on two things, the improvement of his own mind and of the minds of others in the most important and useful knowledge. This comprehends the whole office of a student and pastor.

The business of a student is to be so employed as to be continually making some valuable accessions to his own intellectual furniture. For this five things are necessary:

1. A proper distribution and management of time.
2. A right method of reading to advantage.
3. The order and regulation of studies.
4. The proper way of collecting and preserving useful sentiments from books and conversation.
5. The improvement of one's thoughts when alone.

The Right Distribution and Management of Time

A student should be as frugal of his time as a miser is of his money; he should save it with as much care, and spend it with as much caution. To be careful how we manage and employ our time is one of the first precepts that is taught in the school of wisdom, and one of the last that is learned. And 'tis a prodigious thing to consider that although, among all the talents which are committed to our stewardship, time (upon several accounts) is the most precious, yet there is not any one of which the generality of men are more profuse and regardless. Nay, it is obvious to observe that even those persons who are frugal and thrifty in everything else are yet extremely prodigal of their best revenue, time, of which alone (as Seneca nobly observed) 'tis a virtue to be covetous. And it is amazing to think how much time may be gained by proper economy, and how much good literature may be acquired if that gain is rightly applied. To this purpose, let the following rules be observed:

1. Take particular notice of those things which are most apt to rob you of your time. Upon such an inquest, you will probably detect the following thieves:

• The bed. Never allow yourself above six hours sleep at most. Physicians tell you that nature demands no more for the proper replenishing of health and spirit. All beyond this is luxury, no less prejudicial to the animal constitution than intemperate meals, and no less hurtful to the powers of the mind than to those of the body. It insensibly weakens and relaxes both.

• Ceremonies and formal visits. They may sometimes be necessary, but if they can't be improved to some useful purpose, the shorter they are the better. Much of this time is spent to no purpose, and it is to be feared that not a little of it is spent to bad purpose.

• Indolence is another thief of time. Indulging a slow, heavy, inactive disposition; delaying or deferring necessary business to a future time which ought to be set about immediately; idle musing, or indulging vain, chimeric imaginations—these are very natural to some, and as unnatural to others. They commonly lead to another and greater waste of time . . .

• Sloth and idleness. No man takes more pains than the slothful man. Indolence and ease are the rust of the mind. No habit grows faster by indulgence, exposes to more temptations, or renders a man more uneasy to himself, or more useless to others.

• Reading useless books. And those books may be called useless to you which either you do not understand, or, if you do, afford neither solid improvement nor suitable entertainment. And especially avoid pernicious books, or such as tend to give the mind a wrong turn or bad tincture.

• Much time is often lost by a wrong method of studying, and especially by applying to those branches of learning which have no connection with the great end you propose. Why should a divine affect the civilian, dive into the depths of politics, or be ambitious to excel in the most abstruse parts of mathematical science? He has spent much time and labor in these disquisitions, and at last gained his point. But after all his expense, how is he a better preacher or a better man? In every undertaking (especially when we enter upon a new course of study) we should remember the good to be sought and ask ourselves how far this is likely to improve our usefulness, or add to our reputation under that character we are about to sustain, and wherein we aim at some degree of distinction.

• Last, much time is lost by an unnatural bent of the mind to a study to which it is not disposed, or by which the faculties are fatigued. It will find great relief by a change of employment. A man who rides posts to save time would not choose to be always spurring a jaded horse, but will rather change him for a fresh one whereby he makes a speedier progress with more ease to himself. The activity of the mind is so great that it often finds more relief and refreshment by turning to a new track of thinking, different from that it was tired in, than it does from a total relaxation of thought in mere bodily exercise; this shows that it is not labor that tires it so much as a dull uniformity of employment, since it is more refreshed by variety than by rest.

2. Let your most precious time (that wherein the thoughts are most composed and free) be sacred to the most serious and important studies. Give the morning to composition, or to reading some valuable author of antiquity with whom it is worth your while to be well acquainted. The afternoon will suffice for history, chronology, politics, news, travels, geography, and the common run of pamphlets; and let books of entertainment amuse a dull hour when you are fit for nothing else. To apply your early time or fresh thoughts to these is like drinking wine in the morning; and giving too much of our time and thoughts to them is like drinking the same intoxicating liquor to excess, and will have the same effect on the mind as that has on the body.

3. Remember to be always beforehand with your business. Whatever must be done now as well as hereafter, for that very reason had better be done now. This is a prudent maxim in life, applicable to a thousand cases, and of no less advantage to a student than to a tradesman. Defer nothing to the very last, lest some intervening accident should prevent the execution of an important purpose or put you into a hurry in the prose-

cution of it. And what is done with precipitance and
haste seldom succeeds so well, or is executed with the
same accuracy and discretion, as that which is the effect of more mature and deliberate thought. A traveler
who must reach his home in a given time would not be
thought discreet if by loitering at the beginning of his
journey he is forced to run himself out of breath at the
end.

That time is not lost, but well used, which is spent
in those exercises that are necessary to invigorate and
strengthen the faculties for harder work or to preserve
a good state of health and spirits, such as eating, drinking, sleeping, medicine, bodily exercise, recreation,
and the like. Through a neglect of these, a student may
contract a bad habit of body or mind, or so far impair
his constitution as to render him a long time unfit for
useful service. But an excess of these things defeats
their end, and is as prejudicial to health as a discreet
and moderate use of them is conducive to it.

4. Enter upon nothing but what you are determined
to pursue and finish. Much time is often lost by vain attempts, and by leaving useful designs imperfect. For as
he who begins to build a house, but never completes it,
must set down to his loss the greatest part of his money
thus expended, so a student who desists from a work
wherein he has taken much pains is chargeable with as
fruitless an expense of his time as the other is of his
money.

The Way to Read Authors to Advantage
A student should be as careful what books he reads
as what company he keeps. They both leave the same
tincture on the mind.

1. Don't read indiscriminately, nor indulge a curiosity of perusing every new book that comes out, nor desire to read it till from the known ability of the author, or the information of some judicious friend, lets you know it is worth your reading. The curiosity of Vanillus to be personally acquainted with men and their characters leads him into all company when he is at Bath; and when he hears of a new stranger he is uneasy till he knows him, and is able to give others a description of his person, equipage, and family. By this turn of temper Vanillus loses much time that would be more agreeably and profitably spent in the conversation of a few select friends. He knows men, but not human nature. There is a wide difference between a man of reading and a man of learning. One can't read everything, and, if we could, we would be never the wiser. The bad would spoil the good, filling our minds with a confused medley of sentiments and desires, and the end of reading would be quite defeated for want of time and power to improve and practice. A man who eats from every dish at the table overloads his stomach, is sick, and digests nothing. He would have been better to have fasted.

2. Lay aside the fruitless inclination of reading a trifling author quite through in hopes of finding something better at the end. You are sure of finding something better in another on the same subject. Therefore do not lose a certainty for the sake of a mere possibility. Why should you confine yourself to listening to the impertinence of one man when, by only turning your back, you may be entertained or improved by the more pleasing and instructive conversation of another?

3. Observe the characteristic beauties of your author. Every good author has his peculiar felicity, his distin-

guishing excellence. Some excel in style, entertaining us with easy, natural language, or with an elegance and propriety of expression; some delight us with their florid, smooth, and well-turned periods. Some love a figurative, diffuse, and flowing style. Others love quite a plain, rational, discursive one. Each have their excellence. But the most elegant is that which is most natural, proper, and expressive; it can't then be too short and plain, both to delight and instruct, which are the two great ends of language. A style overloaded with ornaments grows prolix; and prolixity always weakens or obscures the sentiment it would express. No decorations of well-chosen words, or harmony of cadence, can atone for this fault. Such a style is like a lady who, in adorning her person, spoils a good shape by a tawdry dress, and a fine face by paint and patches. And both proceed from the same affectation in preferring the embellishments of art to those of nature, whose charms are infinitely more powerful and pleasing.

Others excel in sentiments. Those sentiments strike us with most pleasure that are strong, clear, soft, sublime, pathetic, just, or uncommon. Whatever has the most weight and brevity finds the quickest way to the heart.

Others excel in method, in a natural disposition of the subject and an easy, free, familiar way of communicating thoughts to the understanding. Nothing is very striking. You approve and are well pleased with your author, and you scarcely know for what. This resembles the agreeableness in the very humor, turn, and air of some people we converse with.

Others are very happy in their manner and way of conveying clear, rational, solid arguments and instructions to the mind, which arrest your attention, command your approbation, and force your assent at once. You see everything in broad day, in a fair, strong, and proper light. A perfect writer has all these excellencies of style, sentiment, method, and manner united. A judicious reader will observe in which of them his author most excels.

4. From all your authors choose one or two for your model, by which to form your style and sentiments, and let them be your pocket-companions. Consult and imitate them every day till you are not only master of their style and sentiments, but imbibe their spirit. But be very cautious in both your choice and imitation lest with their excellencies you adopt their faults, to which an excessive veneration for them may make you blind.

If your author has an established reputation, and you don't relish him, suspect your own taste and judgment. Perhaps something has biased your mind against him; find it out and compare it with those beauties which charm his other readers more than all his blemishes offend them. Or perhaps you do not understand him; then 'tis no wonder you don't admire him. If your judgment is good, 'tis a sure sign your author is so when, the more you read him the more you like him. A good friend and a good book are known by this: they grow in your esteem as you grow in acquaintance with them.

When you meet with such an author on any subject, stick by him, and make yourself master of him. You will discover new beauties in him every time you read him, and regret not that you are unread in the common rubbish. Some books better deserve to be read through ten times than others once.

5. Before you sit down to a book taste it, that is, examine the title page, preface, contents, and index, then turn to the place where some important article is discussed. Observe the writer's diction, argument, method, and manner of treating it. And if after two or three such trials you find he is obscure, confused, pedantic, shallow, or trifling, depend upon it that he is not worth your reading.

6. Last, if the book is your own, make marks in the margin beside those passages where the sentiment is well conceived or expressed and worth your remembering or retaining. Or transfer it into your commonplace book* under the heading your author is treating, or at least a reference to it. In reading an ancient Latin or Greek author, it will be a help to the memory to transcribe the passages that struck you most, in the spare leaves at the beginning or end of the book in English, and by thus skimming off the cream you will have it always ready for use. If you meet with a happy expression, or even one well-chosen word on any subject, which you may have occasion to use (and wish it might occur to you when you are at a loss for expression), mark it and make it your own forever. Thus you will read with taste and profit, and avoid the censure which falls upon some:

> *A bookish blockhead ignorantly read*
> *With loads of learned lumber in his head.*

---

* A commonplace book was something pastors in training kept during their schooling, full of examples from everyday life to be used as illustrations, or of things that were read and could be used later in a sermon.

How to Study to Advantage

Here we must consider both the subject and the method.

As to the subjects of your study, consider what will make you most eminent and useful in your profession; this kind of study is to be your serious business, and daily and diligently prosecuted. In all your reading keep this point in view. A traveler should have his right road and the end of his journey always in his eye, whatever little diversions or excursions he may indulge by the way.

To an acquaintance with books, join the study of human nature. Your own heart, passions, temper, humor, habits, and dispositions will be the books you have most need to consult on this subject. For human nature, in the main strokes of it, is much the same in all the human species. Next to this, your observations on the ways and characters and tempers of men will be of great help to you, together with some books where human nature is strongly and finely painted in its various shapes and appearances.

'Tis not beneath the Christian philosopher to take some pains to be acquainted with the world, or the humors, manners, forms, ceremonies, characters, and customs of men—at least so far as is necessary to avoid singularity and a disagreeable awkwardness, and to preserve a decorum and an easy address in all company.

A student should not think anything unworthy of his attention and notice that has a tendency to make him either more agreeable or more useful to others. Some regard is therefore due to dress, behavior, the usual form of civility, and whatever contributes to the art of pleasing. Among these I would particularly rec-

ommend a habit of expressing his sentiments freely
and properly upon any subject. Let his style and language be studied principally with this view.

As to the method of studying to advantage, pray for a
divine blessing on your studies, that God would guide
you into the most useful knowledge and all-important
truths; direct your subjects, and assist your meditations
upon them.

Procure a collection of the best and most approved
books which treat the sciences you chiefly desire to cultivate, and make yourself master of them in the way previously prescribed.

Consult your own genius and inclination in the
study you intend to pursue; you will otherwise row
against the tide, and make no progress that is either
comfortable or creditable to yourself.

Compose your spirits, fix your thoughts, and be
wholly intent on the subject at hand. Never pretend to
study while the mind is not recovered from a hurry of
cares or the perturbations of passion. Such abrupt and
violent transitions are a discipline to which it will not
easily submit, especially if it has not been well managed
and long accustomed to it.

Let the scene of your studies be a place of silence
and solitude, where you may be most free from inter-
ruption and avocation.

When you have a mind to improve a single thought,
or to be clear in any particular point, don't leave it till
you are master of it. View it in every light. Try how many
ways you can express it, and which is the shortest and
best. Would you enlarge upon it? Hunt it down from author to author, some of whom will suggest hints concerning it which perhaps never occurred to you before;

give every circumstance its weight. Thus, by being master of every subject, as you proceed, though you make but a small progress in reading, you will make a speedy one in useful knowledge. To leave matters undetermined, and the mind unsatisfied in what we study, is but to multiply half-notions, and introduce confusion, and is the way to make a pedant, but not a scholar.

Go to the fountainhead. Read original authors rather than those who translate or retell their thoughts. It will give you more satisfaction, more certainty, more judgment and more confidence when those authors are the subjects of conversation than you can have by taking your knowledge of them second-hand. It is trusting translations, quotations, and epitomes that makes so many half-scholars so impertinently wise.

Finally, be patient of labor. The more you accustom yourself to laborious thinking, the better you will bear it. But take care that the mind is not jaded.

If divinity is your particular study, observe the following rules:

RULE 1. Be critically expert in the original Scriptures of the Bible, and read a chapter in Hebrew and another in Greek every day. Especially observe the different senses in which the same original word is used by the same author; this often throws a great light on his meaning.

RULE 2. When you have found what you take to be your author's own sense, keep to that, and admit no vague, uncertain, or conjectural constructions, whatever doctrine they may discountenance or favor.

RULE 3. Be sure to make the sacred Scripture the source, standard, and rule of all your theological sentiments. Take them from it, bring them to it, and try them by it.

RULE 4. Make yourself master of some short, well-chosen system of divinity, for the sake of method and memory; but take care that you are not swayed by the credit of any human names in matters of divine faith. Let reason, evidence, and argument be the only authorities to which you submit. Remember, 'tis truth you seek; and seek her (as you would do anything else) in the place where she is most likely to be found.

RULE 5. Divest yourself as much as possible of all prepossessions in favor of, or prejudice against, any particular party names and notions. Let the mind be equally balanced, or it will never rightly determine the weight of arguments. Prejudice in one scale will outweigh much solid truth in the other; and under such a prepossession, the mind only observes which balance preponderates, not what it is that turns it.

RULE 6. Cultivate a proper sense of the imbecility of the human mind and its proneness to error, both in yourself and in others. This will guard you against a dogmatic confidence in defense of your own opinions, and will arm you against the influence of it in others. And, on the contrary, endeavor after a meek, humble, teachable temper which, from the highest authority we are sure, is the best disposition of the mind to seek and receive divine truth.

RULE 7. Do not be fond of controversy. Theological altercations have in all ages been the bane of real religion, and the fatal source of unknown mischief to true Christianity. They sour the temper, confound the judgment, excite malevolence, foment feuds, and banish love from the heart. Theological battles are the devil's most successful engine to depreciate and destroy the principles of vital piety. Let the controversies you read be the most important, such as those against the deist and papists. And read only the best authors among them. You will find none to exceed the late bishop of London and Dr. [John] Leland against the deists, and Dr. [John] Tillotson and [William] Chillingworth against the papists.

RULE 8. Avoid theological minuteness. Lay no stress on trifles, as you see many do, from either a wrong education or a weak turn of mind. Reserve your zeal for the most important subjects, and throw it not away upon little things.

RULE 9. Let none but the best writers in divinity be your favorites. And those are the best writers who display together a clear head and a good heart, solid sense and serious piety—where faith and reason, devotion and judgment, go hand in hand.

The Method of Collecting and Preserving Useful Thoughts from Conversation

Whenever it can be done without affectation and pedantry, turn the conversation onto the subject you have been reading last, if you know it to be suitable to your company, and introduce your most mature observations upon it. This will fix it in your memory, especially if it becomes matter of debate. For the mind is never more tenacious of any principles than those it has been warmly engaged in the defense of. And in the course of such debate, you may perhaps view them in a new light, be able to form a better judgment of them, and be excited to examine them with more care. Intercourse awakens the powers, whets the mind, and

rubs off the rust it is apt to contract by solitary thinking. The pump, for want of use, grows dry, or keeps its
water at bottom, which will not be fetched up unless
more is added.

When you have talked over the subject you have
read, think over what you have talked of; and perhaps
you will be able to see more weight in the sentiments
you opposed than you were willing to admit in the
presence of your antagonist. And if you suspect you
were then in an error, you may now retract it without
fear of mortification. That you may at once improve
and please in conversation, remember the following
rules:

RULE 1. Choose your company as you do your
books, and to the same end. The best company, like the
best books, is that which is at once improving and entertaining. If you can receive neither pleasure nor
profit from your company, endeavor to furnish it for
them. If this can't be done (and especially if there is
danger of receiving hurt from them), quit them as decently as you can.

RULE 2. Study the humor and character of your
company. If they are your superiors, or most inclined to
talk, be an attentive hearer. If they are your inferiors, or
more disposed to hear, be an instructive speaker.

RULE 3. When the conversation drops, revive it with
some general topic by starting a subject on which you
have some good things to say, or you know others have.
To this end it will not be amiss to be a little prepared
with topics of conversation suitable to the company you
are going into; and the course of your own thoughts in
conversation will be more free than you ordinarily find
them to be in silent meditation.

RULE 4. When anything occurs that is new or instructive, or that you are willing to make your own, enter it down into your minute or commonplace book if you cannot trust your memory (for in conversation all are free-loaders; whatever you lay your hand on that is worth keeping is lawful prize). But take care that you do not fill either the one or the other with trash.

RULE 5. Never stand for a cipher in company by a total silence. It will appear boorish and awkward, and give a check to the freedom of others. 'Tis ill manners. Better to say a trivial thing than nothing at all. Perhaps you hear a good deal of impertinence uttered by some in the company which you candidly excused; presume upon their candor if you happen to talk in the same manner. You have a right to claim it. You will readily receive it. Something trite and low, uttered with an easy, free, obliging air, will be better received than entire silence, and indeed better than a good sentiment delivered in a stiff, pedantic, or assuming manner. And many good things may arise out of a common observation. However, after a dead silence, it will set the conversation a-going, and the company who want to be relieved from it will be obliged to you. This is a secret that will never fail to please.

RULE 6. Do not join in the hurry and clamor of the talk, especially when a trifling point is disputed and several speak at once; but be a patient hearer till you have made yourself master of the subject and the argument on both sides. And then you may possibly find an opportunity to put in as mediator, with credit to your judgment. Do not repeat a good thing in the same company twice, unless you are sure you were not distinctly heard the first time.

RULE 7. Though you may safely animadvert upon, yet do not oppose, much less rally, the foibles or mistakes of anyone in the company; unless they are very notorious, and there is no danger of giving offense. But remember that he himself sees the matter in a different light from how you do, and with other eyes.

RULE 8. If detraction or profaneness should mingle with the conversation, discountenance it by a severe or a resolute silence, where reproof would be thought indelicate. If this be not sufficient to put a stop to it, make no scruple to withdraw.

RULE 9. Do not attempt to shine in conversation, especially before those who have a good opinion of their own understanding. The surest way to please them is to give them opportunity to show their parts; a monopoly of this kind will scarce ever be endured with patience.

RULE 10. Bear with the impertinence of conversation; something may be learned from the speakers, or some opportunity may be given you to put in a sentiment more appropriate. Besides, what appears low and flat to you may not to another.

RULE 11. Appear perfectly free, friendly, well-pleased, easy, and unreserved. This will make others so, and will draw out many a good thought from them. And this is much more pleasing than a studied politeness and all the usual arts of commonplace civility.

Improving Our Thoughts When Alone

A student (like a philosopher) should never be less alone than when alone. Then it is that (if it is not his own fault) he may enjoy the best of company.

Next to the regulation of the appetites and passions,

the most important branch of self-government is the command of our thoughts, which, without a strict guard, will be as apt to ramble as the other are to rebel. The great difficulty will be to keep them fixed and steadily employed upon your subject. To this end, let the mind be calm and dispassionate; view your theme in every light; collect your best thoughts upon it; clothe those thoughts in words, and consider how any writer you admire would express the same. Guard against vagrancy or dissipation of your thoughts; recall them when they are rambling, observe by what connection of ideas or images they are enticed away from their work, and refix them more diligently. If you have a pen and ink at hand, set down your best sentiments on paper. If your subject is of a religious nature, it may not be amiss to recollect some proper text of Scripture as a standard to which you may recall your vagrant forces.

Let the matter of your meditations be something seasonable, important, or entertaining. Consult the temper your mind is in, or ought to be in at that time, and let your subject be suitable to it.

Take care that nothing vain or vicious steals into your mind when alone. Hereby you may make yourself a very bad companion to yourself, and become your own tempter.

If the place or occasion will admit it, think *viva voce*, or utter your thoughts aloud.

In your evening meditations, go over in your mind the best things you have read or heard that day, and recollect them the next evening.

The great advantage of being alone is that you may choose your company—either your books, your friend, your God, or yourself. There is another who will be ready to intrude if not resolutely repelled. By the turn of your thoughts you may detect his entrance, and by what passage he stole in. You may know him by his cloven foot. And you have the best precept, exemplified by the best precedent, how to eject him.

If books are your subject, or what you lately read and laid up in your memory, your mental employment will be recollection and judgment. Recall to your mind the good things you have read, and use judgment to range them under their proper class. And consider upon what occasion or in what company it may be proper or useful to produce them.

If you choose a friend for the companion of your solitude, let it not be merely for your own pleasure, but consider in what manner you may improve or entertain him, or what it is that you would learn from him, and in what manner you may best behave towards him the next time you come into his company.

When you desire to have the great God for the object of your contemplation (as you should always do in your religious retirements), your mind cannot be too serious, composed, and free. Now it is that the thoughts will be most apt to revolt and ramble, and the utmost efforts must be used to guard and guide them. Two things in this case you should never forget: first, earnestly implore His help, so that you may think not only steadily, but worthily of Him; second, consider Him as present with you, and as witness to all the employment of your mind.

Last, if you are your own companion and self-meditation is your business, you have a large field before you. But be sure not to neglect to sharply and impartially reprove yourself in case of any observable failure;

and resolve to amend your conduct in that particular, especially when the same circumstances recur.

Part 2: The Pastor

The business of a pastor is to do all he can to promote the eternal interest of the souls of men. And to keep his eye continually on this, the great object of the sacred office, will be a good direction to him in the prosecution of it.

He is now to improve, regulate, digest, and apply that stock of knowledge he has taken so much pains to acquire, and examine what part of it will be most helpful to him in his great design.

The duties of the pastor's office may be comprised under the six following general headings:

Preaching

Praying

Administering the sacraments

Visiting the sick

His conduct towards his people in general, and his conduct towards persons of different characters in particular.

Preaching may be divided into two parts: preparation and elocution. Preparation consists of composition and the duties immediately previous to preaching.

Composing Sermons

Besides all the usual academic preparations, the study of languages, sciences, divinity, and so on, there is a particular art of preaching to which, if ministers did more seriously apply themselves, it would extremely facilitate that service, and make it more easy for themselves and more profitable for their hearers. For acquiring this art the rules laid down in this and the three following sections may be helpful to those who are entering upon the sacred employment.

1. The first thing to be considered is the choice of the subject. Here you must consult your own genius, taste, and abilities. Choose those subjects which have most impressed your own mind, for on those you are most likely to succeed, and to produce the most mature and useful sentiments. Consult also the temper, taste, and capacities of your audience. For the more suitable your subject, style, and sentiments are to them, the more likely you will be both to please and to improve them. And therefore a minister should never settle, nor choose to preach, among a people whose opinions are widely different from his own.

Let the most useful and pertinent subjects be your most frequent choice. Those are the most useful which are the most edifying, and those are the most pertinent that are most fitted to the capacities and necessities of the audience, to both of which you ought to have a special regard. If you are at a loss for a text, consult the contents of the several volumes of sermons you have by you. That a man may equip himself for preaching, he ought to take some of the best models, and try what he can do on a text handled by them without reading them, and then compare his with theirs. This will sensibly, and without putting him to the blush, lead him to imitate or (if he can) to excel the best authors. Whatever particular text strikes your mind with more than common force, in the course of your reading or meditating on the Scriptures, pen it down with some useful strictures that may occur to you for the foundation of a future work. By this means you will have a good supply of suitable texts at hand.

A sermon should be made for a text, and not a text found out for a sermon, for to give our discourses weight it should appear that we are led to them by our text. Such sermons will probably have much more effect than a general discourse, to which a text seems only to be added as a decent introduction, but to which no regard is had in the progress of it. Do not attempt an obscure, difficult, or barren text to show your ingenuity in throwing light upon it, or to set others wondering what you can make of it. Discourses from such texts must be either unprofitable or unnatural.

2. Having chosen your subject, your next care is to be furnished with a store of useful and pertinent thoughts upon it. Having fixed the spot on which to build, you are now to prepare materials. To this purpose, carefully peruse your text in both the original and different translations. Attend to its connections and reference, and observe what is the principal subject it points to. Collect from your concordance or commonplace book to the Bible, or from Mr. Clarke's *Annotations*, or from Wilson's *Christian Dictionary* and others, all its parallel places, or the several scriptures that have a reference to it. Pen them down on loose paper, to be properly interwoven into the discourse under any particular heading or branch of it. Consult other authors on the same subject. Use their thoughts, but not their words, unless you quote them expressly— which should never be done unless your author is a writer of eminence and of good repute with your audience. And let it be a sentiment so weighty and well-expressed as deserves to be remembered by them; and

then they will remember it the sooner as coming from him than from yourself.

3. Having thus provided materials, form your plan. Let your method as well as your subject flow from your text. Let the division be easy and natural, and such as the audience would expect. Let it arise from the subject itself, and give a light and just order to the several parts. The division should be such as may be easily remembered, and at the same time may help to connect and retain the whole, a division that shows at once the extent of the subject, and of all its parts.

Avoid a tedious multiplication of particulars under every general heading of your discourse. Let your particular headings be not only few, but distinct; do not try to conceal the number and order of them if they are distinct and natural, as some modern preachers do. 'Tis a false delicacy to aim at reducing a sermon to the form of a polite harangue. The other method, expressing the number of the headings in their proper order, is not only more pleasing to the common sort of hearers, but a help to their understanding and their memory, which a preacher should by all means carefully regard. It will be proper to draw your method or plan on a loose piece of paper laid before you, with the several particulars under their respective general headings; and whatever passage of Scripture or inferences you meet with in reading or meditating, pertinent to any particular point you shall speak to, you may then place them under that particular. For all things may not come to your mind at once, and a thought is so quickly gone (let your memory be never so tenacious and retentive) that you will hardly retain it unless it is in this manner committed to paper. And whatever passage of

Scripture you make use of which you do not well understand, consult the ablest commentators on that passage
for the meaning of it, so that you may not apply it to a
wrong sense.

4. Having thus provided materials and formed your
plan, begin the superstructure, which will now be
raised and adorned with great ease, and will be continually improving upon your hands. For no man can talk
well on a subject of which he is not entirely master.

In the beginning you must endeavor to gain the favor of the audience by a modest introduction, a respectful address, and the genuine marks of candor and pro-
bity. Let your introduction be short, modest, grave, and
striking, either by proposing your method, and entering upon your subject directly, or by a few important
general observations that are connected with or naturally lead to it, or by some short, unexpected remark on
the words of the text.

In your enlargement on particulars, if you find that
your thoughts don't run freely on any point, do not
urge them too much. This will tire and jade the faculties too soon. But pursue your plan. Better thoughts
may occur afterwards which you may occasionally in-
sert.

Let your best sentiments stand in the beginning or
end of a paragraph, and the rest in the middle, which
will pass very well in good company. And let every heading conclude with some striking sentence or pertinent
Scripture.

As every complete sermon resembles a little book,
the method of composing the former may be the same
as what Ringelbergius tells us he used in composing
the latter:

> My first care is to form in my mind a perfect plan
> of the work before me. Then on a large tablet, or a
> sheet of paper, I set down the titles of the chapters,
> or the several headings I am to discourse on. Then
> I look over them to see if they have their proper
> place, connection, and coherence. And I alter
> them as I see occasion. Then, whilst my mind is
> still warm with the subject, I take a brief sketch of
> what is proper to be said under each heading,
> which I write down on a loose piece of paper;
> these I afterwards transfer into my plan, and in a
> fair hand transcribe under their proper heaings. By
> this means, I have the whole subject and method of
> the work under my eye at once. Then I every day
> transcribe a chapter for the press, and add or ex-
> punge as I go along, according as the matter re-
> quires. After this, when I see nothing deficient or
> redundant in the subject, I apply myself to revise
> the language.

Let your application be close, fervent, and animated. To this end get your own heart warmed and penetrated with your subject. For however drowsy or inattentive your hearers may be in the beginning or middle of a discourse, they should be always awakened and warmed at the close. 'Tis oftentimes proper, at the end of a discourse, to make short recapitulation, wherein the orator ought to exert all his force and skill in giving the audience a full, clear, concise view of the chief topics he has enlarged upon. And let the last sentence of the sermon be either your text, some pertinent Scripture, or some weighty thought well expressed and worth remembering.

5. Having thus raised your superstructure on the plan proposed, you must put the finishing hand to the work by decently adorning it. This is the business of re-

vision, wherein you are to reexamine the method, matter, and style.

The method. Here perhaps you may see some small alterations necessary. This heading may come in more naturally before that one; such a sentiment will shine to more advantage at the conclusion of a paragraph; and this particular heading is not sufficiently distinct from that one, and therefore both had better be wrought into one.

The matter. Such a sentiment is expressed before, therefore strike it out here; too much is said upon this part of the subject, too little upon that; add here, retrench there. If any new thought or pertinent Scripture occurs to your mind, search out the proper place where to dispose of it.

The style. This thought is obscurely expressed, explain it; this sentence is equivocal, be more determinate; this is too long, shorten it; here is a jingle, correct it; this disposition of the words is harsh and hard to pronounce, alter it; this expression is too mean and vulgar, substitute a better one.

I shall conclude this section with the following general rules relating to the style of the pulpit.

First, let it be plain, proper, and perspicuous—and then the shorter the better. A concise, full, and succinct style is always most striking, therefore most pleasing. To obscure and weaken the sense by a studied ornament or flow of words is wrong oratory, and nauseous to everyone of true taste.

The words in a sermon must be simple and in common use, not savoring of the schools, or above the understanding of the people. All long sentences, such as carry two or three different thoughts in them, must

The Christian Pastor's Manual

be avoided; for few hearers can follow or apprehend these. Niceties of style are lost before a common audience.

Second, let your rhythm be full and flowing, and carefully avoid all harshness from dissonance in the choice and disposition of your words. This is a part of rhetoric which, though carefully cultivated by the ancients, is too much neglected by the moderns. In reading over a discourse to ourselves, we must observe what words sound harsh, and agree ill together; for there is a music in speaking as well as in singing, which a man, though not otherwise critical in sounds, will soon discover.

Third, observe a medium between a too short and too prolix style. The pithy style is apt to be defective; a prolix one (if the members of a long sentence are not judiciously disposed, and fraught with a weight of sentiment) is tedious and disagreeable; and a low, creeping style is as unbecoming the dignity of the pulpit as a high and pompous one. There is a decency to be observed in our language as well as our dress. With regard to both, a prudent man will consider not only what is decent in itself, but what is most so at certain times.

Fourth, an illustration of your subject by sensible images and apt smiles will always be agreeable.

Fifth, and last, let the conclusion of your sentences be harmonious, and your concluding thoughts the most memorable.

> Expression is the dress of thought, and still
> Appears more decent, as more suitable.
> A low conceit in pompous words express'd;
> Is like a clown, in royal purple dress'd;
> For different styles with different subjects sort,

As several garbs, with country, town and court.
Some by old words to fame have made pretence,
Ancients in phrase, mere moderns in their sense:
Such labour'd nothings in so strange a style,
Amaze th' unlearned, make the learned smile.

—Pope's *Essays on Criticism*

General Rules Related to Preaching

RULE 1. It would be advisable for young preachers to write down every sentence of their sermons in shorthand, and trust nothing to their memories till they are masters of a free, fluent, and proper style, and have acquired a good command of their spirits, a free utterance, and a maturity of sentiments. Then they may venture to leave something to the memory by writing half-sentences, till by degrees they are able to trust to it a good part of the enlargement under every heading. This will be no great burden, provided they take care to be thoroughly masters of their notes before they go up into the pulpit, and will be a great help to a free, decent, and natural elocution.

I would not advise any young minister, though ever so happy in a strength of memory, entirely to lay aside his notes, as it can answer no valuable end, and the inconveniences of it are several. The thoughts may possibly wander; in that case you are bewildered without a guide. This reflection will create a confusion and perplexity in the mind which the hearers will observe with pain, and you will scarcely ever be able to recover the right track in that hurry of spirits without many a trip and much trouble. This will throw a tremor, or at least a diffidence, on the mind which will make it difficult to resume your wonted courage. Besides, when so much attention is bestowed on the memory, you will be apt to pay too little to the judgment and affections. You will not have leisure to observe how much your own heart is affected, or how you may best affect those of your hearers, who are never more pleased than when they see their preacher composed, free, and deeply impressed with his own subject, and never more disgusted than when they observe him to be confused, bewildered, or inattentive to what he himself delivers. Besides, the inaccuracy of diction and the inelegance, poverty, and lowness of expression which are commonly observed in extemporaneous discourses will not fail to offend every hearer of good taste.

RULE 2. Go to the bottom of your subject. Think of everything that ought to be said upon it. Consider what points, or parts of it, your hearers would be glad to have cleared up or most enlarged upon. To skim off only the surface is to put off your audience with froth. The weightiest sentiments often lie at the bottom; take pains, then, to dive deep and bring them up from thence.

RULE 3. On the other hand, take care that you do not torture your subject by aiming to exhaust it. Don't endeavor to say everything that could be said, but everything that ought to be said upon the subject. A preacher's excellence is seen not so much in saying a great deal upon a text as in saying the best things in the best manner.

RULE 4. Don't crowd your thoughts too thick. This will but fatigue and perplex the minds of your hearers, who should always have time to follow you. If you pour water too fast into the funnel, it will run over.

RULE 5. Do not protract your discourse to an undue length. The best sentiments will not be attended to

while your hearers are impatiently waiting and wishing
for the conclusion. It would be better to offend by the
other extreme, provided your matter is solid, well-
disposed, and well-digested. Better to leave your audience longing than loathing. Abstinence is less hurtful
than repletion. I think Luther says in his *Table Talk* that
one necessary qualification of a preacher is to know
when to leave off.

RULE 6. In practical preaching (which should be
your ordinary strain), remember that you preach to
Christians, and let your chief motives to practice be
drawn from Christian principles. It is verily a fault in
too many of the public teachers of our times that their
sermons are moral harangues generally, and Tully's
Offices and Seneca's *Epistles* serve them instead of the
Bible. They are furnished with nothing but moral precepts, as if they were preaching at old Rome or Athens
and their audiences were all infidels.

RULE 7. Be sure to consult the capacity and understanding of your hearers. Remember that you are not
declaiming in the academy, but preaching to an illiterate congregation. Take care, then, that you are not too
learned or too logical; that you do not shoot over the
heads of your hearers in either your doctrine or your
language. Condescend to their capacities, and let it be
your ambition and care while you are treating the
highest subjects to be comprehended by the lowest understanding—wherein Archbishop Tillotson, Archbishop Sharp, and Dr. Sherlock will be your best patterns. 'Tis not easy to conceive how much ignorance of
divine things there is in the minds of the greatest part
of those you preach to.

It was the observation of a late celebrated divine in

the church of Rome that there are always three-quarters of an ordinary congregation who do not know those principles of religion in which the preacher supposes everyone to be fully instructed. It is to be hoped that matters are somewhat mended in our Protestant assemblies; but still there is reason to fear that they who compose the major part in our places of worship are deplorably defective in their knowledge of the true doctrines of Christianity. And as the subject should not be too deep for their conceptions, so neither should the style be too high for their comprehension. Therefore, all scholastic terms, systematic phrases, and metaphysical definitions should be forever banished from the pulpit.

RULE 8. Do not attempt to show your skills by entering upon nice and curious disquisitions, or by a strong portrait of general characters. This is shooting beside the mark, or at least will but very seldom reach it. The chief end it will produce (and which you will be thought to aim at) is your own applause, and not your people's profit. "Too close a thread of reason, too great an abstraction of thought, too sublime and too metaphysical a strain, are suitable to very few audiences, if to any at all," said Gilbert Burnet.

'Tis here that our preachers are defective. Most of their fine sermons contain only philosophical reasonings; sometimes they preposterously quote Scripture only for the sake of decency and ornament. Their sermons are trains of fine reasoning about religion, but they are not religion itself. We apply ourselves too much to the drawing of moral characters and inveighing against the general disorders of mankind, but we don't sufficiently explain the precepts and principles of the gospel.

Cambray wrote, "I love a serious preacher, who speaks for my sake and not for his own, who seeks my salvation and not his own vain-glory. He best deserves to be heard who uses speech only to clothe his thoughts, and his thoughts only to promote truth and virtue. Nothing is more despicable than a professed declaimer who retails his discourses, as a quack does his medicine."

RULE 9. Endeavor to affect your own mind with what you deliver, and then you will not fail to affect the minds of your hearers. There must be a life and power in your delivery to keep up the attention and fix the affection of them who hear you, "for artificial eloquence without a flame within is like artificial poetry; all its productions are forced and unnatural, and in a great measure ridiculous," wrote Burnet. 'Tis said of John the Baptist that he was a burning and shining light. 'Tis a hard matter to affect others with what we are not first affected by ourselves.

RULE 10. When you are called to touch upon controversy (which you should avoid as much as possible in the pulpit), be candid, clear, short, and convicting. Be sure that your arguments are solid, close, and strong, and your answers at least as clear as the objections. For if these are plain and those perplexed, you will but confirm the error you mean to confute. Avoid all needless censures, especially of persons by name. When a censorious spirit is kindled by the preacher, nothing will sooner be caught by the hearers, and that unhallowed flame will quickly be propagated far and wide. Dark debates in divinity are like rocks, not only steep and craggy, but barren and fruitless, and not worth the

pains of climbing to the top. Whatever influence they
have on the spirits of men is commonly a bad one. 'Tis
scarce to be imagined what harm these theological
subtleties do us. As spirits extracted from bodies are always hot, heady, and inflammatory, so divine truths,
made too subtle and too sublimated, heat, intoxicate,
and discompose the minds of men, fire their tempers,
and kindle very hurtful and unruly passions to the dis-
turbance of their own peace and that of others.

RULE 11. Let your great aim in every sermon be to
please God and profit your people, to do them good
rather than gain their applause. Don't covet a reputation for eloquence; it will turn you off from higher
views. Besides, an excessive desire for popularity and
fame will subject you to many secret vexations. As well
may you expect the sea to be undisturbed as the mind of
an ambitious man to be long free from disquietude.

RULE 12. Last, endeavor to get the great principles
of Christianity wrought into your own heart, and let
them shine in your temper and conversation. Ministers
have one great advantage beyond all the rest of the
world in that, whereas the particular callings of other
men prove to them to be great distractions, and lay
many temptations in their way to divert them from
minding their high and holy calling of being
Christians, it is quite otherwise with the clergy. The
more ministers follow their proper callings, the more
certainly they advance their general one; the better
priests they are, they become also the better Christians.
Every part of their calling, when well performed, raises
good thoughts and brings good ideas into their minds,
and tends both to increase their knowledge and to
quicken their sense of divine matters. Cicero,

Quintilian, and Horace all made virtue a necessary qualification in a complete orator. I am sure it is so in a Christian preacher. It is required of a presbyter that he be blameless (Titus 1:6).

When a preacher has the great doctrines that he teaches wrought into his temper, and he feels the influence of them on his own spirit, he will reap from thence these three great advantages in his public ministrations: he will then speak from his own experience; he will, with greater confidence and assurance, direct and counsel others; and he will more readily gain belief of what he says. Without this experimental sense of religion in the heart, and a steady practice of it in the life, all the learning in the world will not make a person either a wise man, a good Christian, or a faithful minister. And to induce him to a wise circumspection in his conduct, he should often consider the influence his own example will have upon his people, for whom he must live as well as for himself, and who will think themselves very justified if they indulge in no other liberties than such as they see their minister takes himself.

Before I close this section, let me add one thing more. A minister, with regard to both his conduct and preaching, should take care not to be too affected with common fame. Though he is not to be absolutely indifferent to the applause and censures of others, yet he should arm himself against the bad influence of both. He must expect to pass through good report and evil report—and both are apt to make hurtful impressions on weak, unstable minds.

As for an evil report, a Stoic will tell you that, when confident of your innocence, you ought absolutely to despise both it and its author. I think Chrysostom's advice is more suited to the character of a Christian minister: "As for groundless and unreasonable accusations (for such a Christian bishop must expect to meet with), it is not right either excessively to fear them or to absolutely despise them. He should rather endeavor to stifle them, though they be ever so false, and the author of them ever so despicable; for a good or a bad report is greatly increased by passing through the hands of the multitude who are not accustomed to examine, but to blab out everything they hear, whether true or false. Therefore we are not to despise them, but to nip those evil surmises in the bud, speak friendly to those who raise them (be their characters ever so bad), and omit nothing that may remove their wrong impressions of us. And if after all they persist in defaming us, we may then despise them."

Duties Immediately Preceding the Work of the Pulpit

To prepare you for this service the following directions may be useful:

1. Before you enter on the public worship of God in His house, be sure to apply yourself to the throne of grace for a divine blessing on your labors. It was a usual saying of Luther, "Good sermons come from good studies." And in these preceding devotions, see that your heart is very sincere and fervent. You must pray for yourself, and pray for your people.

You must pray for yourself, that God would help you to bring your own spirit into a frame suitable to the work you are about to undertake; that the word you deliver may affect your own heart, or that you may first feel the holy flame you would communicate to others; that a door of utterance may be opened to you, and that you may speak as becomes the oracles of God; that He would direct you to speak to the consciences and particular cases of your hearers, or that what you deliver may be a word in season; and that He would especially assist you in prayer, and give you the spirit of grace and supplication.

You are to pray that your people's attention may be engaged to both the evidence and the importance of the things they are to hear; that God would open their hearts to give them a fair and candid reception, and that no bad prejudice may prevent the good effect of the Word; that the grace of God may cooperate with His appointed means to set home divine truths with power on their consciences; that they may be able to retain the good seed that is sown; that it may bring forth its proper fruit in their future lives; and finally that their prayers for you and behavior towards you may strengthen your hands and make you more serviceable to their souls.

2. Let your mind and countenance be very composed and serious, and your gestures grave and decent. To this end, endeavor to bring your spirit into a religious and devout frame before you come into the house of God. Attend to the real importance of the work you are called to, both when you are the mouth of God to the people and when you are the mouth of the people to God. Avoid those objects and avert those thoughts that tend to discompose your mind, or indispose it for the sacred service you are going to engage in. Clear your heart of all vain and worldly cares, and especially of all vexatious and disturbing thoughts, before you enter into the public service of God. Endeavor to attain a

spiritual, holy, and heavenly frame of mind by preparatory prayer, reading, and devout meditation. It will render your sacred work both more agreeable and easy to
yourself and more beneficial to your hearers, if you endeavor to carry into the house of God that serious temper of mind which you desire they should carry out of
it.

3. Before you enter on your work, take time to premeditate and recollect some of the most weighty, pertinent, and important sentiments and expressions you
may have occasion for, in either prayer or preaching.
This will be especially necessary if you entrust anything
to your memory, that you may not be at a loss for those
sentiments when they are to be produced in their
proper place. The mind should be well seasoned with
the discourse before it is delivered. 'Tis not enough to
be master of your notes, but you must enter into the
spirit of your subject. Call in everything that is proper
to improve it, and to raise and animate your mind in
the contemplation of it.

4. Affect your mind with the consideration of the
solemnity and importance of the business you are going about, and how much may depend on a faithful execution of it. Few men ever had more natural courage
than Luther, and yet he was often heard to say that even
to the latest part of his life he never could conquer his
fear when he mounted the pulpit. And St. Chrysostom
used to say that that Scripture in Hebrews 13:17, "They
watch for your souls, as those that must give an account," struck his mind with constant awe.

5. Last, keep up a self-command and a becoming
presence of mind, and get above a low, servile fear of
men. If you are master of your subject, come well-

furnished with suitable materials for their religious improvement, and produce plain Scripture and reason for what you advance, you have no cause to fear either the critic or the censor; but you may with modesty conclude that you are at least as good a judge of the subject you have taken so much pains to understand and digest, as they are, who never gave it so precise or extensive a consideration.

Pulpit Elocution

By this phrase I mean the language, pronunciation, and action that are most becoming the pulpit. The language must be plain, proper, pure, concise and vigorous.

Let your language be plain or perspicuous. 'Tis a nauseous affectation to be fond of hard words, or to introduce terms of art and learning into a discourse addressed to a mixed assembly of plain, illiterate Christians. The silliness of it will appear by supposing that you were to talk to them in that manner in common conversation. Those who don't understand you will dislike you, and they who do will see the affectation and despise you.

Let your words be well chosen, proper, and expressive—not only such as your hearers understand, but such as are most fit to convey the sentiments you mean.

Aim at purity of language. To this end, diversify your style, as far as it is consistent with perspicuity and propriety. Avoid the frequent and near repetition of the same word, unless it is very emphatic, and the reiteration rhetorical. Shun all harsh and jingling sounds. Have an eye to an easy cadence at the close of your sentences, and conclude as often as you can with an emphatic word. Avoid dubious and equivocal expressions, or such as leave the sense indeterminate. Avoid all low, vulgar, and barbarous words. Let your phrases be like your dress: decent, unaffected, and free from gaudy and studied ornaments. Finally, let all your art be to imitate nature.

A concise style very well becomes the pulpit, because long sections do not convey the sense with either so much ease or so much force, especially to uncultivated minds. But do not attempt to speak in proverbs. A short, sententious style, if it is expressive, full, and clear, will be always strong and universally agreeable.

Aim at a striking, vigorous style rather than a diffusive, flowing one. Let the most emphatic words convey the sublimest thoughts; and if there is a glow in the sentiment, it will seldom fail to shine in the expression.

Regarding the pronunciation:

Let it be quite free, natural, and easy. The whole art of good oratory consists in observing what nature does when unconstrained. You should address yourself to an audience in such a modest, respectful, and engaging manner that each of them thinks you are speaking to him in particular. Every sort of affected tone is to be carefully avoided. Suppose your whole audience to be but one person, and that you were speaking to them in your own parlor. Let the nature of your subject direct the modulation of your voice. Be cool in the rational portions, easy in the familiar ones, earnest in the persuasive parts, and warm in the emotional parts of your discourse. Every passion requires a pronunciation proper to itself.

Let the voice be always distinct and deliberate, and give every word its full sound. Attend to your own voice. If it is not strong, full, and clear to yourself, you may be sure it is not so to many of the audience. And to help your voice, address yourself chiefly to the remotest part of the assembly, and then they who are nearer will hear plainly enough. Let your pronunciation be very deliberate. You will be in little danger of speaking too slowly, provided that your voice, your action, and the weight of the sentiment keep up your hearers' attention.

Do not attempt to move the passions by a loud, clamorous voice. This is not powerful preaching, and argues no excellence in the preacher but the strength of his lungs. It is unseemly in a Christian minister to imitate the priests of Delphos, who delivered their oracles with rage and foaming. This noisy, blustering manner shocks a delicate hearer and degrades the dignity of the pulpit. To be a Boanerges it is not necessary to become a Stentor.

However, let your voice be always lively and awakening, though at some times it should be more animated than at others.

Now and then a sudden change from a higher to a lower key (when something remarkable occurs) will wonderfully catch the attention. This is what Quintilian calls "varying airs," which, when well-timed, are not only graceful in themselves, but pleasing to the ear, and give no small relief to the preacher.

Repeat sometimes the most remarkable sentences with a free, decent, easy manner.

Make a pause after some important thought. These pauses (especially near the close of a discourse) will have a very good effect, as they not only render the service more solemn, but give both yourself and your hearers time to compose and recollect; they will mightily awaken the hearers' attention to what follows, which should therefore be always something worthy of it. There are some occasions where an orator might best express his thoughts by silence; for if, being full of some great sentiment, he continues immovable for a moment, this surprising pause will keep the minds of the audience in suspense, and express an emotion too big for words to utter. In a word (as Quintilian observes), the great art of elocution is no more than a proper and natural modulation and variation of the voice, according to the nature of the subject.

As for the action, it must always be adapted to the pronunciation, as the pronunciation to the passions. There are two extremes to be avoided: too much and too little action.

Do not let your action be too much. We have some at home who outdo the French and invent new ways of displaying an apish and uncouth deportment. One is ready every moment to throw himself out of the pulpit, and the people who sit below him are in continual fear that he will really do so. Another reckons up all the headings and particulars on the tips of his fingers, which he exposes to the gazing people. Others, by odd and fantastic gestures of the like nature, delight to give the hearers diversion, and make good the primitive use of the word "pulpit," which was the higher part of the stage where the players and comedians acted. But the serious preacher abhors all displays of this kind, and never attempts to be theatrical.

To be more particular, your action should not be

perpetual. The body, or any part of it, must not be in constant motion. As the preacher should not be like the trunk of a tree, always immovable, so neither like the boughs of it, in continual agitation. Nor must the movement of the body be uniform and unvaried. A steady vibrating swing of the body from the right to the left, like the pendulum of a clock, is very unnatural and faulty. As there is a monotony in the voice, so there is a uniformity in the gesture that is no less nauseous and unnatural, and equally contrary to the good effect that one might expect from decent action.

Again, your action should not be mimical. The hands should seldom stir unless when some passion is to be expressed or some weighty sentiment pointed out. Nor should it be too violent, as when it exceeds the force of the expression and the dignity of the senti-ment—a fault we often see in company among persons of a warm, impetuous temper.

Nor should it be theatrical, pompous, and affected. This becomes neither the dignity of the pulpit nor the solemnity of the work. The chief action should be, first, in the eyes, which should be commanding, quick, and piercing, not confined to your notes, but gently turn-ing to every part of your audience with a modest, grace-ful respect. Second, the head should always regularly turn with the eyes. Third, as for the hands, the right hand should have almost all the action; at least the left hand is never to be moved alone. Fourth, the upper part of the body should always correspond with the motion of the eyes, head, and hands; it should be for the most part erect. Avoid a lazy drooping on the cushion on which your elbows should rarely rest, and when they do rest (e.g., when you make a considerable pause), let it be with an easy, graceful attitude. In a word, let all your pulpit actions be natural, free, decent, and easy—which, by frequent practice and a careful observation of these rules, will be soon attained.

The other extreme to be avoided is too little action. To stand like a statue, stiff and motionless, when you are speaking to your people of the most momentous and affecting things, is as unnatural and as disagreeable as a set, uniform tone in pronunciation, and looks as if you were not in earnest yourself, and cared not whether your people were so. How singular would this appear if you were talking to a friend in private upon any particular affair that very much concerned him, and to which you desire to excite his most earnest attention! How will your hearers be able to keep from sleeping if they see you are scarcely awake yourself? Into this extreme the English preachers are most apt to fall, as the French into the former.

But after all, let it be remembered that the end of a decent, just, and lively pronunciation and action is only to excite and fix the attention of your hearers. Let your chief care be still directed to the propriety and importance of your sentiment, and to the dignity of your subject. For it will never fail to disgust your hearers if you rouse their attention by a solemnity of voice and action, and then put them off with something low, trite, or unaffecting.

Prayer

The next most considerable part of the pastoral office is prayer, which is commonly divided into the grace and gift of prayer.

The *grace*, or the spirit, of prayer signifies either,

first, praying with the heart and spirit, with the intent engagement of all the mental powers, understanding, will, and affections; second, praying with the exercise of those Christian graces that are proper to kindle a devout fervor of mind in that part of worship, such as humility, self-abasement, faith, love, delight, desire, trust in God, hope, and heavenly-mindedness; or, third, praying under the particular aid and influence of the Holy Spirit, who helps our infirmities and teaches us to pray. So the apostle says, "We know not what to pray for as we ought, but the Spirit helpeth our infirmities" (Romans 8:26), by composing our spirits, giving us a greater abstraction from the world and a greater elevation of heart, and calling into lively exercise the graces before mentioned. And this spiritual prayer may be entirely mental, without the use of words; and it is this spirituality that gives our prayers all their effect and power. Without this help from the Spirit, no prayer, though ever so properly composed or decently delivered, will be acceptable to God or available to ourselves; for this help, therefore, we should frequently and earnestly ask at the throne of divine grace. But it is the other kind of prayer which I am at present more particularly to consider.

The *gift* of prayer is an ability to perform this duty *extempore,* in a decent and devout manner, publicly. And to this purpose three things are required, which will take in the matter, method, and manner of prayer.

1. An enlargement of mind takes in the matter of prayer. Whatever we want, desire, or know we ought to desire should be the subject matter of our prayers. In order to attain an enlargement of mind in prayer, and a suitable supply of matter, we must be well acquainted

with the state of our souls, and must attend to our spiritual wants and weaknesses. The Christian's own heart is his best prayer book. The more we converse with it, the better we shall converse with God. It may not be amiss to commit to writing those defects and blemishes we chiefly observe in our characters, as well as the mercies we have received (especially any particular mercies we have received by prayer), either deliverance from evil, direction in difficulties, or the accomplishment of a desired end—each of which will be a proper subject of either petition, confession, or thanksgiving.

When you address yourself to the sacred work, see that the mind is free, composed, and serious. Its conceptions and apprehensions will then be more ready, and proper thoughts will more freely occur.

Possess your mind with an awful reverence of the divine majesty whom you address as the heart-searching God. Let your expression be very deliberate and solemn, so that the mind may have time not only to conceive, but to regulate and contemplate its conceptions. Daily study the Word of God with this view in particular, so that you may be better supplied with materials for devotion.

Endeavor after a comprehensive view of things. Let the mind take a wide scope, and let it freely run on those subjects that most affect it.

Let practical divinity, and a right disposition of heart towards God, be your principal care and study.

Take some time to premeditate and recollect the chief topics of prayer, and commit some few well-chosen expressions and sentences to memory.

Let the subject you have preached upon (and especially those you have found your mind most warmly affected with, and some of the most striking sentiments and expressions in them) be wrought into the composition of your future prayers, ranged under their proper headings. This, in time, will greatly enrich your magazine of materials for prayer, and will lead you to proper thoughts and words on the most important occasions.

2. We should not only aim at comprehension, but observe a method in prayer. The usual method begins with invocation, wherein we are to make a solemn mention of some of the divine attributes. Nor should this be always confined to the beginning of prayer. It may very properly be repeated by way of preface to some of the principal petitions we lift up to God, which, when pronounced with seriousness and reverence, will have a good effect to awaken the devotion of the heart. But always remember to invoke the Almighty under those attributes and perfections that are most suitable to the blessings you ask of Him. For example, when we pray for an accession of divine knowledge and wisdom, the address may be in this form: "O Thou Father and fountain of light, in whom there is no darkness at all, who givest to man the wisdom he asketh of Thee, we beseech Thee to disperse the darkness of our minds, shine into our hearts, and liberally bestow upon us that wisdom which Thou knowest we want."

The second part of prayer is the confession of sin. The transition to this part of prayer will be natural and easy, by taking particular notice of those moral perfections of the divine nature in which we ourselves are most defective. For example, we might pray regarding the righteousness and holiness of God as thus: "O holy, holy, holy, Lord God Almighty, who art of purer eyes than to behold iniquity; wherewith shall we, Thine unholy creatures, presume to appear before Thee, or lift up our eyes or thoughts to heaven, which our iniquities have reached before them!" In public prayer, let these confessions be general; in private, particular, as your consciousness of guilt may suggest.

The third aspect of prayer is petition. The connection here may be properly made by the mention of the divine mercies, the remembrance of Christ's mediatorship, and the promise of grace and pardon to penitent sinners. It most properly begins with petition for pardon, and then for a more perfect renovation, after which it proceeds to beg for other spiritual blessings, such as more light and knowledge, more love for God, more faith and hope, more strength against temptation and sin, more purity and heavenly-mindedness, more indifference to the world, and the like. Then it proceeds to temporal blessings.

The fourth part of prayer is particular intercessions. These it will be best to precompose, committing to memory the expressions and phrases that are most proper to be used on particular occasions. But let the phrase and subject be often varied so that it may not appear to be a form. And in all our prayers upon any particular or special occasions, there's great need of much premeditation.

The final aspect of prayer is thanksgiving. The subjects of this are either general or particular, and as various as our mercies. This part of prayer may perhaps come in more properly after the invocation, and the transition from here to confession may be made by the mention of our unworthiness to receive the divine blessings.

Beside this general method it would be proper to

preserve in your mind a particular method of the several blessings you are to pray for, the sins you confess, and the mercies you commemorate. Let these be laid up in the mind in order to be produced in their proper places. But do not tie yourself down to the invariable use of any method, whether general or particular; for a too close application of the mind to the method or expression of prayer is apt to obstruct the devout employment of the heart. Besides, this will make the prayer appear too formal, artificial, and studied, and bring a drowsiness on the minds of those whose devotion you are called to excite and lead; these persons are never more pleased and edified in this part of worship than when they observe us to be affected with our own prayers. A heart inspired with warm devotion will not be confined to exact methods. A lively start of thought, and a strong, surprising sentiment uttered out of its due place, will strike the minds of our fellow worshippers so strongly that they will not attend to the want of method, or, if they do, will readily excuse it. Enlarge mostly on that part of prayer with which you find your own mind most affected; and let not any occasional deviations from your purposed method interrupt the fervent workings of your spirit. 'Tis good, however, to be master of a regular system of materials, and of pertinent expressions under each heading which may serve instead of a form (but still to be uttered in the most solemn and reverend manner) when the powers of the mind happen to be heavy and inactive, or oppressed by the presence of others at a time when we are called to the performance of this duty.

Next to the matter and method, we should have a regard for the manner of prayer. This respects, first, the gesture of the body, which should be always decent, grave, humble, and expressive of the reverence of the heart: folding the hands, or putting the open palms together, sometimes erect, sometimes declining with the body; sometimes lifing up the eyes, according as the pious or humble motions of the heart direct. Let the eyes be mostly closed, or, if open, steadily fixed; for nothing is more indecent than for the eyes to wander in the performance of this duty.

With respect to the pronunciation, let it be slow, solemn, grave, distinct, and serious. Let not your words follow faster than your thoughts, so that the latter may have time to be maturely conceived and well-expressed. By this means, one thought will more naturally rise out of another, and will be in readiness to be produced while the other is uttering. And when the conceptions are thus aligned beforehand with the expressions, the mind will be free, composed, and serious, and will have time to feel the weight of its own thoughts, which will be a great help to the true spirit of prayer. Due and proper pauses and stops will give the hearer time to conceive and reflect on what you speak, and more heartily to join with you, as well as give you leave to breathe, and make the work more easy and pleasant to yourself. Besides, when persons run on heedlessly with an incessant flow of words, being carried, as it were, in a violent stream, without rests or pauses, they are in danger of uttering things rashly before God; giving no time at all to their own meditation, but indulging their tongue to run sometimes too fast for their own thoughts, as well as for the affections of such as are present with them. All this arises from the hurry of the tongue into the middle of a sentence before the mind has conceived the full and complete sense of it.

Avoid the extremes of a too low and muttering voice, which some use, and a clamorous, strong, noisy tone, which others affect, as if they expected to be heard for their loud speaking, or as if the devotion of the heart consisted in a strength of lungs. This is improperly called "powerful praying," and will be very disgusting to many.

With regard to the expression, let the following rules be observed:

RULE 1. Let your language be plain but proper. Avoid all low, vulgar, and obsolete phrases, but do not attempt an elegant or rhetorical style, much less an obscure and mystical one; for how can the mind feel the weight of that sentiment it does not understand?

RULE 2. Scriptural expressions, if happily chosen, are very ornamental in prayer. It would be of excellent use to improve us in the gift of prayer if in our daily reading of the Word of God we observed what expressions were suited to the several parts of this duty—adoration, confession, petition, or thanksgiving—and let them be wrought into our addresses to God that day. And to be furnished with a body of scriptural expressions to be used in prayer, read Matthew Henry's *Method of Prayer*, Bishop [John] Wilkins's *Discourse on the Gift of Prayer*, or *Closet Devotions*.

But here let the following cautions be observed:

Do not let your prayer be all in Scripture words. Some conceive a prayer of nothing but texts of Scripture tacked together, which prevents the mind from taking a proper scope, and leaves no room for the invention or the utterance of pious thoughts.

Avoid the dark, mystical expressions of Scripture,

which you have reason to believe the greatest part of your hearers do not comprehend the sense of. If we indulge the use of such dark sentences in our speaking to God, we might as well pray in an unknown tongue, which was so much disapproved of by the apostle (1 Corinthians 14:9). Let not the pomp and sound of any hard Hebrew names or obscure phrases in Scripture allure us to be fond of them in social prayer, even though we ourselves should know the meaning of them, lest we confound the thoughts of our fellow worshippers.

If you do not have the faculty of clothing your own ideas in proper and pertinent words, borrow the phrases and expressions of others upon the same subject. Make a collection of them from the best authors, but remember to pick out those which come nearest to your own phraseology, or such as you best approve and would wish to have in readiness when you are speaking on that particular subject. And when you are furnished with a store of such well-chosen expressions, turn them into the form of a prayer, and commit them to memory. This will not only facilitate your expression, but will give room for further invention. 'Tis usual for young students to be very careful in gathering commonplace books; it would be a much greater advantage if they were as diligent to collect under proper references any such particular matter or expressions in prayer wherewith at any time they find themselves to be more especially affected.

'Tis very proper and requisite that your prayer after the sermon be formed on the subject you have been treating, wherein you may go over all the headings of your discourse, touch upon the most important sentiments, and repeat the most striking expressions in it. But as the mind will be then sometimes fatigued, and the powers exhausted and unfit to be put onto the new labor of invention, it may not be amiss to pen down the short concluding prayer verbatim, to be repeated from memory, but without confining yourself to either the precise expressions or the method you had previously conceived, if the mind is able or disposed to enlarge.

Avoid those phrases and modes of expression which you know to be obnoxious or disgusting to your hearers, and prefer those that will give the least offense to any party or denomination of Christians.

Throw your prayer out of a form, as much as you can, by varying both method and phrase, and by a fresh supply of sentiments and expressions; this will be a great help both to your own devotion and to theirs who join with you in this part of worship.

Let your prayers, as well as your sermons, be rather too short than too long.

Avoid preaching prayers. Some persons who affect long prayers are greatly faulty in this respect. They are speaking to the people and teaching them the doctrines of religion, and the mind and will of God, rather than speaking to God the desire of their own mind. They wander away from God to speak to men. But this is quite contrary to the nature of prayer.

Last, do not be too fond of a nice uniformity of words, nor of perpetual diversity of expression in prayer. We should seek indeed to be furnished with a rich variety of holy language, that our prayers may always have something new and something entertaining in them, and not tie ourselves to express one thing always in one set of words lest this make us grow formal, dull, and indifferent in those petitions. But, on the other hand, if we are guilty of a perpetual affectation of new words that we never before used, we shall sometimes miss our own best and most spiritual meaning, and many times be driven to great impropriety of speech. At best, our prayers by this means will look like the fruit of our fancy and invention, and the labor of the head more than the breathings of the heart.

I shall conclude this section with a few general directions how to attain and improve this useful gift.

Accustom yourself to a serious, devout, and decent discharge of this duty every day in private, whereby a readiness of conception and expression will be sooner acquired.

Spare no pains to gain so excellent a talent; for 'tis not to be had (especially by some) without much application—but it is worth it all. And there are few things on which the labor of one who is a student for the sacred ministry can be more usefully employed.

Pray often for this gift of prayer.

Endeavor to get your spirit deeply impressed with the great things of religion; and let those sentiments that most affected you in your most serious frames be wrought into your prayers.

Maintain a manly presence of mind, and use all proper means to conquer that bashfulness and timidity of spirit which young persons are subject to, and which is a great hindrance to a decent discharge of this duty.

Take every opportunity you can to hear others pray, and imitate them in everything you observe to be decent, graceful, and excellent.

Last, vary your concluding doxologies. And that you may herein give no offense to any, it may be proper to confine yourself to those of Scripture, which are very various and such as follow:

Hebrews 13:21: "Through Jesus Christ, to whom be glory forever and ever. Amen."

Romans 16:25–27: "Now to Him that is of power to establish you according to the gospel of Jesus Christ; to God only wise, be glory through Jesus Christ forever. Amen."

Romans 9:5: "Through Jesus Christ, who is our all, God blessed forever. Amen."

Galatians 1:4–5: "Who gave Himself for our sins, that He might deliver us from this present evil world, according to the will of God and our Father. To whom be glory forever and ever. Amen."

Ephesians 3:20–21: "Now unto Him who is able to do exceedingly abundantly above all that we ask or think, according to the power that worketh in us, unto Him be glory in the church by Christ Jesus throughout all ages, world without end. Amen."

1 Timothy 1:17: "Now unto the King eternal, immortal, invisible, the only wise God, be honor and glory forever and ever. Amen."

1 Peter 4:11: "Through Jesus Christ, to whom be praise and dominion forever and ever. Amen."

2 Peter 3:18: "Through our Lord and Savior Jesus Christ, to whom be glory both now and forever. Amen."

Jude 24–25: "Now unto Him that is able to keep us from falling, and to present us faultless before the presence of His glory with exceeding joy, to the only wise God our Savior, be glory and majesty, dominion and power, both now and ever. Amen."

Revelation 1:5–6: "Unto Him who loved us, and washed us from our sins in His own blood, and hath made us kings and priests to God, even His Father, to him be glory and dominion forever and ever. Amen."

Revelation 5:13: "Blessing, and honor, and glory, and power be unto Him that sitteth upon the throne, and unto the Lamb forever and ever. Amen."

The Administration of the Sacraments
 1. Baptism:
A minister ought to instruct his people frequently in the nature of baptism so that they may not go about it merely as a ceremony, as it is too visible that the greater part do, but that they may consider it as dedicating their children to God, offering them to Christ, and holding them thereafter as His, directing their chief care about them to bring them up in the nurture and admonition of the Lord. In the administration of this ordinance it is best to keep to the original institution as your rule and guide. The most natural method to be used in the celebration of it seems to be this:

Recite the express words of the institution found in Matthew 28:28.

Then it would not be amiss to say something in vindication of those two positive institutions of Christianity, baptism and the Lord's Supper, and to show the excellency of the Christian dispensation from its simplicity, that it is not encumbered with those numerous external ceremonies as the Jewish dispensation was.

Make a short discourse on the ordinance as a sacrament of the Christian church, wherein you may offer some useful remarks on the practice of infant baptism. Then add some proper observations relating to the mode and manner in which the ordinance is to be celebrated, laying this down as an undisputed principle: that in the manner of performing divine worship it is always best and safest to keep close to the divine rule, so as neither to go beyond nor fall short of it. For in the former case, we know not whether human and arbitrary additions will be approved of God; but this we are sure of: He will never condemn us for not doing what He never commanded. And therefore the sign of the cross may be safely omitted as nowhere enjoined by God Himself. As to the latter case (neglecting any part of our rule, or those instructions He has given us for the directory of our worship), this must certainly be criminal, and derogatory to the honor of the divine Institutor. But where the circumstance or mode of any religious action is left undetermined in the form and words of the institution, that which is most decent and convenient is to be preferred. Hence, sprinkling or washing the face of the baptized person gently with the hand is to be preferred to plunging the body all over in water, because the former is more safe and decent, and the latter nowhere commanded as the standing, universal mode of baptizing.

Be more particular in explaining the nature, end, and design of this ordinance, and in explaining the typical part of it. Here you may bring in the doctrine of sanctification, the purifying influences of the Holy Spirit represented by the water in baptism, and the relation this Christian institution has to the baptizing of proselytes and to the Jewish ordinance of circumcision.

You may then briefly explain the nature of the present duty of the parents in giving up their child to God, and what is implied therein, that is, their desire that the child should be received into the church of Christ and brought up in the Christian faith. And be very particular in your address to the parents of the infant who is to be baptized, pressing upon them the importance of their charge and the care they are to take in the education of their child, especially in reference to his or her spiritual and eternal concerns. But this may be either before or after the ceremonial part of the ordinance is performed.

Proceed then to ask a blessing upon the ordinance, and pray for the infant in particular.

Then take the infant and, washing him gently with water, baptize him in the name of the Father, and of the Son, and of the Holy Ghost.

Then, last (if the exhortation to the parents does not come in here, but was addressed to them before), conclude with the thanksgiving prayer and the benediction.

2. The sacrament of the Lord's Supper (of the method of performing it, and of taking in communicants):

The most regular method of performing it seems to be to make a short preparatory discourse, tending to explain the nature and design of this sacrament and the necessity and importance of its intention, or to excite some devout affections in the minds of the communicants, especially relating to the love of Christ, the design of His death and sufferings, and the necessity of a frequent commemoration thereof in this sacred institution. But let the address be very serious, and very solemn. Then read distinctly the words of the institution. Then solemnly pray for the divine blessing and presence; give thanks to God for the institution of the visible symbols to affect your mind and assist your faith;

and earnestly pray that the great end of this sacred
solemnity may be visibly answered in every one of the
communicants, and be manifested in their growing
love for the Redeemer and their more steady attach-
ment to His gospel as their only rule of faith and life.
Then break the sacramental bread, and distribute it either personally or by the hands of the deacons. To assist the devotion of the communicants, it is the custom
of some ministers to pronounce now and then some
serious and weighty sentences relative to the love and
sufferings of Christ, or the benefits of His death. But
this is not used by others under an apprehension that,
instead of quickening the devotion of our fellow worshippers, it may interrupt it by diverting the course of
their own meditations.

After the distribution of the bread, make a short
prayer to beg for the continuance of the divine presence and blessing, and that God would graciously forgive the infirmities of our worship; and give thanks for
the element you are about to partake of, praying that it
may answer the design intended by it, which is all that
Protestants mean by the consecration of the elements.
But it is the custom with some to pray for a blessing on
both of the elements in one single prayer.

Then follows the distribution of the cup in the
manner already mentioned. In some churches it is the
custom for the minister to partake of the elements last,
and in others first, pronouncing with an audible voice
these or some such words: "In obedience to Christ's
command, and in remembrance of Him, I take and eat
this bread, as the memorial of His body which was bro-
ken for sin." And so in partaking of the cup: "I take and
drink this cup . . . ."

After the distribution of the elements, the minister sometimes makes a short exhortation to the people relating to the nature of their sacramental obligations, and exhorting them to be faithful thereunto. After this a collection is made for the poor by the deacons from pew to pew, or at the door when the congregation breaks up. Then follows a suitable hymn or psalm. Last, conclude with a short thanksgiving prayer.

In order to furnish your mind with suitable matter for your sacramental exhortations and prayers, it is requisite to read some proper devotional treatise on this ordinance before you enter on the celebration of it.

The method of admitting communicants to the Lord's Table varies in different churches. For direction in this affair these general rules may be of service:

As every particular church is a select religious society, every member of it has a right to be satisfied of the character and qualification of every new member who is admitted into it. This is plain from the very nature and design of such a society, and necessary to preserve the purity and discipline of the church.

The qualifications required in the candidates should be no other than what we have plain warrant from Scripture to demand, and such as are necessary to preserve purity and discipline. For herein (as well as in other parts of Christian discipline and church government) we are strictly to adhere to Scripture as our rule, so far as it affords us any direction in this matter. And, therefore, to require that the spiritual experiences of the candidate be publicly declared by himself or read by another in the presence of the church before he is allowed to take communion with them (which is the practice in some Protestant dissenting congregations) is not only unnecessary, but unwarrantable, and often attended with very bad effects. It is unnecessary because it is found not to answer the end principally designed, the greater purity of the church; it is unwarrantable because we have no shadow of a precept or precedent for it in Scripture or primitive antiquity.

The bad consequences of it are, first, that it bars the way to this ordinance, and discourages meek, humble, and modest persons from presenting themselves to the communion, while it is easily accessible to men of bold, forward, and confident tempers. Second, it is a temptation to the candidates to declare more than they have really experienced, lest the church should reject them, or to describe the animal passions as divine influences, and the workings of the imagination as the operations of the Spirit, which young and inexperienced Christians are too apt to do. Third, it supposes and countenances some very mistaken principles, such as that none have a right to this ordinance but those whose hearts are not only really converted, but who are also sensible of this, and are able to make others sensible of it by describing the time, means, manner, and effects of that conversion. Fourth, it attributes a power to the church which it has no right to, of judging the hearts of others, and that by a very precarious rule: from what they say of themselves. For if the members of the congregation judge by the general character, life, and conversation of the candidate (which is a much better rule), there is no necessity for a public declaration of his experience. It likewise implies a power in the church of excluding from this ordinance all who cannot produce such evidence of their real conversion as will satisfy every member of the church. Upon what foundation so extraordinary a claim is built, it is hard to say. Finally, this practice tends to make the members thus admitted too careless and confident after their admission; for when they have the testimony of the whole church concurring with their own strong imagination that they are true, converted Christians, and look upon the sins they commit after this only as the weakness of God's children, they are in great danger of being betrayed into a false and fatal peace.

Therefore, a creditable profession, and unblemished character and conduct, may be deemed as a necessary and sufficient qualification for Holy Communion. This is necessary in order to keep up the discipline and preserve the purity of the church; and it is sufficient because we do not find that our sacred rule requires anything further.

As soon as the members of the church are satisfied of this general qualification of the candidate, they have no right to refuse their assent to his admission.

Provided that they have this satisfaction, it is not material by what means they receive it. Sometimes the elders of the church are delegated to confer privately with the candidate, and to inquire into his knowledge of the design and nature of this ordinance, and whether his views and ends in desiring to join in it are sincere and right. Sometimes this is left entirely to the minister, whose business it more properly is; if he is satisfied in those points, he may acquaint the church of it at the next ensuing sacrament. And thereupon he declares that if any of the members present do not signify to him (before the next sacrament) any objections against the candidate's admission, he will then (by their consent) be admitted to the ordinance as a member of that church. In other churches members are admitted by the minister only, without any notice given to the church till the very time of their admission; nor even then are they apprised of it in any other way than by a few petitions in the minister's prayer particularly in behalf of the newly admitted member.

The church has an undoubted right to expel irregular and unworthy members. This is generally done at first by suspension, when the minister intimates his desire and that of the church to the delinquent member, that he should refrain from coming to the sacrament till he hears further from him. This is generally sufficient without the solemnity of a formal and public expulsion.

Visiting the Sick

This is a very arduous and delicate office, and especially in some circumstances; and a different method of address and conduct is requisite according to the different characters of the persons you visit.

It will therefore be proper to lay down some general rules to be observed, in order to rightly execute this part of your duty, and to specify some particular cases.

Some general rules to be observed in order to a right execution of this part of your duty would include the following:

1. A previous preparation for it is very proper, by considering what kind of address will be most necessary and suitable to the persons you visit. 'Tis something strange that ministers who take such pains to prepare for the work of the pulpit should generally take so little to prepare for this, which is one of the most

difficult and most important offices in the ministry.

2. It would be advisable to have in readiness a good store of Scripture expressions, adapted to the support and comfort of the afflicted, which may be easily collected from the commonplace book to the Bible; and out of these, choose such as are as most applicable to the case of your friend.

3. Adapt yourself to his taste and understanding, as well as to the circumstances of his case, by making such observations, and using such expressions, as you know are most familiar and agreeable to him. But take care to explain the phrases he makes use of, if you have reason to think he does not understand them.

4. Let your deportment and address be very free, friendly, close, tender, and compassionate.

5. Place yourself in the condition of the person before you, and consider in what manner you would wish a minister or friend to behave toward you in those circumstances.

6. While you are tender, be sure to be faithful, and have a respect to the approbation of your conscience afterwards. Remember that you are a minister of the gospel, and must not sacrifice the cause of truth and godliness to a false shame or tenderness.

7. Let your prayer for the sick person be short but very serious and solemn, and adapted as much as may be to the state of his soul and the danger of his disease. In this function there is great need of much piety, fidelity and wisdom.

Let us now consider how a minister ought to behave in his visitation of the sick, under some particular circumstances.

1. If you have reason to believe that the afflicted person you visit is a real, good Christian, your work will not be very difficult; it may even be pleasant and useful. And you may possibly receive more advantage from him than he does from you. For a Christian's graces are at such a time commonly most lively, and the tongue is very faithful to the sentiments of the heart, so that you will presently see what it is that lies most upon his mind.

And as your present business will be to administer consolation and solve his doubts, your topics of consolation may be taken from his past experience. Direct him to look back to the goodness of God to him, and the sensible experience he has had of the divine love and presence. Bid him think of what God has done for his soul, and thence draw David's conclusion: "The Lord has been my help." Refer his thoughts to the paternal character; bid him think of the compassion of a father to a weak and helpless child. Open the inexhaustible stores of the divine mercy in the gospel. Insist on the mighty efficacy of the Redeemer's blood. Insist on the genuine marks of a true faith and sincere repentance. Last, endeavor to affect his mind with a lively apprehension of the heavenly glory, to which he will very shortly be received.

And as to his doubts, tell him that he is not a proper judge in his own case, under the present weakness of his powers; that the lowness of his animal spirits causes him to look too much upon the dark side, and to see everything through a wrong medium. Tell him that he has no reason to expect his case to be worse now than it was when he had better hopes concerning it; that the best of men have had their doubt; that if it is the sign of a weak faith, it is however the sign of some true faith; that it is much safer to be doubtful than over-confident; that however variable his frame may be, God's regards for His own children are unchangeable. Bid him examine his doubts to the bottom, and trace them up to the true source; and perhaps they may appear to arise from the agency of Satan, who delights to disturb the tranquility of those he cannot destroy. Ask him if he has any hopes, and whether he would part with the little hope he has for the greatest treasures on earth. Bid him examine the foundation of those hopes as well as that of his fears; for he can never judge aright till he looks on both sides, and oftentimes a Christian's weak hope has a better foundation than his strongest fears.

But suppose the character of the sick person you visit is doubtful. Then your business is more difficult, and your address must be more cautious. If there is no apparent danger of death, endeavor to give him just notions of a particular providence—that though men do not so often attend to it as they ought, yet it is most certain from Scripture and reason, that whatever befalls every individual man on earth is under the immediate direction of providence. And as to this affliction in particular, persuade him to regard and consider it as the hand of God.

Then discourse on the wisdom and goodness of God in sending these occasional rebukes of His providence, which, whatever we think, are sent for the best ends. Afflictions are the medicine of the soul, designed to purify and purge it.

Under this view of things, press upon him the exercise of patient submission and a total resignation to the divine will; and direct him to look upon the present dispensation (though grievous) as sent in mercy to him, and as what may hereafter produce the most excellent effects.

Tell him that in the best of men there are sins and follies sufficient to justify the severest dispensations of God's providence; that many good Christians have suffered worse; and what reason he has to be thankful that his case is not more calamitous.

Remind him of the many mercies mixed with the present affliction.

If it should please God to restore him, exhort him faithfully to concur with the design of this visitation by his constant endeavor to amend what his conscience now smites him for.

But if there are apparent symptoms of approaching death, exhort him to seriously review his past life, and to call to mind the most remarkable transgressions of it, for which he should now greatly humble his soul before God, and sincerely renew his repentance. And that his repentance may be sincere and unfeigned, endeavor to make him sensible of the evil and guilt of sin, from its contrariety to the holy nature of God and the inevitable ruin it exposes the soul unto. When he is thus humble and penitent, revive him with the consolations of the gospel, the amazing compassion and goodness of God to a world of sinners in sending His Son to redeem them by His death, and the merits of the Redeemer's sufferings, whose blood cleanses from all sin. Then open to him in a plain and easy manner the gospel method of salvation by Jesus Christ. In a deep self-abhorrence for his sins, and in such a lively faith in Christ, advise him to call upon the Father of mercies for pardon through Jesus Christ, His Son. Remind him

to settle his affairs in this world as well as he can, and
then think no more of it forever. Last, leave with him
some suitable text of Scripture which you apprehend to
be most applicable to the state of his soul.

But if the sick man you visit has been notoriously
wicked, and appears ignorant, insensible, and hardened, your business then is the most difficult of all.

To make any right impression on such a one, you
must pray to God beforehand that you may be enabled
to say something that is suitable to his case and that
may be a means of awakening him to a proper sense of
his danger. And then, when you come into his room,
appear deeply affected with his case. Let him see that
you are more concerned for him than he is for himself,
and that you are more sensible of his danger than he is
of his own. Then, in order to bring him to a proper
sense of his state of danger, put some close questions to
him relating to the holy and righteous nature of God,
His infinite hatred of sin, the absolute impossibility of
being happy hereafter except in His favor, the certainty
of a future judgment when God will render to everyone
according to his works, and the unspeakable importance of the soul's being safe for eternity. Then beg
him not to deceive himself with vain hopes, but to be
willing to see the truth of his case as it is represented to
him in the unerring Word of God, however dangerous
or dreadful it may appear to him; for while he shuts his
eyes against the danger, there's no possibility of escap-
ing it.

If his distemper is likely to be fatal, let him know it,
and that all that can be done to escape everlasting misery must immediately be done; that there is as yet some
hope (though it is but small) that this possibly may be

done; that on this moment depends his future condition forever. Beg him not to lose the last and only chance he has for eternity. If his conscience by this means is awakened, and you observe some genuine relentings of heart, take that occasion to assist its workings, to enforce its reproofs and urge its convictions, till you see something like a true penitential remorse. Then earnestly pray with him and for him, that God would continue to give him a just sense of his sin and danger, and that His grace and Spirit would carry on those convictions till they issue in a real change of heart.

Then take your leave of him in a tender and affectionate manner, not without giving him some hope that, if the same sensible and penitent frame continues, there may be mercy in reserve for him. But beg him, while he has the use of his reason, not to omit any opportunity to cry mightily to God for mercy through the merits of Jesus Christ, His Son.

In your next visit (which should be soon after this), if you find him penitent, exhort him to glorify God by making an ample confession of his sins in private, with all their heinous aggravations, and not to be afraid to see the worst of himself; and if he has in any matter injured or defrauded others, you must insist upon it, as a mark of true repentance, that he immediately make restitution or satisfaction, if it is in his power. Last, if his penitential sorrow still continues, and you have reason to believe him to be sincere, you may begin to administer the consolations of the gospel, and address him as you have been directed in the case of the person already mentioned under the like circumstances.

The Minister's Conduct Towards His People

Here it will be proper to lay down some general
rules to be observed at all times, and some particular
rules applicable to extraordinary occasions.

There are some general rules to be observed at all
times. But prior to laying these down I would desire you
to observe these two things:

First, arm yourself with resolution, and prepare to
meet with difficulties and contempt. The nature of your
office implies the former, and all the dignity of it will
not secure you from the latter. But if you behave prudently and faithfully in it, you will meet with contempt
from none but those who deserve it, and whose esteem
would be no honor.

Second, study the true nature of Christian humility,
and let your mind be clothed with it as its greatest ornament. But distinguish between that dastardly meanness and pusillanimity which makes you ashamed to
look in the face of and speak in the presence of your
superiors (and which may tempt you to an abject compliance with all their humors), and that humility which
arises from a reverence of God, a consciousness of your
own defects, the difficulty of your work, and the knowledge of your character. This will teach you to bear contempt with dignity and applause with decency; the latter perhaps you will find no less difficult than the former. Let the knowledge of yourself be your guard
against that vanity of mind which will be apt to steal
into it when you hear the approbations or commendations of men.

Thus, armed with resolution and humility:

1. Let your principal care be to be faithful to God
and conscience, and take care that nothing betrays you

into such a behavior upon any occasion for which your own mind will reproach you in secret. And a steady regard to this rule will lead you to decline the most usual and dangerous temptations.

2. Let your conduct to all be inoffensive, beneficent, and obliging. Make it your practice, and it will be your pleasure, to do some kind office to everyone to whom you have a power and opportunity to do it with prudence. And let the Emperor Titus's rule of conduct be yours, not to let one day pass, if possible, without doing some good to one person or another.

3. Visit your people in a kind and friendly manner, as often as it suits with your convenience and theirs. This is the business of the afternoon—for the whole morning, and as much time as you can redeem at night, should be devoted to study. Where your visits are most pleasant and profitable, and most expected and desired, pay them most frequently. But where there is any prospect of doing good to any in your flock, there you should sometimes pay your visits, though it be to the poorest persons, and especially when they are in trouble. And in all your visits take some opportunity to make moral remarks, drop some useful instructions, or leave some good rule or religious observation for their benefit. But this must be done not with a magisterial authority or ministerial air, but with all the freedom and ease imaginable, when it rises naturally out of the subject of the conversation.

4. Throw off all affectation, parade, stiffness, morose conceit, reserve, and self-sufficiency. Let your ambition be to be distinguished by nothing but real goodness, wisdom, and benevolence. And be courteous, free, condescending, affable, open, unreserved, and friendly to

all. But amidst all your freedoms, forget not the dignity
and decorum of your character.

5. Circumspectly avoid everything that may give
them unnecessary offense, whether by word or conduct,
though it be in matters of indifference. You may possibly, in point of fidelity, be obliged to give them offense
in some important things; in all others, therefore, you
should endeavor to conciliate their esteem and respect.
It shows much weakness, and little prudence and candor, to be obstinate and tenacious about little things,
whether modes, customs, or phrases, which are offensive to others. It is not walking charitably, nor following the things that make for peace, and is a violation of
the apostle's rule of becoming all things to all men.
But see that your charitable conformity does not
transgress the laws of sincerity.

6. Above all, let your character be a fair copy of the
virtues you preach; and let the documents of the pulpit
be exemplified in the conduct of your life. A minister
should abstain from the appearance of evil, not only
from things criminal, but from those that may be interpreted to his dishonor and reported to his disadvantage.

7. Be much in prayer for wisdom, strength, prudence, and capacity equal to your work and difficulties.
This you will find as necessary as your most important
studies. But take care that your private transactions with
God are very serious, solemn, and sincere; and let your
endeavors go along with your prayers.

I wish to lay down some particular rules applicable
upon extraordinary occasions, or proper to regulate
your conduct towards persons of different characters.

CASE 1. What is a right conduct towards those from whom you have received abuse, contempt, or just cause of offense?

1. Your first care must be to guard your passions. Keep your temper, and banish all vindictive resentments. If possible, never think of it; but be sure not to harbor the thoughts of it, which will but chafe and corrode the mind to no purpose. Be satisfied with a consciousness of your innocence, and consider the injurious person as an object of your pity rather than indignation.

2. As you must endeavor to forget the offense, you must not only cease to think, but forbear to talk of it unless it is with an intimate friend to ask his advice.

3. You may lawfully decline the company of the person who has thus injured you, and break off a familiar commerce with him, as you cannot look upon him as your friend. But take every opportunity to do him good that lies in your power.

4. Embrace the first opportunity and overture to reestablish a good understanding and renew your former amity.

5. Last, in all cases of this nature, let it be remembered that the misconduct of others towards you will not justify yours towards them, and that you are still under the same obligations to walk by the rules of that wisdom from above which is first pure, then peaceable.

CASE 2. What is the right conduct towards narrow, bigoted, censorious Christians, who are proud of their orthodoxy and zealously attached to party notions?

1. These persons must by no means be disputed with or opposed, because, while they have much more zeal than knowledge, they are very apt to be warm and angry

at any argument that is leveled against their favorite
sentiments—and much more so if they cannot answer
it. And while bigotry blinds their minds, they are not
capable of seeing the force of an argument, much less
of being convinced by it. They should therefore be
treated like froward children, or persons in a passion.

2. Take every opportunity to secretly undermine
their false notions (especially if they are dangerous) by
hinting at their bad consequences, or by setting the
opposite doctrine of truth in a strong light from
Scripture. But do not dwell long upon it lest they apprehend themselves particularly to be aimed at, which
they will not fail to resent.

3. Treat them with the utmost marks of freedom,
tenderness, and friendship, to convince them that your
sentiments of doctrine (though opposite to theirs) create in you no disaffection to them.

4. Endeavor to make them sensible of the much
greater importance of those things in which you agree
with them, and press them powerfully on their consciences. And once they come to feel the weight and
force of these, they will gradually abate of their zeal for
the lesser things. And this is the only (at least the best
and safest) way to convince them that these things on
which they have misplaced their zeal are to be reckoned among the minutiae of divinity; for nothing is
more natural and common than for the mind to raise
the importance of a subject in proportion to the zeal it
expresses for it. Otherwise it would lie under the constant self-reproach of being governed by a blind, irregular zeal. And as their zeal for any particular doctrine
has fixed the importance of it before their understanding has precisely weighed it, to go about to argue

against that importance would be to argue against their zeal, that is, their passions, which is a very unequal encounter, and altogether vain.

5. Take occasion often to expose the effects of bigotry in other instances to their view, whereby they may possibly become sensible of their own. But let the instances be so distant (or, if near, so artfully insinuated) that they may not be sensible of your design.

6. Come as near to their sentiments as you possibly can (when your subject leads you that way), and show them the plain reason why you cannot come nearer.

7. Refer to all plain Scripture, and resolve to adhere to that, for both the confirmation of doctrine and the confutation of error; and, by removing their mistaken sense of Scripture, open to them the first source of the errors they have imbibed.

CASE 3. What is a right conduct towards those who are inclined to infidelity?

1. As these are but bigots of another rank, they must be treated with the same tenderness, caution, and prudence. The latitudinarian and narrow bigot will be equally enflamed by a violent opposition; for they both lay an equal claim to superior wisdom, and eagerly demand (and, if you would keep them in humor, you must not be backward to pay it) some compliment to their own understanding.

2. But as these are the greatest champions of reason, and will admit no other weapon in the hand of their antagonist, be sure to be expert at that, and insist upon it that your adversary uses no other—that he does not put you off with sophistry, paralogism, illusion, equivocation, ridicule, buffoonery, clamor, confidence, passion, or grimace, instead of solid argument and plain

reason. Keep him to his point. Admit nothing but what you understand, and nothing but what he understands himself. Take care that he does not entangle you in a wood of words, blind your eyes with dust, prevent your seeing distinctly the point in hand by holding a cloud before it, or lead you from it by diverting to another subject when he is pinched and piqued by an argument he cannot answer.

3. If your adversary is a person of sense, learning, and ingenuity, the most effectual method to draw him to your opinion is by a strong appeal to those good qualities, whereby he will convince himself.

4. If his self-conceit is unsufferable and his ignorance ridiculous, it may not be amiss sometimes to mortify the former by exposing the latter.

5. Insist that if his regard and esteem for natural religion are sincere, that will engage him to think favorably of the Christian institution, which has refined and exalted morality to its utmost perfection; that there is no honest Deist but (whatever he believes) would heartily wish Christianity to be true.

6. Last, if you observe him to be capable of serious impressions, urge him to consider seriously the dreadful risk he runs while he pawns his immortal soul upon the idea that Christianity is an impostor, and how unavoidable his ruin is while he continues willfully to neglect it. For if Christianity is true, the sentence of condemnation pronounced against him (by the great Author of it) for resolving not to believe it must also be true.

CASE 4. How should we conduct ourselves as faithful and judicious ministers towards melancholy, dejected, and doubting Christians? As this is a frequent case, and often attended with no small difficulty, I shall consider it more particularly.

1. The first thing to be considered is the true source and origin of this melancholy gloom and dejection of mind, whether it arises from bodily disorder, worldly losses and afflictions, some grievous sin committed, or an excessive apprehensiveness and timidity of spirit. Perhaps the person himself may impute it to none of these, but to either divine desertion or the buffetings of Satan. But these must carefully be distinguished and explained, because they are frequently mistaken; and then, according to the true source of their spiritual trouble your advice and address to them must be.

If you have reason to believe that the troubled state of their mind is owing principally to a bodily disorder, or some obstruction or disorder of the animal fluids, you should recommend to them a physician, or prescribe for them medicine, cold baths, constant employment, or exercise in the air.

If their sorrow or settled melancholy of mind is the effect of some worldly losses and afflictions, you must endeavor all you can to alleviate it by showing them in how many ways God can (if He pleases) make up to them the loss they have sustained; how many wise and kind ends may be answered by it; and that the scenes of life are variable: after night comes the day. Beseech them to put their hope and trust in God as a gracious and indulgent Father, and urge every topic of consolation proper to be used in a time of worldly adversity.

If the disconsolate state of their mind is the effect of a melancholy constitution, the case is still more difficult, and belongs rather to the physician's department than that of the minister. The latter can have but small hope of administering any proper relief because the person is not capable of reasoning or thinking justly, and there is something within him that obstructs the avenues to his heart. This must first be removed before comfort can find its way to it. All that can be done in this case is to persuade him if you can (of what he will find very hard to believe) that he sees everything in a wrong light, and is not at present a competent judge in his own case, and therefore ought not to believe his own thoughts. Ask him if he ever judged more favorably of his spiritual state heretofore than he does now, and whether he was not a more capable judge of his case then than he is now.

If the trouble of his mind arises from the reproaches of conscience from some grievous sin committed, your way is then more direct and plain. If you have reason to believe that this sorrow of heart is the effect of a true, penitential remorse, you are then to lay before him every proper topic of consolation the gospel admits: the riches of divine mercy, the merits of the blood of Christ, the extent and efficacy of free grace, the precious promises of the gospel, and the examples of God's mercy and wonderful compassion to humble penitents. Then conclude all with an earnest exhortation to trust his soul in the hands of Christ, and to rely on the mercy of God in the way of a steady, conscientious obedience.

If it arises from an excessive apprehensiveness and timidity of spirit, and you have cause to believe that the person's state is much better than he fears, you are then to fortify and encourage his heart by referring him to his own past experience of what God has done for his soul, the various tokens of His favor to him in the former scenes of life, and the several methods of His grace and providence. Urge upon him the exercise of a lively faith encouraged by the grace of the gospel; and convince him that it is no less wrong and prejudicial for a person to think too ill than to think too well of himself; as he is in no danger at all of the latter, advise him, for the honor of God, the credit of religion, and his own peace and comfort, to guard against the former, where his greatest danger lies.

If the melancholy and dejected soul has a pious turn, and imputes his present darkness to what he calls divine dereliction, or the hidings of God's face, explain that affair to him. Tell him that his want of that spiritual joy and comfort he once found in his soul may be owing to other causes: the present low state of his spirits, a distemper of the animal frame, the influence of external objects and accidents, or a concurrence of all these; that nothing is more variable than the frame of the human mind; that we are not to think that God's regards to His own children vary with our minds. Let him know that this is a great mistake, and a mistake that is greatly dishonorable to Him; that while He sees His children upright, sincere, humble, obedient and dependent, His regards to them are always the same, whatever they may think of Him; that God never hides His face from His people till they withdraw their hearts from Him; that unless they forsake Him, He will never depart from them; that the hidings of God's countenance (which the psalmist so often complains of) generally, if not always, refer to the external dispensations of God or outward providential afflictions—not inward, spiritual desertions—when the distress of his circumstances was so great that God might seem to have for-

gotten and forsaken Him, and his enemies might be
ready to put that construction upon it.

Last, if the person imputes the trouble of his mind
to the buffetings of Satan, explain that affair to him.
Let him know that though in some cases that evil spirit
may have an agency in creating some spiritual troubles,
yet he has no more power over the mind than what it
pleases God to give him; that his influence (be it what
it will) is controlled and limited; that the most he can
do is to suggest sinful and troublesome thoughts,
which we may and ought to repel; that the Holy Spirit
has a counter-agency to inspire good and holy affections; that by indulging in excessive grief and gloomy
apprehensions we give the devil an advantage over us,
and even invite his temptations. And finally we ought
to take special care to distinguish between the agency
of Satan and the operation of natural causes, and not to
impute those things to the devil which are owing to our
own folly and weakness, or are the physical effects of
external objects.

CASE 5. What is the right conduct towards the licentious and profane?

1. While you behave toward them with civility and
discretion, it will be advisable to decline a particular intercourse with them. A minister's behavior toward men
should in a good degree be regulated by their moral
characters.

2. In case they seek your more intimate friendship
by kind and benevolent offices, so that gratitude and
good manners will not permit you to forbear your visits,
you will then have a fair opportunity to insinuate some
necessary and gentle admonitions, either by way of
story, simile, repartee, raillery, or reproof suitable to the

subject of the discourse or the temper they may be in; these (if they take effect) will prepare your way for a more free and close remonstrance.

3. Always open a way to the heart on that side where you find the easiest access. Some are most touched with a sense of honor and a regard to their reputation; others have a view to their interest; others must be allured by an easy, gentle, rational address; and others will yield to nothing but close and warm reproof. But take particular care to know the ruling passion of the person you address, and, if possible, to bring that over to your side.

4. Beg them to erect their hopes and extend their views as rational beings designed for an immortal existence, and not to forget their connection with another world; for to provide only for the present, and live from hand to mouth, is to act far below the dignity and design of human nature.

5. If they have any taste for reading, put into their hands such books as are most suited to their capacity, taste, and character.

6. Last, you should frequently address them from the pulpit. But your public address (while it is strong and animated) must be general, and must have nothing in it that is distinguishing or appropriative. Do not give the audience room to think that any person is particularly intended in the animadversion; for though they bear to be preached to, yet no man loves to be preached at.

CASE 6. How are we to behave towards the grossly ignorant and careless?

1. Endeavor to rouse them to a sense of religion and their dependence on God by a seasonable improvement

of some awakening providences: their own sickness, worldly disappointments, the death of a friend, or some public calamity.

2. Represent to them the most important and affecting subjects of religion in the strongest light and plainest language: the shortness of time, the awfulness of eternity, the certainty and near approach of death, and the terrors of the final judgement.

3. If you find that your conversation is agreeable to them, frequently visit them in a free and friendly manner, and take care that there is nothing dogmatic or authoritative in the advice you give them. But let all appear to proceed from a compassionate concern you have for the interest of their souls.

4. As they are but children in understanding, they must be dealt with as such: put the plainest and most affecting books into their hands, and take care not to feed them with strong meat when they stand in need of milk.

5. It will not be amiss in some part of your sermon (especially in the application) to adapt yourself in particular to their capacity and condition, so that they may not only understand but feel what you say. For this sort of hearer (among both the high and the low) perhaps makes a much larger part of our audience than we imagine.

CASE 7. What is the proper behavior towards those who are superior to us in rank and fortune?

1. Readily pay them the respect due to their distinction and character. If their temper and conduct are not altogether such as you would wish, yet that will not excuse you from a civil, decent, and obliging behavior towards them. You must remember your duty to others,

however they may be deficient in theirs to you. But if they treat you with kindness, friendship, and affection, they claim your gratitude, honor, and esteem, which will prompt your endeavors to oblige and serve them in every way you can.

2. But be free, open, conversant, and discreetly unreserved before them. Absence of mind, distance of behavior, formality of address, stiffness of manner, or affected silence is always ungenteel and disgusting, especially in the presence of superiors.

3. Preserve a generosity and manliness of temper and address, and show nothing of a mean, low, timid, servile spirit; that is not only dishonorable to your own character, but infers a bad compliment upon theirs. They are not tyrants, nor, if they were, must you submit to be their slaves. And remember that if they are sensible and genteel, wise and good, they will consider their superiority to you in one respect as balanced by that of yours to them in another; theirs may be most showy, but perhaps yours may be most valuable.

4. Forget not the dignity and decorum of your character. There is something you owe to that as well as to the distinction and opulence of your friends. And while this is your guard against incidental levities and a compliance with sinful customs, it is by no means inconsistent with pure wit, innocent humor, and seasonable cheerfulness, which, if attended with good sense and an obliging, natural behavior, will be no less agreeable in the company of your superiors than in that of your equals.

5. Do and say all the obliging and agreeable things you can, consistent with truth, conscience, and the honor of your function.

6. And then take every opportunity to insinuate something (conformable to the duty of your office) which may be serviceable to their spiritual interest and helpful to their moral character.

7. Last, make a prudent and seasonable use of your interest in them for the relief of your poor neighbors, whose distresses may be better known to you than they are to them.

CASE 8. What is the proper behavior of a minister towards the poor of his congregation?

This must be regulated by their moral character.

1. If their character is immoral or profane, as they will not be very fond of your company, they will take no offense if you forbear to visit them; but they should not be wholly neglected. Genteel, kind, and candid reproof, prudently and seasonably given, may have a good effect when they come to reflect upon it coolly; and a seasonable relief to them in their distress will add weight to your admonitions, and will give them such impressions of your charity as will better dispose them to receive your instructions.

2. But if they are serious and well-inclined, and you find yourself agreeable to them, you should frequently call upon them; and though your visits may be short, they should be free, friendly, condescending, and courteous. Always leave them with some spiritual, moral, or religious instruction suited to their taste, understanding, and circumstances. Be ready to advise and help them in everything you can. If you see a good heart at bottom, and especially a humble spirit, make the greatest allowance for their ignorance, prepossession, or infelicity of temper; and when there is need of reproof, let it be preceded by the sincerest expressions of love, and

by real acts of friendship. If they are willing to open the state of their souls to you, attend to it with patience and care, so that you may administer the most suitable advice and comfort. Have a particular regard to their capacity in your public exhortations. "To the poor the gospel is preached." And as these sometimes make up the bulk of a congregation, and their souls stand as much in need of spiritual nourishment as those of greater knowledge and comprehension, they should be always fed with food convenient for them.

CASE 9. In what manner ought a minister to behave towards those who have fallen into notorious sins?

This must be regulated by the disposition, character, and temper of the offender. The sensible and penitent must be treated in one way, the obstinate and impenitent in another. The following method in general will perhaps be found to be the most prudent and effectual:

1. Previous to all reproof should be a circumstantial knowledge of the fact you reprove.

2. Be sure that it is criminal or indiscreet, and that the person guilty is (or ought to be) sensible of it; for if you reprove him for what he is not guilty of, or what he is not sensible that there is any harm in, he will probably retort upon you the charge of censoriousness. If there is guilt and indiscretion in his conduct, and he is not sensible of it, your business then is to convince him of it, and how much injury he may do his character by inadvertently allowing those things as fit and innocent which are not so in him. And let your arguments in proof of the guilt be taken from the circumstances of the fact, the character and relation he bears in life, the opinions of wise and judicious men, the nature of

things, and the testimony of Scripture.

3. And then see that your reproofs are not too severe. By this I do not mean more severe than the offender would choose, but more severe than the nature and circumstances of the case require, or more severe than is necessary for the justification of your fidelity and the reformation of the sinner.

Too great severity towards tender minds does more harm than good. See Galatians 6:1: "Brethren, if a man be overtaken in a fault, ye which are spiritual, restore such a one in the spirit of meekness, considering thyself, lest thou also be tempted."

4. Take care lest, through fear of offending your brother, you do not offend God by a want of faithfulness. Proverbs 27:6: "Faithful are the wounds of a friend." It is the greatest piece of friendship you can do him, and if he is wise he will think it so, and more highly esteem you for it. Psalm 141:5: "Let the righteous smite me, it shall be a kindness."

5. Let your reproof appear to flow from your love for him, and be administered with the utmost tenderness and wisdom.

6. Last, do not leave your offending brother without proper directions for a better conduct.

The Difficulties a Minister must Expect to Meet With in the Execution of His Office, and His Proper Support and Encouragement under Them

Some of these may arise from your own natural temper, which may render you indisposed or unapt to some particular parts of the ministerial office. But the most difficult duties, by becoming a habit, become easy.

No small difficulty may arise from the resolution

and labor requisite to put some of the aforementioned rules into execution. But this difficulty will in like manner diminish as this course becomes habitual. In all other professions, those who follow them labor in them all the year long, and are hard at their business every day of the week. And shall ours only, which is the noblest of all others, make laboring in our business an objection against any part of our duty?

Another discouragement may arise from the seeming singularity of this character, and the general neglect which ministers of all denominations discover of the duties belonging to the sacred function. What you do out of conscience they may impute to affectation, which, instead of procuring their esteem, may create their envy. But it is a small matter to be condemned in the day when man judges you, since you will be acquitted on another day, when He who judges you will be the Lord (which is the proper import of 1 Corinthians 4:3–4).

Yet another difficulty comes from the little success you meet with, notwithstanding all your most earnest endeavors to promote the spiritual interest and eternal happiness of mankind. But your future acceptance and reward will not be in proportion to the success, but to the sincerity of your endeavors.

Your own weakness and infirmities, both of body and of mind, may throw fresh discouragements in your way. But these will be graciously allowed for; God requires of none more than they have received. If we have received but one talent, He does not expect so much from us as from those on whom He has bestowed ten.

The ministerial character itself may subject you to the contempt of some profane men. But if you adorn it by the useful, upright conduct already described, it is highly unlikely that you will secure their esteem and respect; if not, their continued contempt is your real honor.

Discouragement can also come from the different tempers, tastes, and dispositions of the people. But how you are to behave with regard to these has been shown before, and no small degree of prudence is required in this case.

In a word, every view of the nature, difficulty, and dignity of your office may furnish you with a proper motive and direction to a right behavior in it. No valuable end can be pursued without some obstruction, nor obtained without some difficulty. Your employment is truly honorable and important, and your encouragement, advantage, and assistance more than equal to the labor it requires. If you are found faithful, you shall not fail of a distinguished recompense from the bountiful hand of that good Master in whose service you are engaged. And a careful observation and practice of those rules of pastoral conduct will adorn your character, increase your honor, exalt your present joy, and enhance your future reward.

The Character and Duty of a Christian Preacher

by
Rev. David Bostwick

"For we preach not ourselves, but Christ Jesus
the Lord." 2 Corinthians 4:5

Were I to give a brief summary description of man's original apostasy in a few words, I would choose to say that it was a departing from God, the Author and Fountain of blessedness, and retiring into himself as his last and ultimate end. I would add that the sum of his moral depravity consists in a habitual disposition to treat himself in the same manner that he ought to treat the God of Heaven, that is, to love himself supremely, seek himself ultimately and finally, and set up himself in one shape or another as the grand center to which all the lines of his busy thoughts, anxious cares, and subtle projects bend, and in which they terminate.

While he continued in his original state of moral rectitude, that God who was the Author of his being was his beginning and end, his interest and motivation, his desire and delight, and, in a word, his all. But when sin took its place in his heart, it warped the unhappy creature from his God to himself, insomuch that self has now become all to corrupt and depraved nature, even as God was once all to uncorrupted and undepraved nature. Selfishness has therefore now become the most active and reigning principle in fallen nature, and, like the first wheel in a grand machine, sets the whole world in motion. For if we survey the conduct of busy mortals in the various ranks and degrees, characters and circumstances of life, we shall easily perceive that self is the idol they are naturally disposed to worship, and selfishness the grand interest to which they are by nature entirely devoted.

We find ourselves in the midst of an active, busy world, the inhabitants of which are ever engaged in some vigorous pursuits. But what are they pursuing? What is the governing principle of their action? And what is the center to which they bend, and in which they terminate? Are they laboring for God as their ultimate end, or for themselves? When the merchant compasses sea and land in search of a worldly treasure, does he do this for God or for himself? When the soldier boldly enters the field of battle, faces death in its most hideous forms, and opens his bosom to the most pregnant dangers, does he do this for the honor of God or for the honor of himself? When the industrious tradesman rises early and sits up late, eats the bread of carefulness and fills up his swift succeeding hours with the most painful and assiduous labor, does he labor ultimately for God or for himself? When men of superior rank and greater affluence devote their wasting moments to the fashionable diversions and pleasurable entertainments of life, do they do this to please and glorify God, or to please and gratify self? In a word, what is it in general that men live for, and what are they doing in the world? What are their thoughts spent, their words spoken, their hands employed, and their time used for? Is it for God or themselves? Alas, how easy it is to see the awful prevalence of this corrupt and accursed principle! It is self that rules kingdoms, governs families, drives their trades, and manages their worldly business; that chooses even their religion and influences their whole conduct; that lies at the root and bottom of all their actual sins, makes them ungodly, and keeps them ungodly, and is their very ungodliness itself.

And, oh, that it might be said with undoubted truth that, notwithstanding the general prevalence of this detestable principle among the various ranks and orders of men, there is at least one order exempted from the general charge, and that none who sustain the sacred character are influenced by mercenary principles or selfish motives, but that each individual could safely adopt the language of the apostle in behalf of himself and his brethren: "We preach not ourselves, but Christ Jesus the Lord."

In the preceding chapter to our text, the apostle had been magnifying his office on account of the excellency and glory of that gospel which was the subject of it. And in this chapter, he vindicates the ministry of the apostles and gospel ministers from the unjust accusations of false and Judaizing teachers who had charged them with walking in craftiness, and handling the Word of the Lord deceitfully. He avows their sincerity, that they have renounced the hidden things of dishonesty; and as a proof of their integrity he assures them that their business was to preach Christ and not themselves. "We preach not ourselves," says he, "and therefore are not a set of designing men, as our accusers would insinuate. Self is neither the matter nor the end of our preaching; we neither teach our own notions, passions, or prejudices as the Word of God, nor do we seek ourselves, or the advancement of our secular interest and glory. But we preach Christ Jesus the Lord, and endeavor to make Him known to the world in each of these amiable characters: as the Messiah, the Christ of God, as Jesus, the Savior of men, and as Lord and King in His church; and we seek to advance the interest of His glorious kingdom among men."

From these words, I shall attempt to show what that selfishness is which the apostle here disclaims, or when ministers may be said to preach themselves. I shall consider some of the operations of that selfish principle, in those particular instances that tend to manifest its reigning dominion. Third, I will show what it is to preach Christ Jesus the Lord. Last, I shall give some application of the whole.

Let us then inquire what that selfishness is which the apostle here disclaims. And to set this in a proper light and prevent mistakes, I must observe negatively that it is not that regular self-love that induces ministers to zeal and faithfulness in the discharge of their sacred trust, from the consideration of future rewards and punishments. There is a self-love implanted in human nature that is consistent with complete rectitude, and therefore is not the effect of our moral depravity. This Adam had in his state of perfect innocence, or else the promises of rewards would have been no inducement to obedience, nor would the severest threats have deterred him, in any measure, from disobedience. It is not, therefore, a criminal selfishness for ministers to have a suitable regard to their own future and everlasting interest, and to be influenced to diligence and industry in their great, important work by motives drawn from those future and eternal realities. It was doubtless agreeable to the God of heaven that Ezekiel the prophet should be influenced to faithfulness in giving warning from that awful consideration that the blood of those who perished would otherwise be required at his hand. And when the apostle urged Timothy to take heed to himself and his doctrine, and to continue in them, he would have him be influenced by the considerations that he should save himself and those who heard him. Nor was even St. Paul entirely above the influence of this motive when he gave this reason why he kept his body under subjection: lest when he had preached to others, he himself should be a castaway. It was not an unreasonable selfishness in the prophet Isaiah to take encouragement under all his complaints, and to be animated in his work, from the consideration that though Israel was not gathered, yet he should be glorious in the eyes of the Lord.

This disclaiming ourselves does not imply a total disregard to our reputation and character among men; for on this the success of our ministry, and consequently the advancement of the Redeemer's kingdom, may in some measure depend. If the character of a gospel minister is stained with false and ill-natured aspersions, this tends to mar his influence and, consequently, his usefulness. It is therefore in no way inconsistent with a gospel self-denial to seek a vindication of himself and his abused reputation. The apostle himself does so in this and his other epistles, and says no man shall stop him in this boasting. It ever becomes the ministers of Christ to have a tender regard to their reputation and character as subservient to the great ends of their ministry, and in which the honor of Christ and the interest of religion are nearly concerned. It be-

348   The Christian Pastor's Manual

comes a bishop to be blameless, and an officer in the church of God to be of good report; yea, and to maintain the authority of his sacred character, and to let no man despise him. Indeed, if our reputation among men of carnal, corrupt minds suffers for our faithfulness in the discharge of our sacred trust, and men speak all manner of evil against us falsely for Christ's sake (which is not at all uncommon), in this case our honor, interest, reputation, and even life itself are to be given up, and made a willing sacrifice to the honor and interest of Jesus Christ—not counting our own life (much less our name and reputation) dear, that we may finish our course and the ministry we have received of the Lord Jesus.

But the selfishness here disclaimed is that which stands in direct opposition to the honor of God and the interest of Jesus Christ. It sets up self in the room and place of God in our estimation, affections, intentions and pursuits, and disposes us to love and value ourselves in the same manner as we ought to love and value the God of heaven, to prefer our honor over His honor and our interest to the interest of Jesus Christ; in a word, to regard ourselves supremely, and seek ourselves ultimately and finally, and to be influenced inordinately, in one shape or another, by mercenary views and selfish motives, in all we do. It is therefore nothing less, on the whole, than a direct contending with the God of heaven, and maintaining a dispute with Him over who shall be most loved and regarded by us, Him or us, and whose honor and interest shall be primarily and ultimately pursued, His or our own.

But more particularly, this selfishness in public preaching may be considered both materially and formally, or as it respects the subject matter and the formal manner of our preaching.

First, then, ministers may be said to preach themselves when the matter of their public preaching is such that it tends rather to promote self-honor and self-interest than the honor of God and the interest of Jesus Christ; when the substance of their sermons is only the enticing words of man's wisdom, calculated rather to gratify men's curiosity with pleasing speculations than to pierce the heart with pungent convictions; when their preaching has a greater tendency to please men's fancies than to convert and save their souls; when in the matter of their preaching they conform to men's vitiated taste and corrupt humors, and rather soothe and flatter than strive to awaken and alarm their consciences, endeavoring rather to win them to themselves, and gain them over to their own self-interest, than to win them to Christ and convert them to God. In a word, we are awfully guilty of this criminal selfishness when our sermons have rather a tendency in their matter and composition to commend ourselves than to commend the Lord Jesus Christ, and to beget in the corrupt hearts of our hearers an esteem of our persons, gifts, and abilities rather than of the person, glory, and offices of the great Redeemer, the ever adorable God-man Jesus Christ.

Second, this selfishness respects the form as well as the matter of our preaching, that is, the governing principle from which we act in our public ministry, and the ultimate end we have in view. And this is doubtless the principal thing here intended; for let the matter of our preaching be ever so good, yet self may be the root and bottom of it all, and the object of our principal aim. Nothing is more evident than that we may do the work of God, and that which is really so, as to the matter or thing done, and yet not do it for God, as to the formal manner, but rather for ourselves. Thus Jehu did the work of the Lord when he executed the vengeance of Jehovah on the house and family of wicked Ahab, and when he broke down the images of Baal and restored Israel from idolatry; and yet he did it not for God, but for himself, as appears by his proud boast, "Come see my zeal for the Lord of hosts."

It is not at all inconsistent to say that ministers may calculate their sermons, as to matter, method, and manner of delivery, so as to have an aptitude and tendency to answer the great ends of preaching, and yet may preach themselves, as to the principle from which they act and the ultimate end they have in view. Nor is it at all to be wondered at, in a time when the most zealous, lively, and practical preaching and the most earnest addresses to the heart and conscience are in vogue, and tend most to recommend the preacher and promote his reputation, that mere selfish principles should induce men to attempt these, and even strive to excel therein. So that though we preach ever so well, as to the matter and method of our sermons, and with ever so much apparent zeal and fervor in the delivery of them, yet if we fail as to the formal manner, and aim chiefly and ultimately at ourselves—our honor, interest, and reputation—we are found guilty of that selfishness which the apostle disclaims; we are making idols of ourselves by treating ourselves in the manner in which we ought to treat the great God of heaven and earth. This is the selfishness here disclaimed, and this is what it means for men to preach themselves.

I will next consider some of the operations of this corrupt principle in those particular instances that tend to display its reigning dominion. In every unsanctified heart, self, in one shape or another, is ever uppermost and has an entire ascendancy and governing influence in everything they do. When, therefore, men of this character take upon them the office of the gospel ministry, self must be their grand motive and their principal inducement. For, though a faithful discharge of this important trust requires more self-denial than any employment under the sun, yet there are many things in the sacred office that may be alluring baits to men of corrupt and selfish minds. A tolerable maintenance or comfortable subsistence in the world may be an inducement to such as know not better how to provide for themselves—who, like the unjust steward, are unwilling to dig and ashamed to beg, and therefore choose this rather than a meaner employment. Thus, in the degenerate times of the church of old, men would crouch for a piece of silver, and say, "Put me, I pray thee, into the priest's office, that I may eat a piece of the bread." And hence that bitter complaint came that "the priests taught for hire, and the prophets divined for money." And on this account they were called greedy dogs that could never have enough, and shepherds that did not understand, looking every one for his gain from his quarter.

Let none understand me as though I insinuated that ministers have no right to insist on a sufficient maintenance and an honorable support; for whatever a carnal, selfish world may imagine, it will be found true at last that God (and not man) "hath ordained that they who preach the gospel should live of the gospel." Nor do I in the least doubt but that the too general neglect of this duty among people to their ministers is one of the crying and God-provoking sins of the present day (see Malachi 3:8–10). What I am proving is that self, in its reigning dominion, may influence men to undertake the sacred employment with such sordid views. And this is necessarily supposed in the apostle's frequent exhortations to ministers not to be greedy of filthy lucre, nor be given to filthy lucre, nor teach things for filthy lucre's sake. The inducement of the apostle himself (as of every other faithful minister) was vastly different: "A necessity is laid upon me, and woe is me if I preach not the gospel." And he could say with the utmost sincerity to the Corinthian church, "I seek not yours, but you."

Again, a life of study, and an opportunity to furnish the mind with the various improvements of human science, may be an inducement to those who have a turn for speculation, and who would be willing to shine and make some figure in literature, from mere selfish principles to undertake the ministry. And—would you believe it, sirs—the supposed ease and indolence of a minister's life, for those who know nothing of the many cares, fatigues, and perplexities of it, may possibly induce a selfish man, who is willing to favor the flesh, to enter upon it. Nor is it at all unlikely that the reverence and respect shown to the sacred character among men may influence those who are chiefly seeking themselves. 'Tis agreeable to a proud, selfish mortal to be looked upon and respected as the leader and guide of the people, and to have others dependent upon him and receiving the law from his mouth.

Now when such alluring baits as these are the prin-

cipal inducements to the ministry, the reigning dominion of a selfish principle is exceedingly evident.
And as these undertake the sacred employment for
themselves and not for God, so they will ever preach
themselves and not Christ Jesus the Lord. For the same
principle, while uppermost in their hearts, will tend to
govern them in every branch of their ministerial conduct. It will go with them into their private studies, and
there will choose their subject, form and methodize
their sermons, and oftentimes make them more attentive to mere words and ornaments than to the sacred
truths of God. And hence, instead of plain and serious
addresses that might tend to melt and change hard and
unchanged hearts, they will abound with trifling speculations, set off with glittering toys, with figures of
rhetoric and arts of elocution. Or, instead of instructing their people in the great things that concern their
everlasting welfare, they go beyond their capacity and
teach them nothing but what they are able to speak
unprofitably and unintelligibly. Self will often dispose
them to take off the edge and dull the life of their
teachings, under a pretense of filing off the roughness
and smoothing the diction. And if a plain and cutting
passage occurs, self will cast it away as too rustic and
ungrateful. Thus, in their preparations for public service, instead of consulting seriously, "What shall I say,
and how shall I say it, so as best to please and glorify
God, and do good to the souls of men?" self will make
them consult, "What shall I say, and how shall I deliver
it, so as to be thought an excellent preacher, and to be
admired and applauded by all who hear me?"

And when self has done its work in their study, and
made their sermon, it will attend them even to the pul-

pit, and there it will form their very countenance and gesture, modulate their voice, animate their delivery, and put the very accent and emphasis upon their words and syllables so that all may be calculated to please rather than profit, and to recommend themselves and secure a vain applause rather than recommend Jesus Christ and secure His interest in the hearts of men.

And when the sermon is ended, self goes home with the preacher and makes him much more solicitous to know whether he is admired and applauded than whether he has prevailed for the awakening and conversion of souls. And so powerful is this principle in some that they could even be glad in their heart (were it not for shame) to ask their hearers, in direct terms, whether they like, admire, and applaud their labors, and have a good opinion of them. But as this will not do, self will put them on some topic of conversation with their hearers that will tend, if possible, to draw out their own commendation; and if they can perceive that they are highly thought of, they rejoice greatly as having attained their end. But if they find they are esteemed as but weak (or at best but common) preachers, they are dejected and disappointed as having missed what they think is the grand prize of the day.

And hence this false, self-seeking heart can be very easy and contented with a general approbation and applause without seeing any saving fruit of ministerial labor from year to year. Or, if he desires success in the awakening and conversion of sinners, yet self may lie at the bottom of this too; and though it may work differently from the manner described above, yet it may terminate in the same thing in the end. Self may make such as these strive to excel in appearances of real godliness, and in zealous, fervent, practical preaching; yea, it may dispose them to desire success and to affect and change the hearts of their hearers, and they may calculate their discourses for that purpose and yet aim ultimately at themselves and the advancement of their own reputation. What can be more agreeable to a man who ultimately seeks himself than to see people throng around him, crowd in multitudes to hear him, and appear to be affected with what they hear? What is more pleasing to him than to find that he is able to command their attention and move their passions and affections, or to hear himself cried up by them as the most able and godly preacher in the land, and famed through the whole country as a man of the highest spiritual excellencies and most successful labors?

I do not mean to insinuate that men of such mercenary and corrupt principles are likely to be very successful, though it is possible that they may do good, and God may bless what means He pleases; yet it seems more probable that, as they labor not for God but for themselves, He will leave them to themselves for the success, that their labors will have no greater blessing than they themselves are able to give, and that their words, however pungent, will reach no farther than their own strength is able to make them. But what I have asserted is that self may make men desire success so far as it may tend to advance their reputation.

Sometimes this selfish disposition will work up envious and bitter thoughts against all those who they imagine stand in their light or, by outshining them, eclipse their glory and hinder the progress of their idolized reputation. Hence they are inwardly vexed and mortified when a preference is given to the names and parts of their brethren, as if all the praise given to others was injuriously taken from them, and that they themselves were not so particularly noticed, respected, and esteemed as their partial, selfish judgment imagines they ought to be. And this often lays a foundation for jealousy, suspicion, and alienation, as if they were carrying on two different and contrary interests. It is this also that makes some so tenacious of their own opinions that they almost claim infallibility, and are ever impatient of contradiction or control. They esteem and value the man who will say as they say, be of their opinion, and promote their reputation; but he who will dare to differ from or contradict them is not to be borne with. O sirs, it is impossible to trace out all the corrupt workings of this detestable and pernicious principle, or to mention the innumerable mischiefs it has occasioned in the church of God. It was this that raised antichrist, by several gradual and progressive steps, to his present tyrannical dignity. It was this that kindled the flames of persecution in the several periods of the Christian church, and stained the earth with the crimson gore of human blood; and it is this that disturbs and rends Christian societies, divides them into different interests and different parties, and fills them with bitterness against one another. Oh, may the Lord in mercy deliver us from ourselves as our worst enemy, and from the power and dominion of selfishness as the sorest plague that can befall us on this side of hell!

But I have dwelt too long on this disagreeable subject, and shall therefore pass to the third general heading, what it is to preach Christ. "We preach not ourselves, but Christ Jesus the Lord." And this also must be considered both materially and formally, or as it respects the subject matter and the formal manner of our preaching.

As it respects the matter. It includes in general the whole sum of the gospel doctrine relating to man's salvation by Jesus Christ: the original contrivance, meritorious impetration, and actual application of it, through His blood and spirit; the fall of man by one man's disobedience, and the guilt and ruin of a fallen state necessarily supposed; the original purposes of God's love and grace that issued in the gift of His dear Son; the glory of His person as God, the eternal relation He sustained to the Father, His substitution as a Surety and designation to the office of Mediator, and His voluntary contract in the covenant of redemption, which made way for His mysterious incarnation; His holy life, His meritorious and cruel death, His powerful resurrection, triumphant ascension, and perpetual, prevailing intercession; the complete atonement He made, and the everlasting righteousness He has brought in, together with the various offices He sustained in both His state of humiliation and His exaltation. It includes the methods of divine operation in the work of effectual calling; the nature and use of divine faith to apply His blood and righteousness; and the blessings consequent on believing, justification, adoption, sanctification, perseverance in grace, consummation in glory, perfection of holiness at death, and the complete happiness of soul and body at the resurrection in the full enjoyment of God to all eternity. These and all other gospel truths supposed by them, included in them, and consequent upon them, relating to Jesus Christ, are to be the subject matter of our preaching. All of these are summarily comprehended in the three characteristics mentioned in the text: "Christ Jesus the Lord"—Christ the Messiah, the anointed of God, qualified for, and set apart for, the office of Mediator; Jesus the Savior of men, who saves His people from their sins, from both the guilt and power and, finally, from the punishment of them by working out for them a righteousness to be imputed; and, by working in them a righteousness implanted, the Lord, the great Head and King of His church, who has its government on His shoulders, to whom all power is given in heaven and upon earth, to whom all homage and obedience are due, and to whom is committed, as a Person in every way qualified and worthy, the sole management of the solemn transactions of the grand and final judgment.

But, particularly, to preach Christ is to hold Him forth not merely as a Lawgiver to be obeyed, but chiefly as a Law-fulfiller, to be believed in for pardon, righteousness, and everlasting life. It is to represent Him to poor, perishing sinners as a Surety who has undertaken in their place to pay the debt of duty and of penalty, for which divine justice has them under arrest. He has atoned for the crimes for which they are under sentence, and worked out for them a complete and perfect righteousness, answerable to the strict demands of His unchangeable law. However honorably we may speak of Christ Jesus as a Ruler to be obeyed and as a Pattern to be imitated, yet if we do not exhibit Him to view as the great Law-fulfiller to be believed in, and as the end of the law for righteousness, we do not properly preach Christ, but conceal a most essential branch of His mediatorial excellency. It is the grand, fundamental article of the religion of Christ, and the ground of all our hopes, that He suffered for us, the just for the unjust,

that He might bring us to God; that He not only died
for our good (as the Socinians say, to set us an example
how to suffer with patience), but that He died in our
place and stead, and was made sin for us by imputation,
that we by imputation might be made righteous in the
sight of God through Him.

To preach Christ is to exhibit to view His infinite,
divine fullness and the freeness of His unbounded
grace, His almighty power to save, and His willingness
to exert that power. It is to declare that in Him is to be
found all that righteousness which the law requires,
and all that grace which the gospel promises—in short,
everything that a poor, guilty, helpless, sin-burdened,
and law-condemned sinner can possibly want—and
that all the blessings of His atonement are freely offered without money and without price.

To preach Christ is to make Him the grand center
of all the variety of subjects we enter upon, in the whole
credenda and agenda of religion. If we treat the nature
and perfections of the Deity, we are to consider them as
displayed most eminently in the face of Jesus Christ. If
we exhibit to view the divine law, and its strictness and
spirituality, we are to remember Christ as the end of the
law for righteousness. If we pronounce its dreadful
curses against everyone who "continues not in all
things written in the book of the law to do them," it is
so that the law, as a schoolmaster, may bring them to
Christ, so that they may be justified by faith. If we speak
of gospel promises and gospel blessings, we must consider them as purchased by the blood, and distributed
by the bounty and grace, of Christ. If we discourse upon
divine faith, Christ must be considered as the Author
and Finisher, as well as the direct object of it. If we

speak of repentance, it is Christ exalted at the right
hand of God who must give it and the remission of
sins, and it is Christ crucified, and viewed by faith, who
must be the first spring of it. If we treat gospel obedience, it must be considered as the genuine fruit of faith
in Christ and union with Him, springing from constraining love for, and performed by strength and grace
derived from, the Lord Jesus Christ, and accepted altogether on account of the merit of His obedience and
death. In a word, Christ must be considered as all and
in all, as the Alpha and Omega, the beginning and the
end, the Fountain from which all is derived and the
center in which all must terminate. His righteousness
is all in justification, His spirit and grace all in sanctification, and the enjoyment of Him all in glorification.
This is to preach Christ as to the matter of our preaching.

As it respects the manner. The formal manner implies
that we aim at the honor and glory of Christ, and the
advancement of His interest, as our ultimate and final
end. This is doubtless the principal thing intended, in
opposition to those mercenary views and selfish aims
that were mentioned before. Men may speak much
about Jesus Christ in their sermons and yet not properly preach Christ; yea, they may preach Christ too as to
the matter of their preaching in all the instances described above, and yet not do it for Christ, but for themselves. And thus they make Christ Himself, and the precious doctrines of the gospel, only subservient to the
advancement of the grand idol, self. To preach Christ,
then, is to make His honor and interest the center of
all our labor and industry, the mark on which we fix
our eye and towards which we endeavor to steer, in all

our private studies and public administrations and in every instance of our ministerial conduct. Our business is to commend Christ and not ourselves; to win the hearts of men to Him and not to ourselves; and to attach them to His interests rather than our own.

And as this must be the ultimate, proposed end, so those means must be chosen that have the most natural tendency to accomplish it, even such methods and manner of address as will tend to pierce the obdurate hearts and wound the stupid consciences of sleepy, secure sinners, by making them feel the ruin of their fallen state, their guilt and condemnation by the law, and the absolute impossibility of obtaining a personal, legal righteousness, so that they may effectually see their need of Christ, both as a Surety to pay their law-debt and as a Fountain to wash from sin and from uncleanness.

The rich and unbounded treasures of gospel grace are also to be laid open, and gospel invitations to be exhibited in their free and definite terms, urged with the most powerful motives and persuasive arguments that can be drawn from love, from wrath, from heaven, or from hell, and from all the glorious and dreadful things of an unseen, eternal world.

Let me now endeavor to apply this subject by an inference or two from each of the principal foregoing headings, and then conclude with a particular application.

First, if ministers are not to preach or to seek themselves in the execution of the sacred office, then none can ever discharge this important trust acceptably in the sight of God who are under the reigning dominion of mercenary and selfish principles. I have observed before that, when man fell from God by original apostasy, he retired, as it were, into himself, and is ever since disposed supremely to love, and ultimately to seek himself as his last and final end. Selfishness, then, in one shape or another, is now the reigning, active principle in fallen nature, and has the entire dominion in every heart that is unrenewed and unsanctified. Therefore, since unsanctified men have no governing principle but self, and can act from no higher principles than they have, how can they be qualified for a faithful discharge of that work which requires so much self-renunciation? If such as these undertake the ministry, their views must be altogether selfish; they study, pray, and preach for themselves, and make themselves the grand center of all they think, speak, and do! They seek their own things and not the things of Christ Jesus; they prefer their honor to His honor, and their interest to His interest; and, therefore, they are guilty of idolatry by setting themselves uppermost in their estimation, affections, designs, and pursuits. And if I should grant that such as these may be useful in the ministry, yet surely the undertaking will be hazardous to the souls committed to their charge, and the consequence extremely dreadful to themselves, for when they have preached to others, they themselves will be finally rejected and cast away.

Second, if the business of gospel ministers is to preach Christ, hence see the honor and dignity of their office. No other than a glorious Christ, the anointed of God, the darling of heaven, and the beloved of angels and saints, is the subject of their ministry; from Him their authority and commission are derived; in His valuable interest they are engaged to speak, as ambassadors in His name and stead. Their office is, therefore, honorable in some proportion to the dignity of the Sovereign from whom they receive commission, the grandeur of the court in whose interest they are employed as ambassadors, and the important errand they have to transact with guilty men. And as they are engaged for Christ, and employed by Him to act as ambassadors in His name, He has declared that He will regard the treatment they meet with as if done to Himself: "He that receiveth you, receiveth Me; and he that despiseth you, despiseth Me, and Him that sent Me." Were we acting a part for ourselves, speaking in our own name, and driving on our own self-interest, men might treat us as they pleased; but if we act as ambassadors for Christ, in pursuit of His interest, and in His name and stead, let them take heed how they despise the sacred character we sustain or neglect the solemn messages we bring. But I must not dwell on these inferences for too long.

Permit me, therefore, now, with all humility, to address myself particularly to the venerable members of this synod, with all others of the sacred character here present. My reverend fathers and dear brethren! The subject I have now been handling will necessarily lead me to great freedom and plainness of speech, yet I will not entertain so dishonorable a thought of any of you as to imagine an apology to be necessary. Nor will I doubt your candid acceptance of what shall now be said, though by one of the meanest of the sacred character, who would gladly sit at your feet and learn, and who is willing to stand corrected and reproved by you.

Let what we have heard lead us into our own hearts, to examine in the presence of an all-seeing God whether we have too much of this abominable, selfish principle still lurking within us, and too little singleness of heart for God and Jesus Christ. Do we never shrink into the diffidence of neglect in cases of duty, through the power and prevalence of that soothing temptation, "Spare thyself"? Do we never find this detestable enemy striving to encroach on the rights of the Godhead, and to assume the honor and regard that are due to Jesus alone? Does it never creep into our studies, and seek to have a hand in our preparations for the sanctuary of the Lord, and dispose us to consult how to please rather than how to profit, and how our own interest may be secured in the esteem and affections of our hearers rather than how the interest and kingdom of Christ may be advanced? And when we enter the sacred desk, with a message from heaven for guilty men, are we never too thoughtful of the notices and observations of our poor fellow mortals round about us, too little sensible of the all-seeing eye of Jehovah upon us and the vast and inexpressible weight of the errand on which we come? Are we never too solicitous about mere external appearances that attend our delivery, and too little so about the spiritual frame of our hearts in the sight of God? Are we never tempted by this pernicious principle to play the hypocrite before our hearers, with a greater show of zeal, fervor, and devotion than is answerable to the inward state and frame of our minds?

If at any time we find ourselves dead and barren, and have but little clearness or freedom, we are dejected; our hearts are depressed and sunk within us—but from whence is this dejection? Is it because we have done so poorly for God, and been so miserably deficient in His service? Or is it only because we have made so indifferent a figure in the eyes of our fellow men? On the other hand, when we find some enlargement and freedom, a readiness of thought and fluency of expression, and feel some suitable degree of zeal and fervor, does a selfish, deceitful heart never prompt us to a sort of self-complacency and delight in ourselves? And if we are pleased that God has enabled us, in any measure, to be faithful, yet are we never too elated with the approbation and applause of those who have heard us?

And when our public performances are ended, what is the object of our greatest solicitude? Whether sinners are awakened and won to Christ, or whether we ourselves are held in high esteem? Whether the Word preached has gained their hearts for God, or whether it has gained for us their pleasing approbation? And does this selfish principle never direct or influence our conduct among the people of our charge? Are we not often best pleased with the company and society of those (perhaps too partial in our favor) who may gratify our vanity with their professions and tokens of esteem and friendship? And do we not, from the same principle, shun or too much neglect those who appear less friendly, though they need our instruction and advice as much as others? Do we not too much neglect the duties of private and particular applications for fear of offending, and yet frame excuses for our neglects that have too much selfishness in them?

In a word, what did we undertake the ministry for? What do we study, preach, pray, live, and labor for? Is it ultimately for God or for ourselves? I beseech you, reverend and dear sirs, bear with this plainness and freedom, and let me not be looked upon in the light of an arrogant accuser. Far be it from me to lay any of these things to your charge, or to harbor a doubt of your disinterested zeal for God and your victory over self. There is but one heart among us, that I have reason to suspect, and over that I find it necessary to keep a continual watch and guard. And, oh, how many are the secret windings and turnings, and different shapes and appearances, of this pernicious adversary, self! How often does it beset us, when and where we have little expected it, and given us occasion to lament and say, "Hast thou found me, O mine enemy?"

If we find, then, on the above-mentioned inquiry, that our self-denial and deadness to ourselves are yet very imperfect, let us bitterly bewail it before God with the deepest humiliation. For what can be more detestable, or carry a greater malignity in its very nature, than that disposition that would exalt self in the place of God and Jesus Christ, and, as it were, contend with Him for the preference, and dispute the point with Him, who shall be most loved and regarded by us, He or we; and whose honor and interest shall be primarily pursued, His or our own? And how inconsistent is this selfishness with that lesson of self-denial that we are obliged to preach to others, and which Jesus has taught us, both by precept and by example. Nay, with what force can we recommend self-denial to others while we are selfish, or how can we reprove or condemn the sin in others that we harbor too much in ourselves? We tell the drunkard, the swearer, the profane sinner that, unless he is converted and changed, he cannot be saved; and is it not as true of us that we cannot be the true disciples or faithful ministers of Christ unless we deny ourselves? Does not our Lord Himself lay this down as the grand criterion by which He submits His own doctrine and mission to trial, whether it was of God or whether He spoke of Himself? "He that speaketh of himself seeketh his own glory; but he that seeketh the glory of him that sent him, the same is true."

I make no doubt, sirs, but that selfishness in its reigning dominion is a greater sin than drunkenness or whoredom. The one dishonors God by breaking His law, but the other strikes at the very relation of sovereign and subject, contends with Him, as it were, for the rights of the Godhead, and insists upon being above Him in the estimation, affections, intentions, and pursuits. Now, it is one thing to break some particular laws of a prince, and another to set up to be above him, or to exalt a rival in his place and stead. The first indeed is transgression, but the other is downright treason and rebellion, and therefore the most heinous. And, indeed, whatever we do in religion, and however good it is as to the matter or thing done, yet if self is the reigning principle, it tarnishes, corrupts, and debases all. And as it is the very essence of holiness to live to God and to act entirely for Him, so it is horrible wickedness, in the very nature of it, to live for ourselves and act ultimately for ourselves. If, therefore, we find the remains or secret workings of so corrupt and detestable a principle, let us mourn and be humbled before God, and repair by faith to Him who once died, "that they which live should not live to themselves, but to Him who died for them, and rose again."

Let us ever be watchful against this enemy of God and our souls, and endeavor to suppress the first risings of it. Let us ever remember that we are not our own, and therefore have no business to live for ourselves, or regard our interest or reputation, any further than the

honor of Christ and the interest of religion are concerned. If God has made us, if Christ has redeemed us,
if in our ordination vows we have solemnly given up
ourselves and our all to Him, then certainly we are not
our own; and therefore to appropriate our time and talents to our own interest and reputation is a sacrilegious
robbing of God.

Further, let us guard against that fear of man that
selfishness would prompt us to, and which would make
us too fond to please, and too fearful to displease; for if
we thus seek to please men, and by that means to advance ourselves, we cannot be the faithful servants of
Jesus Christ. And yet such are the perverse tempers of
many we have to deal with that we are often reduced to
an unhappy dilemma, and must either offend God or
offend them. Poor, guilty mortals love to be soothed
and flattered, but do not love to be plainly dealt with.
Hence, such pointed addresses as tend to discover them
to themselves often excite their resentment. Thus,
when our Lord was representing to His hearers, by several parables, the awful destruction that would shortly
come upon the final rejecters of the gospel Savior and
the gospel salvation, it is said, "the chief priests and
Pharisees perceived that He spake of them." A heinous
business indeed, as if it were intolerable insolence for
Him to speak of them! It is true, they perceived rightly,
He did speak of them, and of all others like them. And
what then? Why, they were exasperated, and would have
laid hands on Him, and treated Him in a manner they
thought He deserved, had it not been that they feared
the multitude. And when this is the case, that we must
offend either God or men, whose displeasure shall we
most regard? If carnal self is consulted, it will influence

us to displease God, and to soothe and flatter our fellow men. But, alas, should we make such an awful sacrifice to their corrupt humors, will they undertake to answer it for us? Will they defend us from the displeasure of Jehovah when He shall send for us by death, or sentence us to hell by His righteous judgment? No, they dare not attempt this, nor dare we trust them in this matter. We have one God and one Master to please, and He must be obeyed whether men like or dislike it. Our errand to them is on matters of life and death, the vast importance of which must engage all the powers of our souls. Poor, Christless sinners are not in a state to be soothed and flattered, or jested and trifled with. Heaven and hell are not matters to be trifled with. Heaven and hell are not matters to be talked of in a careless, indolent strain. It is plain dealing that such want, however they may take it—such as will tend to make them feel their wretched, miserable state, and awaken their solicitude for deliverance.

Again, our business is to preach Christ Jesus the Lord, and to exhibit Him to view in His personal glory and divine fullness as the Law-fulfiller and Savior of sinners; to urge them compassionately to come to Him that they might have life, and, on their final refusal, to pronounce against them the terrors of eternal death. And besides the inexpressible importance of these things, every consideration from the present providences of God suggests an awakening call to the utmost diligence and most painful industry. The God of heaven is now thundering an alarm on every side; our country is groaning under ravages and devastations, and all the frightful calamities of war and blood! The enemies of Zion are forming a confederacy, saying,

"Let us raze it, let us raze it to the foundation." And who can tell how soon our churches may be demolished and beaten into rubbish, and we ourselves called to prison and to death. And what in the name of God shall we do in a day of suffering if we have not learned to deny ourselves and account our honor, interest, and even life itself to be nothing in comparison to the interest and kingdom of Jesus? Or should God in mercy yet spare His church from the ravages of popish and pagan adversaries, yet, as for us, we know our time is short, and the night of death will soon come when no man can work. We live in a dying world and dwell in regions of mortality, and have lately had frequent and awful notices of the uncertain tenure of human life.

The last year in particular, with respect to ministers, may very properly be called the dying year, in which the God of heaven has smitten His church in these parts with repeated strokes of sore bereavement in a close and awful succession! Scarcely had we time to dry our weeping eyes for the loss of one of eminent character and usefulness [The Reverend Mr. Aaron Burr, President of the College of New Jersey]. but the streams of grief were called to flow down afresh for the loss of another [The Reverend Mr. James Davenport, Minister at Hopewell, NJ.], whose zeal for God and the conversion of souls was scarcely to be paralleled. And yet, for all this, the anger of Jehovah was not turned away, but His hand was soon lifted up again, and with a dreadful aim and resistless stroke has brought down to the dust perhaps the greatest pillar in this part of Zion's buildings.* Oh, how does the whole fabric shake and totter!

---

* The Rev. Jonathan Edwards, President of the College of New Jersey, of whom the Rev. Gilbert Tennant of Philadelphia wrote:

"On Wednesday the 22nd instant, departed this life the reverend and worthy Mr. Jonathan Edwards (formerly of Northampton, in New England, but lately of Stockbridge), president of the College of New Jersey; a person of great eminence both in respect of capacity, learning, piety, and usefulness; a good scholar, and a great divine. As his genius was extraordinary, so it was greatly improved by long and hard study, by which he treasured up much useful knowledge, both divine and human, and was thus uncommonly prepared for the arduous and important province to which he was called. Divinity was his favorite study, in the knowledge of which he had but few if any equals, and no superior in these provinces. The humility, gravity, and modesty of his behavior rendered him amiable to all who feared God, who had the pleasure and privilege of his acquaintance. But nothing appeared with greater luster, and with more striking charms in his conduct, than his candor to man and his fidelity to his God. These virtues are very rare in this degenerate age, wherein piety, integrity, and bravery are ready to breathe their last—an age wherein "All flesh have corrupted their way" and there is none (or almost none) upright among men. This man of God was favored with an unshaken firmness in the cause of his great Master, nor would his noble soul stoop to vulgar prejudices, or meanly blend with the crowd. His judicious and magnanimous defense of the principles of the Christian reformed religion, against the plausible pretexts and cavils of Arminians, in a late volume upon the liberty of the human will—a volume in which their cause is with great force of argument entirely baffled—is thought by some professors of divinity in Europe, and by divers divines here, to exceed anything that has been written on the subject; and his excellent writings in behalf of the power of piety (which some time since happily spread in this sinful land) deserve esteem, and make his memory blossom in the dust. Others of his writings, likewise, deserve to be mentioned with honor; it is as a comfort to us, in the midst of grief, that this ascending Elijah has left behind him the mantle of so many valuable

And what a gloomy aspect do these providences wear, as

---

volumes, by which, though dead, he speaks with wisdom and warmth, in favor of truth and holiness; hereby, though without design, he has erected to his memory a bust, not only preferable to fulsome funeral panegyrics, but even to the most durable monumental marble.

As this wise and faithful servant of Christ glorified his blessed Master, with uprightness and intrepidity of heart, by a conversation becoming his gospel; so it pleased God to put great honor upon him, living and dying, by crowning his honest and unwearied labors with surprising success in the conversion of many, and by giving him great calm in his soul at the time of his exit. When eternity drew near, he with undisturbed composure desired his daughter to request her mother and his wife not to indulge excessive grief on the occasion of his departure from her, but to consider that the spiritual relation between them would not be dissolved by death, and that he hoped to see her again; and likewise that she should tell the other children that he requested them to observe the instructions he had from time to time given them, and that if they did so good would come to them. After he had spoken to the above purpose, he looked about, and said, "Where is Jesus of Nazareth, my true and never failing Friend?" and so he fell asleep, and went to the Lord he loved and left a bereaved society to sit in the dust, and mourn the unspeakable, (yea, in some respects) the irreparable loss of so wise, experienced, and faithful a head; and that in a time of great necessity, general calamity, great and growing danger to the church and state. Oh! when a holy God takes away such righteous persons, such invaluable jewels, in thick succession from our guilty land and nation to His own bosom, His own cabinet—and that in the beginning of a dark gathering tempest, big with the fate of nations—is it not an awful omen? May we not, with some variation, lament the death of this excellent man, in the language of David over Saul and Jonathan, O Princeton, the 'beauty of Israel is slain upon thy high places'? Or, as it was once said over brave Abner, 'Know ye not this day that a great man is fallen in Israel?' Or, in the pensive strains of Elisha over a departed Elijah, 'My father, my father, the chariot of Israel, and the horsemen thereof?' "

if God, by calling home His ambassadors, was about to quit the affair of negotiating peace with mankind any more!

Shall not we then who survive double and redouble our diligence, knowing that our time is short, and that in proportion to the decrease of laborers, the work increases upon our hands? O sirs, are heaven and hell glorious and dreadful realities? Are sinners despising the one and sleeping over the mouth of the other, and are we sent from God to awaken them and show them their danger? Are we sent to offer them a Savior and invite them to flee from the wrath to come to His atoning blood? Why, then, oh, why do these important realities not swallow up our whole attention? Why do we not make more haste in plucking sinners as brands from everlasting burning? Why do we not pray more fervently, preach more zealously, and lay out our whole life, soul and strength in this great work? What! Are the interest and happiness of deathless, immortal souls worth no more pains? Can we do no more for the honor and interest of our glorious Master than this comes to? Shall the men of this world be more painful and industrious in seeking themselves than we are in seeking the glory of Christ and the salvation of souls? God forbid! We are on matters of life and death; we pray, preach, and labor for eternity. Surely it becomes us then to do it with all our might. Shall we not be solemn and serious when we are so near that state and place where all are serious? Believe it, sirs, there is no trifling in the eternal world; there are none in jest in either heaven or hell. God forbid, then, that we should jest and trifle with immortal souls who are just at the door and upon the borders of an eternal state!

A Letter on the Propriety of a Ministerial Address to the Unconverted

by
Rev. John Newton

Sir,

In a late conversation, you desired my thoughts concerning a scriptural and consistent manner of addressing the consciences of unawakened sinners in the course of your ministry. It is a point on which many eminent ministers have been and are not a little divided; and it therefore becomes me to propose my sentiments with modesty and caution, so far as I am constrained to differ from any from whom in general I would be glad to learn.

Some think that it is sufficient to preach the great truths of the Word of God in their hearing; to set forth the utterly ruined and helpless state of fallen man by nature, and the appointed method of salvation by grace through faith in the Lord Jesus Christ; and then to leave the application entirely to the agency of the Holy Spirit, who alone can enlighten the dark understandings of sinners and enable them to receive, in a due manner, the doctrines of either the law or the gospel. And they apprehend that all exhortations, arguments, and motives addressed to those who are supposed to be still under the influence of the carnal mind are inconsistent with the principles of free grace and the acknowledged inability of such persons to perform any spiritual acts; they therefore believe that the preachers who, avowing the doctrines of free grace, do, notwithstanding, plead and expostulate with sinners usually contradict themselves, and retract in their application what they had labored to establish in the course of their sermons.

There are others who, though they would be extremely unwilling to derogate from the free grace and sovereign power of God in the great work of conversion, or in the least degree to encourage the mistaken notion which every unconverted person has of his own power, yet think it their duty to deal with sinners as rational and moral agents, and as such, besides declaring the counsel of God in a doctrinal way, to warn them by the terrors of the Lord, and to beseech them by His tender mercies, that they receive not the grace of God in a preached gospel in vain. Nor can it be denied but that some of them, when deeply affected with the worth of souls and the awful importance of eternal things, have sometimes, in the warmth of their hearts, dropped unguarded expressions, and such as have been justly liable to objection.

If we were to decide to which of these different methods of preaching the preference is due by the discernible effects of each, it will perhaps appear in fact, without making any invidious comparisons, that those ministers whom the Lord has honored with the greatest success in awakening and converting sinners have generally been led to adopt the more popular way of exhortation or address, while they who have been studiously careful to avoid any direct application to sinners as unnecessary and improper, if they have not been altogether without seals to their ministry, yet have seen their labors bear fruit more in building up those who have already received the knowledge of the truth than in adding to their number. Now as "he that winneth souls is wise," and as every faithful laborer has a warm desire to be instrumental in raising the dead in sin to a life of righteousness, this seems at least a presumptive argument in favor of those who, besides stating the doctrines of the gospel, endeavor, by earnest persuasions and expostulations, to impress them upon the hearts of their hearers, and entreat and warn them to consider how they shall escape if they neglect so great a salvation. For it is not easy to conceive that the Lord should most signally bear testimony in favor of that mode of preaching which is least consistent with the truth, and with itself.

But not to insist on this, nor to rest the cause on the authority or examples of men, the best of whom are imperfect and fallible, let us consult the Scriptures which, as they furnish us with the whole subject matter of our ministry, so also afford us perfect precepts and patterns for its due and orderly dispensation. With respect to the subject of our inquiry, the examples of our Lord Jesus Christ, and of His authorized ministers, the apostles, are both our rule and our warrant. The Lord Jesus was the great preacher of free grace, "who spake as never man spake." And His ministry, while it provided relief for the weary and heavy laden, was eminently designed to stain the pride of all human glory. He knew what was in man, and declared that none could come unto Him unless drawn and taught of God (John 6:44–46). And yet He often speaks to sinners in terms which, if they were not known to be His, might perhaps be censured as inconsistent and legal (see John 6:27; Luke 13:24–27; John 12:35). It appears from both the context and the tenor of these passages that they were immediately spoken not to His disciples, but to the multitude. The apostles copied from their Lord; they taught that we have no sufficiency of ourselves even to think a good thought, and that "it is not of him that willeth, or of him that runneth, but of God who showeth mercy." Yet they plainly call upon sinners (and that before they had given evident signs that they were pricked to the heart, as in Acts 2:37) to repent, and turn from their vanities to the living God (Acts 3:19; 14:15; 17:30). Peter's advice to Simon Magus is very full and express to this point; for though he perceived him to be in the very gall of bitterness, and in the bond of iniquity, he exhorted him to repent, and to pray, if perhaps the thought of his heart might be forgiven. It may be presumed that we cannot have stronger evidence that any of our hearers are in a carnal and unconverted state than Peter had in the case of Simon Magus; and therefore there seems no sufficient reason why we should hesitate to follow the apostle's example.

You have been told that repentance and faith are spiritual acts, for the performance of which a principle of spiritual life is absolutely necessary, and that therefore to exhort an unregenerate sinner to repent or believe must be as vain and fruitless as to call a dead person out of his grave. To this it may be answered that we might cheerfully and confidently undertake even to call the dead out of their graves if we had the command and promise of God to warrant the attempt; for then we might expect that His power would accompany our words. The vision of Ezekiel (chapter 37) may be fitly

accommodated to illustrate both the difficulties and
the encouragement of a gospel minister. The deplorable state of our hearers may often remind us of the
Lord's question to the prophet, "Can these dry bones
live?" Our resource, like that of of the prophet, is entirely in the sovereignty, grace, and power of the Lord.
"O Lord, Thou knowest, impossible as it is to us, it is
easy for Thee to raise them unto life; therefore we renounce our own reasonings; and though we see that
they are dead, we call upon them at Thy bidding, as if
they were alive, and say, 'O ye dry bones, hear the Word
of the Lord!' The means is our part, the work is Thine,
and to Thee be all the praise." The dry bones could not
hear the prophet, but while he spoke, the Lord caused
breath to enter into them and they lived. But the word
was spoken to them when they were considered dry and
dead.

It is true, the Lord can, and I hope He often does,
make that preaching effectual to the conversion of
sinners wherein little is said expressly to them, and
where only the truths of the gospel are declared in
their hearing; but He who knows the frame of the human heart has provided us with a variety of the topics
that have a moral suitableness to engage the faculties,
affections, and consciences of sinners—so far at least
as to leave them condemned if they persist in their sins,
and by which He often effects the purpose of His grace,
though none of the means of grace by which He ordinarily works can produce a real change in the heart unless they are accompanied with the efficacious power of
His Spirit.

Should we admit that an unconverted person is not
a proper subject of ministerial exhortation, because he

has no power in himself to comply, the just consequence of this position would perhaps extend too far,
even to prove the impropriety of all exhortation universally. For when we invite the weary and heavy laden to
come to Jesus so that they might find rest; when we call
upon backsliders to remember from whence they are
fallen, to repent and to do their first works; yea, when
we exhort believers to walk worthy of God, who has
called them to His kingdom and glory, in each of these
cases we press them to acts for which they have no in-
herent power of their own. And unless the Lord, the
Spirit, is pleased to apply the Word to their hearts, we
do but speak into the air, and our endeavors can have
no more effect in these instances than if we were to say
to a dead body, "Arise and walk." For an exertion of divine power is no less necessary to the healing of a
wounded conscience than to the breaking of a hard
heart, and only He who has begun the good work of
grace is able either to revive or to maintain it.

Though sinners are destitute of spiritual life, they
are not therefore mere machines. They have a power to
do many things which they may be called upon to exert.
They are capable of considering their ways; they know
they are mortal; and the bulk of them are persuaded in
their consciences that after death there is an appointed
judgement. They are not under an inevitable necessity
of living in known and gross sins; that they do so is not
for want of power, but for want of will. The most profane swearer can refrain from his oaths while in the
presence of a person whom he fears, and to whom he
knows it would be displeasing. Let a drunkard see poison put into his liquor, and it may stand by him un-
tasted from morning to night. And many would be

deterred from sins to which they are greatly addicted by
the presence of a child, though they have no fear of
God before their eyes. They have a power likewise of attending upon the means of grace; and though the Lord
alone can give them true faith and evangelical repentance, there seems no impropriety to invite them, upon
the ground of the gospel promises, to seek Him who is
exalted to bestow these blessings, and who is able to do
that for them which they cannot do for themselves.
And He has said, "Him that cometh unto Me, I will in
no wise cast out." Perhaps it will not be easily proved
that entreaties, arguments, and warnings formed upon
these general principles, which are in the main agreeable and adequate to the remaining light of natural
conscience, are at all inconsistent with those doctrines
that ascribe the whole of a sinner's salvation, from first
to last, to the free, sovereign grace of God.

We should undoubtedly endeavor to maintain a
consistency in our preaching; but unless we keep the
plan and manner of the Scriptures constantly in view,
and attend to every part of it, a desire for consistency
may fetter our sentiments and greatly preclude our usefulness. We need not wish to be more consistent than
the inspired writers, nor be afraid of speaking as they
have spoken before us. We may easily perplex ourselves
and our hearers by nice reasonings on the nature of
human liberty and the divine agency on the hearts of
men; but such disquisitions are better avoided. We
shall, perhaps, never have full satisfaction on these subjects till we arrive in the world of light. In the meantime, the path of duty, the good old way, lies plain before us. If when you are in the pulpit the Lord favors
you with a lively sense of the greatness of the trust and

the worth of souls committed to your charge, and fills your heart with His constraining love, many little curious distinctions which amuse you at other times will be forgotten. Your soul will go forth with your words, and, while your bowels yearn over poor sinners, you will not hesitate for a moment whether you ought to warn them of their danger or not. That great champion of free grace, Dr. [John] Owen, has a very solemn address to sinners, the running title to which is "Exhortations unto Believing Forgiveness." It is in his *Exposition of the 130th Psalm*, which I recommend to your attentive consideration [*The Works of John Owen,* Banner of Truth Edition, Volume 6, pages 515–41].

Thoughts on
1 Timothy 4:13

by
Rev. Thomas Scott
(in a letter to Rev. G. Knight)

Aston Sandford, June 17, 1816

My Dear Sir,

As wholly unable to meet you in person, I send you my proxy in a paper of hints on your most important question.

Should any brother undertake to form a paper for publication from the whole result of the discussion, he is perfectly at liberty to use my hints for that purpose; but if this is not determined on, I shall be glad to receive them back again, as probably I may make some use of them hereafter. And I shall also gladly receive any of the remarks which my brethren make on them, or on the general subject.

I hope I shall not forget to pray for a large blessing on the company and the congregations, for my heart will be with you. And I trust you will be particular, both when together and when separate, in praying for me, and for my life, or health, or even ease, so that I may be upheld and enabled to act consistently in my closing scene, and may finish my course with joy. For I feel myself a poor, weak, and sinful creature, in constant danger of falling or fainting unless upheld by the power and grace of the Lord Jesus. With my kind remembrances to Mrs. Knight, prayers for a blessing on you and your family, and Christian love to all the assembled brethren, I remain your faithful and affectionate brother,

Thomas Scott

Thoughts on the words of St. Paul to Timothy, "Give thyself wholly to them," considered as an instruction to all ministers of Christianity, in every age and nation

The context of this expressive clause should be considered with peculiar attention in explaining the words made use of. "Let no man despise thy youth, but be thou an example of the believers in word, in conversation, in charity, in spirit, in faith, in purity. Till I come, give attendance to reading, to exhortation, to doctrine. Neglect not the gift that is in thee, which was given thee by the laying on of the hands of the presbytery. Meditate upon these things; give thyself wholly to them, that thy profiting may appear to all. Take heed unto thyself, and unto the doctrine; continue in them, for in doing this thou shall both save thyself and them that hear thee" (1 Timothy 4:12–16). Each expression, when closely examined, is as it were a sermon; and the whole comprises such a mass of appropriate instruction, warning, and encouragement to ministers as can rarely be found in so few words. Let us then meditate on these things continually.

Two particulars seem especially to call for our notice in the clause more immediately under consideration: the things which the apostle intended, and what it is to give ourselves wholly to them.

1. The things intended: The apostle doubtless referred to those exhortations which he had just before given to his beloved son Timothy, respecting his personal conduct and example; his ministerial office, as a talent entrusted to him; the exercise of this ministry; the preparation for that exercise; and the ends to be proposed in the whole. "Continue in them, for in so doing thou shalt both save thyself and them that hear thee," that is, those who so hear you as to believe and obey the doctrine taught by you.

A few hints may then be here dropped on some of the particulars relating to our important ministry; for we cannot too much magnify our office, and should have high and honorable thoughts of it as the best of all good works, the most beneficial service which man can perform to man, and the most immediately connected with the glory of God our Savior—yet attended with the most awful responsibility. It is a gift conferred on us when we are set apart to that service. To us it is given to preach the unsearchable riches of Christ. It is a talent entrusted to our stewardship which demands faithful improvement. It opens the way to the cultivation of the mind for purposes peculiar to the minister, to purposes that are of the highest importance, and in which, if he does not neglect it, his profiting may appear unto all men, not only when he sets out as a young and inexperienced minister, but even if he had attained to Timothy's competency, nay, to that of Paul the aged himself (except as inspiration and miraculous powers are concerned, and from these the gift here spoken of, at least in applying it to us, should be considered as entirely distinct).

He who would be apt to teach must be apt to learn, and always learning to the end of his life; else (as is, alas, too often the case) he will be like those who spend much and gain little, and are always in debt. In this general office and stewardship, the apostle would probably, if he spoke to us in modern language, and according to our situation as pastors, point out the public exercise of our ministry, in season and out of season, instant, with many things concerning our doctrine, our motives, our spirit, and so on. He would advert to the more private exercise of our ministry from house to house, according to the various openings which are afforded us of privately warning, instructing, counseling, and comforting the healthy and the sick (and those around the sick), or in teaching children, and in various other ways. He would note those things that we should attend to in the study by reading and writing and preparing for our public ministry, or aiming at practical usefulness by our studies and publications. The fisherman, when not fishing, is employed in washing or mending his nets, repairing his boat, so that he may be ready for the next expected opportunity, or to seize on one that he did not expect. The apostle would especially point out what is to be done in the closet by our earnest and constant prayers and supplications (see Colossians 2:1; 4:12). He would go with us into our families, and lead us to consider the importance of so commanding our children and our households (Genesis 18:19), and so governing them that everything, as far as we possibly can, may bear the holy stamp of our sacred office. Here a large field opens before us of family instruction and worship, of educating our children, of our conversation before them and our friends, in order that by every means we may fix the impression that we deeply mean all that we deliver from the pulpit. For, alas, too often the conduct and conversation of the dining and drawing room render this impression at least very doubtful to those who more narrowly inspect our conduct. The apostle would even attend us on our visits, our journeys, and our seasons of relaxation, and remind us that we must never forget not only our Christian, but our ministerial character. All must be stamped with its holiness; all must be a part of a system, strictly adhered to, of being constantly learning, and awaiting the opportunity of imparting what we have learned in the things of God.

I might go into all our needful intercourse with those outside the church, and our concerns in the world as they relate to temporal things, or to any employments in which it may be expedient to engage in connection with our ministry—in short, to our whole example, an example not only to the world, but to believers. But these hints must suffice.

2. The import of the words rendered: "Give thyself wholly to them." I remember that Demosthenes somewhere uses the same (or an entirely similar) expression concerning himself and his application to public affairs. He was always the statesman; his time, his talents, his heart, his all were swallowed up, as it were, in this one object. And in fact no man ever became very eminent in any line when this was not his plan. It is noted by some writer concerning Bonaparte that he never went to any new town, city, or country but immediately he was examining and considering where would be the best place for a castle or a camp, for an abush or an at-

tack, for the means of defense or annoyance. He thus, in his line, entered into the spirit of the clause, "always the general." Our Lord says of Himself, "My meat is to do the will of Him that sent me, and to finish His work," and His whole time and soul were engaged in it. The apostles say, "We will give ourselves continually to prayer and to the ministry of the Word." In other words, "We will not suffer even things good in themselves (such as serving tables) to take us off from these grand and essential employments." Much less would they have left them for secular interests or trivial pursuits. They entered into the spirit of the clause under consideration.

Let these things then have our whole time; let even recreation and refreshment be so regulated, moderated, and subordinated that they may not interfere with our grand employment, or make us unfit for it, but rather recruit and prepare us for it so that they may all become subservient to our main object. Prudent men of the world know how to do this in respect of their object, and will let neither meals, sleep, visits, nor diversions interfere with it, but will endeavor in all these to promote it by means of them. They enter into the spirit of this clause, and of the words used elsewhere, "redeeming the time."

Let these things have our whole mind, our capacity, natural ability, genius, and learning; whatever we have or are, or can attain to, let these things have the whole. Wherever the bees collect the honey, they bring it all to the hive. Let us give all our powers and talents to our highly important service, and not for a moment admit an idea of employing genius or learning to other purposes foreign to our ministry. The vows of God are upon us. At least I feel this to be my case, for, almost forty years ago, I solemnly vowed before God not to engage in any literary pursuit or publication, however creditable or lucrative it might be, which had not the religious instruction of mankind for its immediate object.

All our reading ought to be subservient to this. We may read any books, ancient or modern, sacred or profane, infidel, heretical, or what not, but always as ministers, to note such things as may better enable us to defend and plead for the truth as it is in Jesus; never merely for amusement, curiosity, or love of learning simply for its own sake, or for the credit or advantages derived from it.

Let these things have our whole heart. We shall never fall in with the apostle's counsel unless our ministry and its employments are our pleasure and delight, unless our warmest affections are excited by it and our sweetest gratifications derived from it. Connected with this, however, our keenest sorrows and regrets will also thus be stirred. But our whole soul and heart must be in it. We must count it both our work and our wages, our business and our pleasure, our interest and our honor, and, in connection with saving ourselves along with those who hear us, our all. Nothing moved the apostle in his various pursuits; he did not think even his life dear to himself, so that he might finish his course with joy, and the ministry which he had received of the Lord Jesus, to testify to the gospel of the grace of God. And neither the smiles nor the frowns of men, neither worldly gain or loss, nor privations, hardships, delays, or disappointments will move us if we enter into his spirit and copy his example.

We must, as has been said, remember that we are the ministers of the holy Jesus, the shepherds of His flock, the stewards of His mysteries. We are His messengers of reconciliation to perishing sinners, and we must never go anywhere or do anything so as to lay aside this sacred character. Is a man invited by neighbors or superiors? Let him decline the invitation, if he cannot in such a visit speak and act as a minister, studying that dignified yet meek and unaffected manner in which Christ improved such seasons and opportunities as openings to most important instruction. Does he journey? Let even the coach, the inn, or the ship be seized as an opening for communicating, in one way or another, useful instruction; and if this should prove impracticable, let him at least learn some lessons concerning the human heart, and the aims and pursuits of worldly men, which may render him more competent to meet the thoughts, plans, and consciences of his hearers. He may thus be learning when he cannot teach, and gleaning when he cannot reap. Does he, for the sake of recruiting health and spirits, retire to some watering place or other scene of relaxation? Let him not divest himself of his ministerial character, as is sometimes done, if not (alas!) of the Christian character also; but let him still be prompt at learning and apt to seize any opportunity for teaching, and let him at least preserve himself, and those belonging to him, from giving any countenance to the festivity, frivolity, and dissipation of such scenes.

Does he teach pupils privately or at a public seminary? Still let him do it as a Christian minister, and endeavor, by wise (James 1:5) and persevering endeavors, to train up his pupils for Jesus Christ. In reading with them the classics, for instance, let him intersperse remarks on the falsity of their principles, the fallacy of their reasoning, and the tendency of their writings, comparing their maxims with those of Solomon, and with the words of Christ and His apostles on similar subjects and occasions. And in every way let it appear in his conduct respecting them that he is far more earnestly desirous of imparting good to them than of deriving advantage from them, remembering our Lord's saying, "It is more blessed to give than to receive."

The same principles are applicable to a variety of other particulars, but I have already too much enlarged. These things adverted to will effectually keep the ministers of Christ from meriting the charge brought against the priests by Malachi 1:10, and even from exciting a feeling in those of decided zeal like St. Paul's when he said, "All seek their own, and not the things of Jesus Christ." Love of filthy lucre, and of empty praise and popularity, will not then warp their minds, but they will feed the flock of God, taking the oversight of it "not by constraint, but willingly; not for filthy lucre, but of a ready mind; neither as being lords over God's heritage, but as examples to the flock. And when the chief Shepherd shall appear, ye shall receive a crown of glory that fadeth not away" (1 Peter 5:2–4).

P.S. When Nehemiah had related the progress made in a short time in building the wall of Jerusalem, in the midst of dangers and opposition, he said, "The people had a mind to work." They were not paid for their work, but incurred expense and danger about it. But the object was so near to their hearts that they had a mind to work, and thus great things were done in a little time. Oh, if all Christians and ministers had thus a mind to work for nothing when good might be done, how much might be effected! He who is willing to work for nothing will never complain that he has nothing to do. Yet the principle that made the apostles determine not to serve tables, though a good work in itself, should render ministers in this day very careful not so to give their services even to the most useful societies, and to attending the meetings of them, as to prevent their giving themselves continually to the Word of God and prayer. A danger at present seems to arise on this side.

Mr. [Richard] Cecil used to say that the devil does not care how ministers are employed, as long as it is not in their proper work; whether in hunting and field sports, at cards and assemblies, in writing notes on the classics, or in politics. It is all the same to him; each might please his own taste.

The Snares and Difficulties Attending the Ministry of the Gospel

by
Rev. John Newton

Dear Sir,

I am glad to hear that you are ordained, and that the Lord is about to fix you in a place where there is a prospect of your being greatly useful. He has given you the desire of your heart, and I hope He has given you likewise a heart to devote yourself, without reserve, to His service, and to the service of souls for His sake. I willingly comply with your request, and shall, without ceremony, offer you such thoughts as occur to me upon this occasion.

You have doubtless often anticipated in your mind the nature of the service to which you are now called, and made it the subject of much consideration and prayer. But a distant view of the ministry is generally very different from what it is found to be when we are actually engaged in it. The young soldier who has never seen an enemy may form some general notions of what is before him, but his ideas will be much more lively and diversified when he comes upon the field of battle. If the Lord were to show us the whole beforehand, who, with a due sense of his own insufficiency and weakness, would venture to engage? But He first draws us by a constraining sense of His love and by giving us an impression of the worth of souls, and leaves us to acquire a knowledge of what is difficult and disagreeable by a gradual experience. The ministry of the gospel, like the book which the Apostle John ate, is a bittersweet one; but the sweetness is tasted first, and the bitterness is usually known afterwards, when we are so far engaged that there is no going back.

Yet I would not discourage you; it is a good and noble cause, and we serve a good and gracious Master who, though He will make us feel our weakness and vileness, will not suffer us to sink under it. His grace is sufficient for us, and if He favors us with a humble and dependent spirit, a single eye and a simple heart, He will make every difficulty give way, and mountains will sink into plains before His power.

You have known something of Satan's devices while you were in private life, how he has envied your privileges, assaulted your peace, and laid snares for your feet. Though the Lord would not allow Him to hurt you, He has permitted him to sift and tempt, and to shoot his fiery arrows at you. Without some of that discipline, you would have been very unfit for that part of your office which consists in speaking a word in season to weary and heavy-laden souls. But you may now expect to hear from him, and to be beset by his power and subtlety in a different manner. You are now to be placed in the forefront of the battle, and to stand, as it were, as his mark. So far as he can prevail against you now, not only you yourself but many others will be affected. Many eyes will be upon you, and if you take a wrong step, or are ensnared into a wrong spirit, you will open the mouths of the adversaries wider, and grieve the hearts of believers more sensibly, than if the same things had

happened to you while you were a layman. The work of
the ministry is truly honorable, but, like the post of
honor in a battle, it is attended with peculiar dangers.
Therefore the apostle cautions Timothy, "Take heed to
thyself, and to thy doctrine." To yourself in the first
place, and then to your doctrine; the latter without the
former would be impracticable and vain.

You need to be on your guard in whatever way your
first attempts to preach the gospel may seem to operate.
If you should (as may likely be the case where the truth
has been little known) meet with much opposition, you
will perhaps find it a heavier trial than you are aware of.
But I speak of it only as it might draw forth your corruptions and give Satan advantage over you. And this may
be in two ways. The first is by embittering your spirit
against opposers so that you speak in anger, to set them
at defiance or retaliate upon them in their own way.
Besides bringing guilt upon your conscience, this
would of course increase your difficulties and impede
your usefulness. A violent opposition against ministers
and professors of the gospel is sometimes expressed by
the devil's roaring, and some people think no good
can be done without it. It is allowed that men who love
darkness will show their dislike of the light; but I believe that, if the wisdom and meekness of the friends of
the gospel had been always equal to their good intentions and zeal, the devil would not have had opportunity to roar so loudly as he has sometimes done. The
subject matter of the gospel is offense enough to the
carnal heart; we must therefore expect opposition. But
we should not provoke or despise it, or do anything to
aggravate it. A patient continuance in well-doing, a
consistency in character, and an attention to return

kind offices for harsh treatment will, in a course of time, greatly soften the spirit of opposition; and instances are to be found of ministers who are treated with some respect even by those persons in their parishes who are most averse to their doctrine.

When the apostle directs us, "If it be possible, and as much as in you lies, live peaceably with all men," he seems to intimate that, though it is difficult, it is not wholly impracticable. We cannot change the rooted prejudices of their hearts against the gospel, but it is possible, by the Lord's blessing, to stop their mouths and make them ashamed of discovering it when they behold our good conversation in Christ. And it is well worth our while to cultivate this outward peace, provided that we do not purchase it at the expense of truth and faithfulness; for ordinarily we cannot hope to be useful to our people unless we give them reason to believe that we love them and have their interest at heart.

Again, opposition will hurt you if it should give you an idea of your own importance and lead you to dwell with a secret self-approbation upon your own faithfulness and courage in such circumstances. If you are able to stand your ground uninfluenced by either the favor or the fear of men, you have reason to give glory to God; but remember that you cannot thus stand for an hour unless He upholds you. It shows a wrong turn of mind when we are so ready to speak of our trials and difficulties of this kind, and of our address and resolution in encountering them. A natural stiffness of spirit, with a desire to have self taken notice of, may make a man willing to endure those kinds of hardships, though he has but little grace in exercise. But true Christian fortitude, from an awareness that we speak the truths of God

and are supported by His power, is a very different
thing.

If you should meet with but little opposition, or if
the Lord should be pleased to make your enemies into
your friends, you will probably be in danger from the
opposite quarter. If opposition has hurt many, popularity has wounded more. To say the truth, I am in some
pain for you. Your natural abilities are considerable;
you have been diligent in your studies; your zeal is
warm and your spirit is lively. With these advantages, I
expect to see you become a popular preacher. The more
you are so, the greater will your field of usefulness be.
But, alas, you cannot yet know to what it will expose
you. It is like walking upon ice. When you shall see an
attentive congregation hanging upon your words;
when you shall hear the well-meant but often injudicious commendations from those to whom the Lord
shall make you useful; when you shall find, upon an in-
timation of your preaching in a strange place, people
thronging from all parts to hear you—how will your
heart feel? It is easy for me to advise you to be humble,
and for you to acknowledge the propriety of the advice;
but while human nature remains in its present state,
there will be almost the same connection between
popularity and pride as between fire and gunpowder:
they cannot meet without an explosion, at least not unless the gunpowder is kept very damp. So unless the
Lord is constantly moistening our hearts (if I may so
speak) by the influences of His Spirit, popularity will
soon set us ablaze.

You will hardly find a person who has been exposed
to this fiery trial without suffering loss. Those whom
the Lord loves, He is able to keep, and He will keep

them upon the whole, yet by such means and in a course of such narrow escapes that they shall have reason to look upon their deliverance as no less than miraculous. Sometimes, if His ministers are not watchful against the first impressions of pride, He permits it to gather strength; and then it is but a small thing that a few of their admirers may think them more than men in the pulpit if they are left to commit such mistakes when out of it as the weakest of the flock can discover and pity. And this will certainly be the case while pride and self-sufficiency are ascendant.

Beware, my friend, of mistaking the ready exercise of gifts for the exercise of grace. The minister may be assisted by God in public preaching for the sake of his hearers; and there is something in the nature of our public work, when surrounded by a concourse of people, that is suited to draw forth the exertion of our abilities, and to engage our attention in the outward services, when the frame of the heart may be far from being right in the sight of the Lord. When Moses smote the rock, the water followed; yet he spoke unadvisedly with his lips and greatly displeased the Lord. However, the congregation was not disappointed due to his fault, nor was he put to shame before them; but he was humbled for it afterwards. They are happy whom the Lord preserves in some degree as humble, without leaving them to expose themselves to the observation of men, and to receive such wounds as are seldom healed without leaving a deep scar. But even these have much to suffer. Many distressing exercises you will probably meet with upon the best supposition, to preserve in you a due sense of your own unworthiness, and to convince you that your ability, your acceptance, and your usefulness depend upon a power beyond your own. Sometimes, perhaps, you will feel such an amazing difference between the frame of your spirit in public and in private, when the eyes of men are not upon you, as will make you almost ready to conclude that you are no better than a hypocrite, a mere stage-player, who derives all his pathos and exertion from the sight of the audience. At other times you will feel such a total emptiness and indisposition of mind that former seasons of liberty in preaching will appear to you like the remembrance of a dream, and you will hardly be able to persuade yourself that you shall ever be capable of preaching again. The Scriptures will appear to you like a sealed book, and no text or subject will afford any light or opening to determine your choice. And this perplexity may not only seize you in the study, but accompany you in the pulpit. If you are enabled at some times to speak to the people with power, and to resemble Samson when in the greatness of his strength he bore away the gates of the city, you will, perhaps, at others appear before them like Samson when his locks were shorn and he stood in fetters. So you need not tell the people that you have no sufficiency in yourself, for they will readily perceive it without your information. These things are hard to bear; yet successful popularity is not to be preserved upon easier terms; and if they are but sanctified to hide pride from you, you will have reason to number them among your choicest mercies.

I have just entered upon the subject of the difficulties and dangers attending the ministry. May the Lord make you wise and watchful! And that He may be the light of your eye, the strength of your arm, and the joy of your heart, is my sincere prayer for you.

Remarks on Subjects Connected with the Christian Ministry

by
Rev. Richard Cecil

The Assistance Which a Minister has Reason to Expect in the Discharge of His Public Duty

Men have carried their views on this subject to extremes. Enthusiasts have said that learning, studying, and writing sermons, have injured the church. The learned men have said, "Go and hear one of these enthusiasts hold forth!" But both classes may be rendered useful. Let each correct its evils, yet do his work in its own way.

Some men set upon exorbitant notions about accuracy. But exquisite accuracy is totally lost on mankind. The greater part of those who hear cannot be brought to see the points of the precise man. The Scriptures are not written in this manner. I should advise a young minister to break through all such cobwebs as these unphilosophical men would spin around him. A humble and modest man is silenced if he sees one of these critics before him. He should say, "I am God's servant. To my own Master I stand or fall. I will labor according to the utmost ability that God gives, and leave all consequences to Him."

We are especially taught in the New Testament to glorify the Spirit of God; and, in His gracious operations in our ministry, we are nearer the apostolic times than we often think ourselves to be. But this assistance is to be expected by us as laborers in the vineyard, and not as rhapsodists. Idle men may be pointed out who have abused the doctrine of divine assistance; but what has not been abused? We must expect a special blessing to accompany the truth—not to supersede labor, but to rest on and accompany labor.

A minister is to be such in season and out of season, and, therefore, everywhere a minister. He will not employ himself in writing secular histories; he will not busy himself in prosecuting mathematical inquiries. He will labor directly in his high calling, and indirectly in a vast variety of ways as he may be enabled. And God may bless that word in private which may have been long heard in public in vain.

A minister should satisfy himself in saying, "It matters not what men think of my talents. Am I doing what I can?" For there is great encouragement in that commendation of our Lord's, "She hath done what she could." It would betray a wrong state of mind to say, "If I had discharged my duty in such and such a way, I would have succeeded." This is a carnal spirit. If God blesses the simple manner in which you spoke, that will do good; if not, no manner of speaking could have done it.

There is such a thing in the religious world as a cold, carnal wisdom, according to which everything must be nicely weighed in the scales and exactly measured by the rule. I question if this is not worse in its consequences than the enthusiasm which it opposes. Both are evil, and are to be shunned. But I scarcely ever knew a preacher or writer like this who did much good.

We are to go forth expecting the excellency of God's power to accompany us, since we are but earthen vessels; and if, in the apostolic days, diligence was necessary, how much more requisite is it now!

But, with regard to the exercise of this diligence, a sufficiency in all things is promised. What does a minister require? In all these respects the promise is applicable to him. He needs, for instance, courage and patience; he may, therefore, expect that the Holy Spirit will enable him to exercise these graces.

A minister may expect more superintendence, more elevation, than a hearer. It can scarcely be questioned that he ought to pray for this; if so, he has a ground in Scripture thus to pray.

I have been cured of expecting the Holy Spirit's influence without due preparation on our part, by observing how men preach who take up that error. I have heard such men talk nonsense by the hour.

We must combine "Good oration comes from good study" with St. Paul's words, "Meditate upon these things; give thyself wholly to them, that thy profiting may appear to all." One errs who says, "I will preach a reputable sermon." And another errs who says, "I will leave all to the assistance of the Holy Spirit," while he has neglected a diligent preparation.

On Preaching Christ

"We preach Christ crucified" (1 Corinthians 1:23). Christ is God's great ordinance. Nothing ever has been done or will be done to purpose, except so far as He is held forth with simplicity. All the lines must center in Him. I feel this in my own experience, and therefore I govern my ministry by it; but then this is to be done according to the analogy of faith, not ignorantly, absurdly, and falsely. I doubt not, indeed, but that excess on this side is less pernicious than excess on the other, because God will bless His own special ordinance, though partially understood and partially exhibited.

There are many weighty reasons for rendering Christ prominent in our ministry:

1. Christ cheers the prospect. Everything connected with Him has light and gladness thrown around it. I look out of my window, and the scene is scowling, dark, frigid, and forbidding. I shudder, my heart is chilled. But let the sun break forth from the clouds and I can feel, I can act, and I can spring.

2. God descending and dwelling with man is a truth so infinitely grand that it must absorb all others. You are his attendants! Well—but the King! There He is, the King!

3. Outside of Christ God is not intelligible, much less amiable. Such men as Clarke and Abernethy talk sublime nonsense. A sick woman said to me, "Sir, I have no notion of God. I can form no notion of Him. You talk to me about Him, but I cannot get a single idea that seems to contain anything." I replied, "But you know how to conceive of Jesus Christ as man! God comes down to you in Him, full of kindness and condescension." And she said, "Ah, sir, that gives me something to lay hold on. There I can rest. I understand God in His Son."

But if God is not intelligible outside of Christ, much less is He amiable, though I ought to feel Him so. He is an object of horror and aversion to me, corrupted as I am! I fear, I tremble, I resist, I hate, I rebel.

4. A preacher may pursue his topic without being

led by it to Christ. A man who is accustomed to investigating topics is in danger. He takes up his topic and pursues it. He takes up another and pursues it. At length Jesus Christ becomes his topic, and then he pursues that. If he cannot so feel and think as to bend all subjects naturally and gracefully to Christ, he must seek his remedy in selecting such as are more evangelical.

5. God puts peculiar honor on the preaching of Christ crucified. A philosopher may philosophize his hearers, but preaching Christ must convert them. John the Baptist will make his hearers tremble; but, if the least in the kingdom of heaven is greater than he, let him exhibit that peculiar feature of his superiority, Jesus Christ. Men may preach Christ ignorantly, blunderingly, and absurdly, yet God will give it efficacy because He is determined to magnify His own ordinance.

6. God seems, in the doctrine of the cross, to design the destruction of man's pride. Even the murderer and the adulterer sometimes beome subjects of the grace of the gospel, because the murderer and adulterer are more easily convinced and humbled; but the man of virtue is seldom reached, because the man of virtue disdains to descend. "Remember me" saved a dying malefactor! "God, I thank Thee . . ." condemned a proud Pharisee!

Every minister should therefore inquire, "What is for me the wisest way of teaching Christ to men?" Some seem to think that in the choice of a wise way there lurks always a trimming disposition. There are men, doubtless, who will sacrifice to self even Christ Jesus the Lord; but they, of all men, are the farthest from the thing. There is a secret in doing it which none but an

honest man can discover. The knave is not half wise
enough.

We are not to judge one another in these things.
Sufficient it is to us to know what we have to do. There
are different ways of doing the same thing, and that
with success and acceptance. We see this in the apostles
themselves. They not only preached Christ in different
ways, but, what is more, they could not do this like one
another. They declare this fact themselves, and acknowledge the grace of God in their respective gifts.
Our beloved brother Paul writes, says Peter, according
to the wisdom given unto him. But there are Peters in
our days who would say, "Paul is too learned. Away with
these things, which are hard to understand. He should
be more simple. I dislike all this reasoning." And there
are Pauls who would say, "Peter is rash and unguarded.
He should put a curb on his impetuosity." And there
are Johns who would say, "They should both discharge
their office in my soft and winning manner. No good
will come of this fire and noise." Nothing of this sort!
Each has his proper gift from God, one after this manner and another after that; and each seems only desirous to occupy faithfully till his Master comes, leaving
his brethren to stand or fall to their own Master.

Too much dependence is often placed on a system
of rational contrivance. An ingenious man thinks he
can so manage to preach Christ that his hearers will
say, "Here is nothing of Methodism! This has nothing
to do with that system!" I will venture to say that if this
is the sentiment communicated by his ministry, he has
not delivered his message. The people do not know
what he means, or he has kept back part of God's truth.
He has fallen on a carnal contrivance to avoid a cross,

and he does no good to souls. The whole message must be delivered, and it is better that it should be delivered even coarsely than not at all. We may lay it down as a principle that if the gospel is a medicine, and a specific one too, as it is, it must be gotten down such as it is. Any attempt to sophisticate and adulterate will deprive it of its efficacy, and will often recoil on the man who makes the attempt, to his shame and confusion. The Jesuits tried to render Christianity palatable to the Chinese by adulterating it, but the Jesuits were driven with abhorrence from the empire.

If we have to deal with men of learning, let us show learning so far as to demonstrate that it bears its testimony to the truth. But accommodation in manner must often spring from humility. We must condescend to the capacity of men and make the truth intelligible to them.

If this is our manner of preaching Christ, we must make up our minds not to regard the little caviler who will judge us by the standard of his favorite author or preacher. We must be cautious too, since men of God have been and ever will be the butt and scorn of the world, of thinking that we can escape its sneers and censures. It is a foolish project to avoid giving offense, but it is our duty to avoid giving *unnecessary* offense. It is necessary offense if it is given by the truth, but it is unnecessary if our own spirit occasions it.

I have often thought that St. Paul was raised up peculiarly to be an example to others in laboring to discover the wisest way of exhibiting the gospel; not only was he a great pattern in other points, but he was designedly raised up for this very thing. How he labors to make the truth reasonably plain! How he strains every

nerve and ransacks every corner of the heart to make it
reasonably palatable! We need not be instructed in his
particular meaning when he says, "I became all things
to all men, if by any means I might save some." His history is a comment on the declaration.

The knowledge of Jesus Christ is a wonderful mystery. Some men think they preach Christ gloriously because they name Him every two minutes in their sermons. But that is not preaching Christ. To understand,
enter into, and explain His various offices and characters—the glories of His person and work, His relation
to us, and ours to him, and to God the Father and God
the Spirit through Him—this is the knowledge of
Christ. The divines of the present day are stunted
dwarfs in this knowledge compared with the great men
of the last age. To know Jesus Christ for ourselves is to
make Him a consolation, delight, strength, righteousness, companion, and end.

This is the aspect in which religion should be presented to mankind; it is suited above all others to produce effect, and effect is our object. We must take human nature as we find human nature. We must take
human nature in great cities as we find human nature
in great cities. We may say, "This or that is the aspect
which ought to have the most effect. We must illumi-
nate the mind; we must enlist the reason; we must attack the conscience." We may do all this, and yet our
comparative lack of success in begetting and educating
the sons of glory may demonstrate to us that there is
some more effective way, and that sound sense and philosophy call on us to adopt that way because it is most
effective.

Our system of preaching must meet mankind; they

must find it possible to live in the bustle of the world and yet serve God. After being worried and harassed with its concerns, let them hear cheering truths concerning Christ's love, care, and pity which will operate like an enchantment in dispelling the cares of life and calming the anxious perturbations of conscience. Bring forward privileges and enforce duties in their proper places and proportions.

Let there be no extremes. Yet I have arrived at this conviction: Men who lean toward the extreme of evangelical privileges in their ministry do much more for the conversion of their hearers than they do who lean toward the extreme of requirement. And my own experience confirms my observation. I feel myself repelled if anything chills, loads, or urges me. This is my nature, and I see it to be very much the nature of other men. But let me hear, " 'Son of man, thou hast played the harlot with many lovers; yet return again to me,' saith the Lord," and I am melted and subdued.

On Visiting Deathbeds

I have found it in many cases a difficult thing to deal with a deathbed. We are called unto deathbeds of various kinds:

The true pilgrim sends for us to set before him the food on which he has fed throughout his journey. He has a keen appetite. He wants strength and vigor for the last effort, and then all is forever well! He has gone home and is at rest!

Another man sends for us because it is decent, or his friends importune him, or his conscience is alarmed. But he is ignorant of sin and salvation. He is either indifferent about both, or he has made up his mind in his own way. He wants the minister to confirm him in his own views and smooth over the wound. I have seen such men mad with rage while I have been beating down their refuge of lies and setting forth to them God's refuge. There is a wise and holy approach to be observed in treating such cases: "I am not come to daub you over with untempered mortar. I am not come to send you to the bar of God with a lie in your right hand. But neither am I come to mortify you, to put you to unnecessary pain, to embitter you, or to exasperate you." There is a kindness, affection, tenderness, meekness, and patience which a man's feelings and conscience will condemn him with while he opposes! I have found it a very effectual method to begin with myself; it awakens attention, conciliates the mind, and insinuates conviction: "Whatever others think of themselves, I stand condemned before God; my heart is so desperately wicked that if God had not shown me in His Word a remedy in Jesus Christ, I would be in despair. I can only tell you what I am, and what I have found. If you believe yourselves to be what God has told me I am and all men are, then I can tell you where and how to find mercy and eternal life. If you will not believe that you are this sort of man, I have nothing to offer you. I know of nothing else for man besides that which God has shown me."

My descriptions of my fallen nature have excited perfect astonishment. Sometimes my patients have seemed scarcely able to believe me, but I have found that God has fastened, by this means, conviction on the conscience. In some cases, an indirect method of addressing the conscience may apparently be, in truth, the most direct; but we are to use this method wisely and sparingly. It seems to me to be one of the characteristics of the day in the religious world to err on this subject. We have found out a circuitous way of exhibiting truth. The plain, direct, simple exhibition of it is often abandoned, even where no cirumstances justify and require a more insinuating manner. There is dexterity indeed, and skillful address in this, but too little of the simple declaration of the testimony of God, which St. Paul opposes to excellency of speech or of wisdom, and to enticing words of man's wisdom. We have done very little when we have merely persuaded a man to think as we do.

But we have to deal with a worse deathbed character than with the man who opposes the truth. Some men assent to everything we propose. They will even anticipate us. And yet we see that they mean nothing. I have often felt when with such persons, "I would they could be brought to contradict and oppose! That would lead to discussion. God might, peradventure, dash the stony heart in pieces. But this heart is like water. The impression dies as fast as it was made." I have sought for such views as might rouse and stir up opposition. I have tried to irritate the torpid mind, but all in vain. I once visited a young clergyman of this character, who was seized with a dangerous illness in a coffeehouse in town, where some business had brought him. The first time I saw him we conversed very closely together, and, in the prospect of death, he seemed solicitous to prepare for it. But I could make no sort of impression upon him. All I could possibly say met his entire approbation, though I saw his heart felt no interest in it. When I visited him a second time, the fear of death was gone and, with it, all solicitude about religion. He was still civil and grateful, but he tried to parry off the business on which he knew I came: "I will show you, sir, some little things with which I have worn away the hours of my confinement and solitude." He brought out a quantity of pretty and tasty drawings. I was at a loss how to express, with suitable force and delicacy, the high sense I felt of his indecorum and insipidity, and to leave a deep impression on his conscience I rose, instantly, said that my time was expired, wished him well, and withdrew.

Sometimes we have a painful part to act with sincere men who have been carried too much into the world. I was called in to visit such a man. "I find no comfort." he said. "God veils his face from me. Everything round me is dark and uncertain." I did not dare to act the flatterer. I said, "Let us look faithfully into the state of things. I would have been surprised if you had not felt thus. I believe you to be sincere. Your state of feelings evinces your sincerity. Had I found you exulting in God, I would have concluded that you were either deceived or a deceiver; for, while God acts in His usual order, how could you expect to feel otherwise on the approach of death than you do feel? You have driven hard after the world. Your spirit has been absorbed in its cares. Your sentiments and your conversation have been in the spirit of the world. And have you any reason to expect the response of conscience and the clear evidence which await the man who has walked and lived in close friendship with God? You know that what I say is true." His wife interrupted me by assuring me that he had been an excellent man. "Silence!" said the dying penitent, "It is all true!"

Soon after I came to St. John's, I was called on to visit a dying lady whom I saw many times before her death. I found that she had taken God for her portion and rest. She approached Him with the penitence of a sinner grateful for His provision of mercy in Christ. She told me she had found religion in her *Common Prayer Book*. She blessed God that she had "always been kept steady to her church, and that she had never followed the people called Methodists, who were seducing so many on all sides." I thought it would be unadvisable to attempt the removal of prejudices which, in her dying case, were harmless, and which would soon be removed by the light which would beam in on her glorified soul. We had more interesting subjects of conversation from which this would have led us away. Some persons may tax her with a want of charity; but, alas, I fear they are persons who, knowing more than she did of the doctrines of the gospel, have so little of its divine charity in their hearts that, as they cannot allow for her prejudices, neither would they have been the last to stigmatize her as a dead formalist and a pharisee. God knows those who are His, and they are often seen by Him where we see them not.

Some Rules Given to a Young Minister Going Into a Situation of Peculiar Difficulty

As I know you have received much good advice, I would suggest to you a few hints, with a view to admonishing you to be careful, while you are doing your work, not by any mistakes of your own to hinder your success:

1. Do not forget that your success with others is very much connected with your personal character. Herod heard John gladly, and he did many things because he knew the preacher to be a just and holy man. Words uttered from the heart find their way to the heart by a

holy sympathy. Character is power: "A good man seen, though silent, counsel gives."

If you would make deep impressions on others, you must use all means to have them first formed on your own mind. Avoid, at the same time, all appearances of evil, such as a covetous, worldly deportment, a vain or assuming one, or a careless or indevout one. Never allow jesting about sacred persons or things. Satan will employ such antidotes as these to counteract the operation of that which is effective and gracious in a minister's character.

2. Do not place your dependence on any means, qualities, or circumstances, however excellent they are in themselves. The direct way to render a thing weak is to lean on it as strong. God is a jealous God, and will utterly abolish idols as means of success. He designs to demonstrate that men and creatures are what He makes them, and that only. This also should be your encouragement: if you look, in the diligent and humble use of means, to that Spirit of life and power without whose influence all your endeavors will be to no purpose, you have reason to expect help suited and adequate to all your difficulties.

3. Do not unnecessarily appear in dangerous or improper situations. It is one thing to be humble and condescending; it is another to render yourself common, cheap, and contemptible. The men of the world know when a minister is out of his place, when they can oppress him by numbers or circumstances, when they can make him laugh while his office frowns. Well will it be for him if he is only rendered absurd in his future public admonitions by his former compliances; well if, being found like St. Peter on dangerous ground,

he is not seduced, virtually at least, to deny his Master.

4. Let there be no suspicious appearances in your family. As the head of your household you are responsible for its appearances. Its pride, sloth, and disorder will be yours. You are accountable for your wife's conduct, dress, and manners, as well as those of your children, whose education must be peculiarly exemplary. Your family is to be a picture of what you wish other families to be; and, without the most determined resolution, in reliance on God, to finish this picture at any cost, your recommending family religion to others will but create a smile. Your unfriendly hearers will recollect enough of Scripture to tell you that you ought, like the primitive bishop, to be one that "ruleth well his own house, having his children in subjection with all gravity; for if a man know not how to rule his own house, how shall he take care of the church of God?"

5. Do not meddle beyond your sphere in temporal matters. Your aim and conversation, like your sacred calling, are to be altogether heavenly. As a man of God, you have no concern with politics and parties and schemes of interest, but you are to live above them. There is a sublime spirit in a devoted minister which, as one says of Christianity itself, pays no more regard to these things than to the battles of rooks, the industry of ants, or the policy of bees.

6. Do not venture off general and acknowledged ground in spiritual matters. Giving strong meat instead of milk to those who are yet but babes; giving heed to fables, which minister questions rather than godly edifying; amusing the mind, but not affecting the heart—these practices are often disturbing and bewildering, but seldom convincing. They frequently raise a smile,

but never draw a tear.

7. Maintain acknowledged truth in your own spirit. Both food and medicine are injurious if administered scalding hot. The spirit of a teacher often affects more than his matter. Benevolence is a universal language, and it will apologize for a multitude of defects in the man who speaks it; while neither talents nor truth will apologize for pride, illiberality, or bitterness. Avoid, therefore, irritating occasions and persons, particularly disputes and disputants, by which a minister often loses his temper and his character.

8. Do not be too sharp-sighted, too quick-eared, or too ready-tongued. Some evils are irremediable; they are best neither seen nor heard. By seeing and hearing things that you cannot remove, you will create implacable adversaries who, being guilty aggressors, never forgive. Avoid speaking meanly or harshly of anyone, not only because this is forbidden to Christians, but because it is to declare war as by a thousand heralds.

9. Avoid the temptations arising from the female sex. I need not mention what havoc Satan has made in the church by this means, from the Fall to this day. Your safety, when in danger from this quarter, lies in flight; to parley is to fall. Take the first hint from conscience, or from friends.

In sum, be watchful in all things; endure afflictions; do the work of an evangelist; make full proof of your ministry. And then, whether or not those around you acknowledge your real character now, they shall one day know that there has been a prophet among them!

Questions Proper for Young Ministers Frequently to Put to Themselves

(Chiefly borrowed from the Epistles to Timothy and Titus)

by

Dr. Isaac Watts

Of Faithfulness in the Ministry

Do I sincerely give myself to the ministry of the Word (Acts 6:4)? And do I design to make it the chief business of my life to serve Christ in His gospel in order to obtain the salvation of men?

Do I resolve, through the aids of divine grace, to be faithful to Him who has put me into the ministry, and to take heed to the ministry which I have received in the Lord, that I may fulfill it (1 Timothy 1:12; Colossians 4:17)?

Do I honestly and faithfully endeavor by study and prayer to know the truth as it is in Jesus (Ephesians 4:21)? And do I seek my instructions chiefly from the Holy Scriptures, which are able to make me wise unto salvation, through the faith that is in Christ, that I may be thoroughly furnished unto every good word and work (2 Timothy 3:14, 17)?

Do I hold fast the form of sound words, as far as I have learned them from Christ and His apostles (2 Timothy 1:13), that I may by sound doctrine exhort and convince gainsayers (Titus 1:9)? And do I determine to continue in the things which I have learned, knowing from whom I have learned them (2 Timothy 3:14)?

Do I resolve to give the people the true meaning of Christ in His Word, so far as I can understand it, and not to handle the Word of God deceitfully, but by manifestation of the truth to commend myself to every man's conscience in the sight of God (2 Corinthians 4:2)?

Am I watchful to avoid profane and vain babblings (1 Timothy 6:20)? And do I take care to shun foolish questions, which engender strife, and disputing about words, which are to no profit but the subversion of the hearers (2 Timothy 2:14, 23)?

Do I study to show myself approved unto God, rightly dividing the Word of truth (2 Timothy 2:15), giving to everyone, that is, to saints and sinners, their proper portion?

Do I make it my business to testify to all men, whether Jews or Greeks, the necessity of repentance towards God and faith in Christ Jesus, and that there is no other name under heaven given whereby we may be saved, making this gospel of Christ the subject of my ministry (Acts 20:21; 4:12)?

Do I constantly affirm that those who have believed in Christ Jesus should maintain good works and follow after holiness, without which no man shall see the Lord (Titus 3:8; Hebrews 12:14)?

Do I teach those who hear me to observe all that Christ has commanded us, and do I not shun to declare to them at proper seasons the whole counsel of God (Matthew 28:20; Acts 20:27)?

Do I preach to the people not myself, but Christ Jesus the Lord, and myself as their servant for Christ's sake (2 Corinthians 4:5)?

Do I, in my study and my preaching, take heed to my doctrine and my exhortations, so that I may save myself and them who hear me (1 Timothy 4:16)?

Do I watch over the souls of men as one who must give an account, being solicitous that I may do it with joy and not with grief (Hebrews 13:17)?

Of Diligence in the Ministry

Do I give attendance to reading, meditation, and study? Do I read a due portion of Scripture daily, especially in the New Testament, and that in the original Greek, so that I may be better acquainted with the meaning of the Word of God (1 Timothy 4:13)?

Do I apply myself to these things, and give myself wholly to them, so that my profiting may appear to all (1 Timothy 4:15)?

Do I live constantly as under the eye of the great Shepherd, who is my Master and my final Judge, and so spend my hours as to be able to give a good account of them at last to Him?

Do I neglect to stir up any of those gifts which God has given me for the edification of the church (1 Timothy 4:14; 2 Timothy 1:6)?

Do I seek, as far as possible, to know the state and the wants of my audience, so that I may speak a word in season (Isaiah 50:4)?

Is it my chief design, in choosing my subject and composing my sermon, to edify the souls of men?

Am I determined to take all proper opportunities to preach the Word in season and out of season, that is, in the parlor or the kitchen or the workhouse as well as in the pulpit, and to seek opportunities to speak a word

for Christ and to help forward the salvation of souls
(2 Timothy 4:2)?

Do I labor to show my love for our Lord Jesus by
feeding the sheep and the lambs of His flock (John
21:16–17)?

Am I duly solicitous for the success of my ministry?
And do I take all proper methods to inquire what effects my ministry has had on the souls of those who
hear me?

Where I find or hope the work of grace is begun in
the soul, am I zealous and diligent to promote it?

Of Constant Prayer and Dependence

Do I give myself to prayer, as well as to the ministry
of the Word (Acts 6:4)?

Do I faithfully pray daily in secret so that I may
thereby maintain holy converse with God, and also that
I may increase in the gift of prayer (Matthew 6:6)?

Do I make it my practice to offer prayers, supplications, and intercessions for all men, particularly for our
rulers, for my fellow laborers in the ministry, for the
church of Christ, and especially for those to whom I
preach (1 Timothy 2:1; Romans 1:9–10; Philippians 1:4)?

Do I seek by prayer for divine direction and assistance in my studies, and in all my preparations for the
public? And do I plead for the success of my ministry
with God, in whom are all our springs (Ephesians 3:14–
19; Philippians 1:8–9)?

Do I always keep upon my spirit a deep sense of my
own insufficiency for these things, so that I may ever
depend and wait on the power of Christ for aid and
success (2 Corinthians 2:16; 3:5; 2 Timothy 2:1)?

Of Self-denial, Humility, Mortification, and Patience

Do I endeavor to please all men for their good, and not make it my business to please myself (Romans 15:2), but to become all to all, that I may win their souls, so far as is consistent with being true and faithful to Christ (1 Corinthians 10:23; 9:19, 22)?

Do I behave myself before men, not as a lord over God's heritage, but as a servant of all for Christ's sake? And do I treat them not as having dominion over their faith, but as a helper of their joy (2 Corinthians 4:5; 1:24)?

Am I gentle and patient towards all men, in meekness instructing those who oppose themselves (2 Timothy 2:24–25)?

Do I approve myself in all things as a minister of God, in much patience possessing my own soul, and having the government of my own spirit (2 Corinthians 6:4)?

Do I, as a man of God, whose business is heavenly, flee from covetousness and the inordinate desire for gain, not seeking my own things so much as the things of Christ (1 Timothy 6:10–11), but, having food and raiment, have I learned therewith to be content (1 Timothy 6:8)?

Am I willing to endure hardship as a good soldier of Jesus Christ? And am I learning to bear whatsoever God calls me to for the sake of the elect, that they may obtain salvation with eternal glory (2 Timothy 2:3, 10)?

Am I more and more fortified against shame and suffering for the testimony of my Lord Jesus Christ (2 Timothy 1:8–12)?

Am I willing to spend myself and to be spent for the good of the people, or even to be offered up as a sacrifice for the service of their faith? And do I count nothing dear to me so that I may fulfill the ministry which I have received of the Lord Jesus (Philippians 2:17; 2 Corinthians 12:15; Acts 20:24)?

Of Conduct

Is it my constant endeavor to hold fast the true faith and a good conscience together, lest making shipwreck of one I should lose the other also (1 Timothy 1:19)?

Do I so walk as to be an example of a Christian in word, in conversation, in charity, in faith, in purity (1 Timothy 4:12), so that in all things I may show myself to be a pattern of good works (Titus 2:7)?

Do I endeavor to walk uprightly among men, and to do nothing by partiality (1 Timothy 5:21)?

Is my conversation savory and religious, so as to minister edification to the hearers (Ephesians 4:29)?

Do I shun youthful lusts and follow after righteousness, faith, charity, and peace with all those who call on the Lord out of a pure heart (2 Timothy 2:22)?

Do I avoid, as much as possible, the various temptations to which I may be exposed, and watch against the times, places, and company that are dangerous?

Do I practice the Christian duty of love and charity to those who differ from me in opinion, and even bless and pray for them who are my enemies (Romans 12:14; 14:1)?

Do I behave blamelessly as a steward of God, not self-willed, not soon angry, not given to wine nor filthy lucre, no brawler, no striker, a lover of hospitality, a lover of good men, sober, just, holy, and temperate (Titus 1:7–8)?

Do I daily endeavor to give no offense in anything, that the ministry is not blamed (2 Corinthians 6:3)?

Do I watch over myself in all times, places, and conversations, so as to do and to bear what is required of me, to make a full proof of my ministry and to adorn the doctrine of God my Savior (2 Timothy 4:5; Titus 2:10)?